Artistic Ambassadors

ARTISTIC AMBASSADORS

Literary and International Representation of the New Negro Era

BRIAN RUSSELL ROBERTS

University of Virginia Press
CHARLOTTESVILLE AND LONDON

University of Virginia Press

Printed in the United States of America on acid-free paper

First published 2013

9 8 7 6 5 4 3 2 1

LIBRARY OF CONGRESS CATALOGING-IN-PUBLICATION DATA

Roberts, Brian Russell.

Artistic ambassadors : literary and international representation of the new negro era / Brian Russell Roberts.

p. cm.

Includes bibliographical references and index.

ISBN 978-0-8139-3367-2 (cloth : acid-free paper)

ISBN 978-0-8139-3368-9 (pbk. : acid-free paper)

ISBN 978-0-8139-3369-6 (e-book)

1. American literature—African American authors—History and criticism. 2. African American diplomats. 3. African Americans—Intellectual life—19th century. 4. African Americans—Intellectual life—20th century. I. Title.

PS153.N5R57 2013

810.9'896073—dc23

2012032767

THE AMERICAN LITERATURES INITIATIVE

A book in the American Literatures Initiative (ALI), a collaborative publishing project of NYU Press, Fordham University Press, Rutgers University Press, Temple University Press, and the University of Virginia Press. The Initiative is supported by The Andrew W. Mellon Foundation. For more information, please visit www.americanliteratures.org.

For Norma

Contents

Acknowledgments

I have written *Artistic Ambassadors* only by contracting large intellectual and personal debts. During the project's early life, I found an unmatched mentor in Deborah McDowell, whose intellectual rigor and attention to detail have been inspiring. Conversations with her shaped the project and pushed *Artistic Ambassadors* in ways I could not have anticipated. Marlon Ross's generous comments and conversations helped to contextualize, redirect, and enrich numerous lines of argument. Eric Lott has had a profound influence on this project—from his 2003 postnationalist American studies seminar to his crucial comments on an early draft of chapter 4. Lawrie Balfour's perspectives were also helpful as I worked to transform the project into a book.

Several others have made important contributions to this project. Early on, Marion Rust directed my attention to the ways in which various forms of representation have intersected in American history. Walter Benn Michaels, Jennifer Ashton, Trent Hickman, and Ben Fagan offered helpful commentary on the project's framing. John Ernest, Kathy Pfeiffer, Leonard Robinson, and John Alba Cutler's enthusiastic and incisive questions regarding James Weldon Johnson's work in diplomacy forced me to tighten and complicate an article-length version of chapter 2, which is published here in revised form with the permission of *Modern Fiction Studies.* David Krasner, Heather Nathans, Michael Chaney, Harry Stecopoulos, and Lotta Löfgren made important suggestions on chapter 3's treatment of Henry Francis Downing, which in article form received the 2009 Darwin T. Turner Award for best essay of the year in *African American Review* (published in issue 42.2). Conversations with Sarah Silkey and Melissa White offered perspective as I drafted chapter 5, and a long-running conversation with Adele Logan Alexander proved crucial to this chapter's treatment of Ida Gibbs Hunt. Her willingness to share work-in-progress on the Hunts' biography made this chapter possible. George Handley, John Carlos Rowe, and especially Keith Foulcher made useful suggestions on chapter 6's treatment of Richard Wright in Indonesia. David Hill, Brent Edwards, Hilmar Farid, Jennifer Lindsay, and Paul Tickell helped in identifying and tracking down sources for this chapter. My research assistants Eric Teng and Anggita Putri, as well as Keith Foulcher, helped translate several Indonesian sources. I am also indebted to Cathie Brettschneider and the anonymous readers for UVA Press.

More generally, Ben Bateman, Jay Bishoff, Nathan Boyack, Frank Christianson, Nate Cox, Jesse Crisler, Gloria Cronin, Aaron Cummings, Katy Cummings, Dennis Cutchins, Ed Cutler, Jason Daniel, Emron Esplin, Billy Hall, Jared Hickman, Keith Lawrence, Peter Leman, Suzanne Lundquist, Nick Mason, Kristin Matthews, Frank Meeuwis, Rosemary Millar, Erich Nunn, Susan Owen, Dennis Perry, LeeAnn Reynolds, Jamin Rowan, Jill Rudy, Scott Samuelson, Phil Snyder, Michelle Stephens, Jackie Thursby, and Matt Wickman offered crucial intellectual and moral support along the way.

I am grateful for the help of archivists at the National Archives, the Library of Congress, Howard University's Moorland-Spingarn Research Center, Yale University's Beinecke Library, the Chicago Historical Society, the University of Chicago's Special Collections, Fisk University's Franklin Library, and Emory University's Manuscript, Archives, and Rare Book Library. Early on, Barbara Foley offered helpful commentary on the uses of archival materials. I am also grateful to the Jefferson Scholars Foundation, the English Department at the University of Virginia, and the College of Humanities at Brigham Young University for the funding that made this archival research possible. UVA's Graduate School of Arts & Sciences and BYU's English Department provided a fellowship and course releases that afforded me time to write.

My family has been the starting point. To my parents, Cathy and Roland, and my siblings, David, Emily, Whitney, and Michael: thanks for making smart comments about the materials and historical moments I have described to you. Thanks also to Evelyn for your enthusiastic support. William and Sierra, you have been hearing about this book and drawing on the back of marked-up manuscript pages for a few years now. Thank you for cheering me on. My greatest gratitude goes to Norma, my brilliant and talented wife, who has read and commented on every page more than once. I would not have written this book without you.

Abbreviations

Archival Sources

AnGP Angelina W. Grimké Papers, Manuscript Division, Moorland-Spingarn Research Center, Howard University, Washington, DC

ArGP Archibald H. Grimké Papers, Manuscript Division, Moorland-Spingarn Research Center, Howard University, Washington, DC

CGWP Carter Godwin Woodson Papers, Part I, Library of Congress, Manuscript Division, Washington, DC

CWCC Charles W. Chesnutt Collection, Franklin Library, Fisk University, Nashville, TN

DF Decimal File 1910–1929, Record Group 59, National Archives, College Park, MD

FGP Francis J. Grimké Papers, Manuscript Division, Moorland-Spingarn Research Center, Howard University, Washington, DC

IACFR International Association for Cultural Freedom Records, University of Chicago Special Collections, Chicago, IL

IMGP Irene McCoy Gaines Papers, Chicago Historical Society, Chicago, IL

JWJP James Weldon Johnson Papers, JWJ MSS 1, Beinecke Rare Book and Manuscript Library, Yale University, New Haven, CT

KBFP Kendrick-Brooks Family Papers, Library of Congress, Manuscript Division, Washington, DC

LHP	Langston Hughes Papers, JWJ MSS 26, Beinecke Rare Book and Manuscript Library, Yale University, New Haven, CT
MFP	Michel Fabre Papers, MSS 932, Manuscript, Archives, and Rare Book Library, Emory University, Atlanta, GA
RG 59	Record Group 59, National Archives, College Park, MD
RG 84	Record Group 84, National Archives, College Park, MD
RWP	Richard Wright Papers, JWJ MSS 3, Beinecke Rare Book and Manuscript Library, Yale University, New Haven, CT
WHHP	William Henry Hunt Papers, Manuscript Division, Moorland-Spingarn Research Center, Howard University, Washington, DC

Microfilm and Other Published Papers

BTWP	*The Booker T. Washington Papers.* 13 vols. Ed. Louis R. Harlan and Raymond W. Smock. Urbana: U of Illinois P, 1972–1989.
DBP	*The Papers of W. E. B. Du Bois (1877–1963).* Microfilm. Sanford, NC: Microfilming Corporation of America, 1980–1981.
DUSCSD	*Despatches from United States Consuls in Santo Domingo.* Microfilm. Washington, DC: National Archives, 1959–1962.
DUSMH	*Despatches from United States Ministers to Haiti, 1862–1906.* Microfilm. Washington, DC: National Archives, 1944.
DUSCSP	*Despatches from United States Consuls in St. Paul de Loanda, 1854–93.* Microfilm. Washington, DC: National Archives, 1962.
GCP	*Grover Cleveland Papers.* Microfilm. Washington, DC: Library of Congress, 1958.
PRFR	*Papers Relating to the Foreign Relations of the United States, with the Annual Message of the President, Transmitted to Congress, December 4, 1893.* Washington, DC: GPO, 1894.

Artistic Ambassadors

Introduction: The Politics of New Negro Literary Culture and the Culture of US International Politics

The end of the 1930s found African American writer Richard Wright conceiving of his literary predecessors via the trope of international diplomacy. In his famous 1937 essay "Blueprint for Negro Writing," he wrote, "Generally speaking, Negro writing in the past has been confined to . . . prim and decorous ambassadors who went a-begging to white America. They entered the Court of American Public Opinion dressed in the knee-pants of servility, curtsying to show that the Negro was not inferior, that he was human, and that he had a life comparable to that of other people. For the most part these artistic ambassadors were received as . . . French poodles who do clever tricks" (53). In referring to his predecessors as "artistic ambassadors," Wright drew negative attention to the African American literary tradition that looked toward black authorship as a mode of speaking on behalf of the race. To Wright's mind, the old structures of artistic ambassadorship threatened to obstruct the cultural and literary (re)construction project that he himself envisioned for the future of African American writing. Yet in spite of the anti-ambassadorial stance Wright upheld in "Blueprint," this era did not find him uniformly hostile to the ambassadorial tradition. Within a few years, he would praise Langston Hughes, whose role had been "that of a cultural ambassador." "Performing his task . . . almost casually," Wright glowingly reported, Hughes had "represented the Negroes' case, in his poems, plays, . . . and novels, at the court of world opinion" ("Forerunner" 600). Hughes had "carried on a manly tradition in literary expression" (601).

Clearly, in Wright's eyes, the black writers who preceded him had at some moments acted heroically and at other moments pathetically, but the notion of ambassadorship brought coherence to their range of performances.

In Wright's deployment of the metaphor of ambassadorship as he issued both stinging criticism and high praise, he was reaching for a performance category adequate to accessing the nexus of racial and literary representational concerns that culminated in what has been conceptualized as the New Negro era.[1] Running from the late nineteenth century through the 1930s, the New Negro era is a cultural and literary-historical designation encompassing the famed Harlem or New Negro Renaissance of the 1920s and 1930s and extending back to claim much of what Charles W. Chesnutt and others have described as African America's "Post-Bellum–Pre-Harlem" era.[2] Especially from the 1890s through the 1930s, black US writers and cultural figures foregrounded discussions of themselves and their colleagues as speaking for and to other constituencies. They saw themselves as elite spokespersons on behalf of the black masses, and they sought an audience with white America specifically and the international world more generally. Alternately artistic and cultural, casual and prim, solicitous and assertive, they were ambassadors seeking to expound on and negotiate African America's case in the courts of American and world opinion. Consequently, as Wright's narratives implicitly theorized, African America was a national actor in an international world. In uneven ways, New Negro writers and cultural figures assumed the role of statesmen speaking to an international community of states and national populations.

This book takes its title from the language Wright used as he gestured toward the similarities between New Negro writers and international diplomats, elucidating a widely misrecognized yet profoundly influential tradition of African American internationalism. Structural similarities between the performances of international diplomats and New Negro writers were not simply casual or coincidental; rather, these similarities arose out of a largely unacknowledged set of political, racial, and literary circumstances that promoted an intense interweaving of the politics of New Negro literary culture and the culture of US international politics. From the 1860s through the 1930s, the United States deployed scores of black diplomatic ministers, consuls, and other officials to locales in Africa, Asia, Europe, the Caribbean, and Latin America. This unprecedented era of black work in US diplomacy began with the postbellum appointment of black ministers to Liberia and Haiti in the late 1860s and early 1870s.[3] As the nineteenth century advanced, so too did US presidents' interest in courting and rewarding black voting constituencies. This interest led the State Department of the late nineteenth century to offer broadened opportunities to African Americans who were willing to represent the United States in nations and colonies of color. With the initial years of the twentieth century, the era of New Negro work in diplomacy reached its heyday as the Theodore Roosevelt administration counseled with Booker T. Washington, who helped arrange for consular appointments that sent African Americans to posts throughout the world. The black presence in US diplomacy was largely maintained during the William Howard Taft administration, but it came under siege with the Woodrow Wilson State Department's mixture of party politics and race prejudice. New Negro work in official diplomacy further waned during the interwar years of the 1920s and 1930s.[4]

Among the scores of influential black professionals who traveled internationally on behalf of the State Department were numerous writers of prominence whose work during the New Negro era evinced a vibrant interest in experimenting with the structural overlaps and homologies among the spheres of literary, racial, and international representation. Frederick Douglass's description of his diplomatic work in Haiti from 1889 to 1891 offered the nascent New Negro era an 1893 edition of *Life and Times* that became the first autobiography to describe the representationally fraught experiences of a black US diplomat. James Weldon Johnson's work as a US consul in Venezuela and Nicaragua (from 1906 to 1913) aided him in transitioning from the career of a popular songwriter to life as a prominent member of the black intelligentsia. During his six years as a consul, Johnson published his novel *The Autobiography of an Ex-Colored Man* (1912) and drafted most of his first volume of poetry, *Fifty Years & Other Poems* (1917). Famed literary and cultural arbiter W. E. B. Du Bois also made his appearance on the roster of US diplomatic representatives. From December 1923 through January 1924, Du Bois spent a month as President Calvin Coolidge's envoy extraordinary and minister plenipotentiary to Liberia, and Du Bois's 1928 novel *Dark Princess* brought his theorizations of international representation into conversation with his project of literary representation.[5]

As prominent race men such as Douglass, Johnson, and Du Bois represented the United States internationally, they did so side by side with dozens of other influential (if currently lesser-known) African American cultural figures, many of whom complemented their careers in international representation with corresponding work in literary and racial representation. Douglass's 1893 edition of *Life and Times*, for instance, was followed by autobiographies by John Mercer Langston (minister to Haiti from 1877 to 1885) and Mifflin Wistar Gibbs (consul in Madagascar from 1898 to 1901). Like Douglass, Langston and Gibbs devoted important attention to describing the ironies and difficulties of being a black US representative abroad. Johnson's *The Autobiography of an Ex-Colored Man* shares a representational genealogy with novels by John Stephens Durham (minister to Haiti from 1891 to 1893) and George Washington Ellis (secretary of legation in Liberia from 1902 to 1910). Like Johnson, Stephens and Ellis brought international diplomacy to bear on the literary project of racial diplomacy. Du Bois's *Dark Princess* shares diplomatic and Pan-Africanist preoccupations with the poetry of Ida Gibbs Hunt, who was the wife of black US consul William Henry Hunt and who co-organized with Du Bois the Pan-African Congresses of 1919 and 1923. Meanwhile, the types of diplomatic scripts that Douglass, Johnson, and Du Bois followed and departed from found literary theorization in the dramatic works of playwrights Henry Francis Downing (consul in Angola from 1887 to 1888) and Angelina Weld Grimké, daughter of Archibald Grimké (consul in Santo Domingo from 1894 to 1898).

This constellation of New Negro artistic ambassadors is not a political and literary community created ex post facto by the present imposition of the ambassadorial metaphors that Wright deployed at the end of the 1930s. This generation of black writer-diplomats and their families generally hailed from a cohesive African American middle class. They tended to know and keep track of others of African descent who, like themselves, found their way into a mode of New Negro racial representation that relied on intersecting lines of literary and international representation. Mifflin Wistar Gibbs, consul in Madagascar, was the father of Pan-African Congress organizer Ida Gibbs Hunt, who married her father's consular successor. Ida and William Henry Hunt's marriage was attended by Angelina and Archibald Grimké. Henry Francis Downing was the nephew of Douglass's friend George T. Downing and claimed to be Douglass's godson. John Mercer Langston was the great-uncle and namesake of Wright's cultural ambassador, Langston Hughes. Archibald Grimké's brother, Francis Grimké, with whom Angelina was left during Archibald's consular work in Santo Domingo, was Ida Gibbs Hunt's pastor and friend before she left Washington to join her husband in Madagascar. John Stephens Durham preceded Archibald as a consul in Santo Domingo and succeeded Douglass as minister in Haiti, and it was a conflict over the same bridge in Santo Domingo that brought Durham into contact with José Martí and brought Archibald his greatest consular success. Ida Gibbs Hunt reviewed Downing's novel in the pages of the *Journal of Negro History*, and James Weldon Johnson's friends Charles Anderson and Booker T. Washington sought to remove Ida's husband from his post in France so they could request that Johnson be sent in his stead. After Johnson's consulships, his literary work shared space in the *Crisis*'s monthly "List of Selected Books" with the works of Downing and Ellis. Meanwhile, Downing, in an aside within his novel, referred to Ellis's office in Liberia as "a sinecure of the most scandalous kind," and Ellis, writing to black politician Theophile T. Allain, omitted Downing's name while listing Douglass, Durham, Langston, Hunt, Johnson, and others as African Americans who had distinguished themselves in US diplomacy.[6] Whether or not their fame has persisted into the early twenty-first century, these diplomats and their family members were almost uniformly distinguished and influential cultural arbiters of the New Negro era.

Recovering and analyzing the mutually shaping literary and diplomatic dossiers produced by this cadre of black writer-diplomats, *Artistic Ambassadors* is a meeting place for a variety of texts and cultural formations that have not traditionally come into contact. On one hand, famous and little-known writers and texts enter into dialogue: novels by Du Bois, Durham, Johnson, and Ellis cross paths with Downing's farce-comedy, Gibbs Hunt's lyric poetry, Angelina Grimké's lynching drama, Wright's travel writings, and autobiographical writings by Douglass, Gibbs, and Langston. On the other hand, literary texts meet with unsuspected diplomatic and political contexts, as letters to the State Department meet with the aesthetic concerns of New Negro arts and letters, as gaps in the diplomatic archive speak to gaps in literary narration, as dramatic scripts negotiate with diplomatic scripts, and as the poetry of revolution shakes hands with the political poetics of revolution.

By orchestrating such meetings, *Artistic Ambassadors* traces the epoch-shaping intersections of literary, racial, and international representation that both Americanized and internationalized the trope of the New Negro. This is a decades-long dialogic relationship between the politics of African American literary culture and the culture of the United States' official international politics. As US presidents courted their black voting constituencies by appointing black men to diplomatic posts, black work in US diplomacy changed the complexion of the United States' interactions with nations and colonies of color. Many of the black writer-diplomats cut their representational teeth in the service of a United States that flexed its postbellum muscles in the Caribbean and certified its imperial status via the Spanish-American War. They contemplated international and literary representation as the United States invigorated its hemispheric presence by means of the Roosevelt Corollary and as the country moved toward international leadership in the wake of the First World War. State-sponsored black travel and international involvement gave rise to literary and other writing that pivotally imported foundational structures of international representation into New Negro discourse on aesthetic and racial representation. Over the course of six chapters, then, *Artistic Ambassadors* outlines the ways in which black work in diplomacy played previously unsuspected roles in shaping major African American representational concerns, including the capacity of New Negro race men to speak for the nation's black masses, the methods of race representation under dispute in the Booker T. Washington–W. E. B. Du Bois debate, and the signifying status of women and the black diaspora within domestic and international African American cultures. These important representational currents culminated in what I (borrowing from Langston Hughes) refer to as *hip-to-macy*, or a hip racial, aesthetic, and political formation that attempted to draw on and reconfigure the logic of official internationalism for the benefit of African America, black diasporan populations, and the West more generally. The hip-to-matic practices of the New Negro era eventually came to play formative and destabilizing roles in the racial logic of the United States' Cold War development of a cultural diplomacy that contributed to an incipient neoliberal order. Access to this complex legacy of the New Negro era has special urgency during a post-9/11 moment that has seen the United States' first two black secretaries of state and the election of its first black president, who is at once the country's chief international representative and the writer of an international bestseller that has drawn the attention of literary writers and scholars.[7]

Diplomatic Encounters and Weak Ambassadorship

Interrogating the international and literary projects of New Negro figures ranging from the hypercanonical to the nearly forgotten, this book offers a conceptual meeting place for encounters among three scholarly fields that frequently overlap in terms of subject matter: African American literary studies, studies in black transnationalism, and the new American studies. In recent years, these fields have come into productive dialogue with one another, and critical focus on the New Negro diplomats requires an intensification of this dialogue along specific lines. Running from Robert Stepto's classic *From Behind the Veil* (1979) to Candice M. Jenkins's *Private Lives, Proper Relations* (2007), African American literary studies have often looked within US borders to analyze the constitution of a literary tradition that is both black and American. In complement to such studies, my project brings critical attention to a distinctly American literary and cultural tradition that has been contingent on travel beyond the borders of the United States. This is a vibrant tradition produced by African American intersections and preoccupations with locales including Haiti, the Dominican Republic, Nicaragua, Venezuela, Sierra Leon, Liberia, Angola, Madagascar, England, France, Russia, and Indonesia, among others.

In many ways, then, New Negro artistic ambassadorship was a transnational literary and cultural formation. Yet studies in black transnational thought and travel—ranging from Paul Gilroy's *The Black Atlantic* (1993) to Nicole A. Waligora-Davis's *Sanctuary* (2011)—have tended to situate black planetary consciousness as existing in marked conflict with the nation-state. My project, meanwhile, interrogates a major mode of black transnational engagement that took place precisely under the nation-state's auspices. Here, the nation-state became a mechanism that promoted—sometimes unwittingly and sometimes by diplomatic design—a series of transnational identifications among African Americans and people of color living in various parts of the world. Transnational connections, frequently unpredictable and surprising in their offshoots, could at some moments undercut US diplomatic intentions; at other moments, however, these connections could be used as a means of promoting the imperial sway of the United States.

Critiquing the United States' imperial relations with the larger world has emerged, during the past two decades, as a major preoccupation within the field of American studies. As scholars have sought to shed the legacies of American studies' disciplinary roots in Cold War American exceptionalism, they often have approached the United States' continental expansion and international engagements via an anti-imperialist hermeneutics of suspicion. Fittingly, when US imperial interests have come under critique within Americanist scholarship, African American literary writers have found prominent representation as intellectual forerunners of the current scholarly milieu's ethical stance against imperialism.[8] But how might scholars go about describing black work in literary and racial representation that grew out of an international diplomacy aimed at shoring up the United States' imperial influence? Even as I am inspired by the trend toward anti-imperialist critique, this book draws complementary energy from the project of cultural recovery that is more characteristic of African American literary studies and studies in black transnationalism. An interpretive crosshatching—accountable to both suspicion and recovery—offers critical access to a previously unrecognized black internationalist tradition produced as African American and US imperial cultures have met and shaped one another.

As *Artistic Ambassadors* orchestrates dialogues among these three fields, it assumes an ambivalent relationship to official internationalism's convention of the diplomatic encounter, or the meeting held among representatives of nation-states. "Diplomatic encounters," suggests M. M. Bakhtin, are the most noteworthy and emblematic of "real-life chronotope[s]" because they are "always strictly regulated" in "time, place, and makeup." Replete with strictures, Bakhtin explains, diplomatic encounters shift in their spatial and temporal configurations according to protocols that are dependent on the diplomatic ranks and positions of those participating in the meetings (99). Structurally, *Artistic Ambassadors* alludes to the diplomatic encounter's strict regulation inasmuch as the book is divided into three parts, with each part offering two chapters and an introduction discussing the chapters' thematics in relation to important conceptual issues pertaining to the project's major fields. The introductions to parts 1, 2, and 3 are oriented toward conversations surrounding New Negro culture, black transnationalism, and American studies, respectively. While these introductions situate each of the book's parts as conceptually engaged with a specific field, however, the individual chapters nonetheless operate on practical levels that eschew the diplomatic encounter's spirit of strict regulation. For instance, even as part 1 is framed as concerned with the problematic of New Negro representation, the part's chapter on James Weldon Johnson also speaks to issues taken up by studies in black transnationalism and American studies. The other chapters also speak out of turn, denying the diplomatic encounter's insistence on regulation as they weigh in on topics relevant to African American and diplomatic history as well as international politics and modernism. Thus, this study of the New Negro writer-diplomats both resembles and unravels the diplomatic meeting's traditional strictures.

Artistic Ambassadors's operation inside and outside the parameters of the diplomatic encounter is emblematic of the project's importance not only to understanding the engagements of New Negro diplomatic insiders but also to assessing the internationalisms of a broader array of

African American cultural figures and populations who have seemed to work outside of official internationalism. If black diplomats have participated in a strong and formally sanctioned type of ambassadorship, then informal modes of black international travel and commentary have functioned in reference to what might be termed weak ambassadorship. Elucidating the way in which nongovernmental international travel is ineluctably connected to the nation-state's diplomatic apparatus, Jamaican American Harlem Renaissance figure Claude McKay once explained, "An American seaman (white or black) on [a foreign] beach is always treated with a subtle difference by his beach fellows. He has a higher face value than the rest. . . . He has the assurance that, when he gets tired of beaching, his consulate will help him back to the fabulous land of wealth and opportunity" (19). The US citizen (white or black) has a weak ambassadorial privilege that flows through the diplomatic matrices of the US consulates and embassies that dot the planet. This privilege is contingent on what Walter D. Mignolo describes as "imperial and colonial differences," with "consulates and embassies act[ing] like frontiers" that classify and thereby ascribe meaning to these differences ("Citizenship" 323–24). Experiencing the sway of diplomacy's governmental frontiers while living in Paris during the 1950s, Richard Wright came to recognize the demands placed on those who accrue the weak ambassadorial privilege produced by US embassies, consulates, and citizenship. Having once disparaged New Negro writers for speaking as artistic ambassadors, Wright now expressed discomfort with his own set of compromising circumstances. He explained that the State Department was attempting to coerce "any American going abroad" into acting "like an ambassador." "In other words," said Wright, "he's not expected to voice any criticism which might reflect on American policy. If he does, then the State Department [tries] to get him back home as quickly as possible" (Henriques). Wright was experiencing the exigencies of weak ambassadorship.

Of course, the performance imperatives of weak ambassadorship are a far cry from the rigid imperatives of diplomatic delegation, which Edmund Burke once outlined as requiring "ambassadors" to receive "*authoritative* instructions [which they are] bound blindly to obey . . . and to argue for, though contrary to the clearest conviction of [their] judgment and conscience" (110). Rather, weak ambassadorship moves away from mandate-based representation and toward standing symbolically and informally for others on one's own terms. And yet because the weak ambassadorial tradition of unofficial African American internationalism inevitably draws on and reconfigures the logic of official internationalism, a study of the New Negro writer-diplomats promises to have ramifications for international currents in broader spheres of black internationalist writing and travel. During the New Negro era, such writing ranges from Sutton E. Griggs's *Imperium in Imperio* (1899) to Eric Walrond's *Tropic Death* (1926) to Jessie Redmon Fauset's *Comedy: American Style* (1933) to Zora Neale Hurston's *Tell My Horse* (1938). Spanning the longer temporal trajectory of African American letters, relevant internationalist moments extend from Phillis Wheatley's decorous eighteenth-century poetic address to England's secretary of state for North America, to Amiri Baraka's post-9/11 poem "Somebody Blew Up America," which is not inclined toward decorum as it links the United States' first two black secretaries of state to domestic and international terrorism (epigraph, and 189–90). Strong and weak, formal and informal, connections between official internationalism and African American culture have been pervasive, with canonical and lesser-known New Negro writer-diplomats functioning as major shuttles between the two. In tracing the resulting interconnections, *Artistic Ambassadors* speaks to the expansive arenas in which peripatetic black writers and texts have found uneasy constituencies and audiences in African America and white America, in the black diaspora and in wider worlds of color.

PART I

Representative Characters

The New Negro's Representative Elements and Official Internationalism

Arriving on the heels of the nineteenth-century heyday of blackface minstrelsy, the years of the 1890s through the 1930s witnessed a struggle on the part of many African Americans to wrest the role of black race representation from white America. This was a struggle against what came to be known as the Old Negro, a myth and formula that circulated as the condensation of minstrelesque figures ranging from Jim Crow to Zip Coon, from Rastus to Sambo, and from Uncle Tom to Aunt Jemima. Calling on black writers and artists to combat the degrading legacies of the Old Negro, W. E. B. Du Bois proposed the following thought experiment: "Suppose the only Negro who survived some centuries hence was the Negro painted by white Americans in the novels and essays they have written. What would people in a hundred years say of black Americans? Now turn it around. Suppose you were to write a story and put in the kind of people you know and like and imagine" ("Criteria" 296). For many black American writers of this era, the kind of people to know and like and imagine circulated under the banner of the New Negro, a discursive formation seeking to supplant "the Negro painted by white Americans." The trope of the New Negro offered an image conflating blackness with urban sophistication, educational attainment, middle-class poise, and economic success. For many members of the black intelligentsia, using writing and art to evoke these qualities—and indeed performing these qualities bodily—was supposed to argue for a black humanity meriting the full rights of US citizenship.

If middle-class poise was less than typical among the masses of black US citizens who were only one generation removed from slavery, then the comparatively elite cultural arbiters of the New Negro era sought ways to privilege their own middle-class attributes and performances in the construction of the race's public face. As Alain Locke wrote the introduction for his influential anthology *The New Negro* (1925), he reached for terminology that could, in apparently salutary ways, confuse the category of the demographically typical with the category of the demographically exceptional, which Du Bois famously referred to as the race's talented tenth.[1] Capitalizing on the slippage between *representative* as typical and *representative* as elect, Locke referred to New Negro society as made up of "the more intelligent and representative elements" of the race (9). This play on the term *representative* was a shrewd instance of demographic legerdemain, as on a discursive level it operated to move the talented tenth from the race's margins to the race's center, supplanting the masses' representative character (based on perceived status as typical) with a representative character evoked by exceptional presentability.[2]

Locke, of course, was not alone in working to construct the race's elite as representative, and several scholars have offered genealogies that trace the production of the New Negro's representational relationship to the black masses. Intriguingly, this scholarship points in unexpected ways to the foundational roles played by official international diplomacy in evoking New Negro race representation. J. Martin Favor has astutely pointed toward New Negro writers who sought to write themselves "into a folk positionality" which thereby created an aura of authenticity linking them to the larger racial constituency they sought to represent (12). Favor describes a New Negro culture in which individuals attempted to speak *as* rather than *for* Negroes, a pose permitting speakers to "assert their own unique set of circumstances . . . rather than adhering to a specific representational protocol" (11). If, as Favor implies, the New Negro era saw an impulse toward individual expression that competed with a demand for following representational protocol, then I would argue that the demands of protocol arose in part through numerous New Negro interactions with the strictures of official international relations. Through years of work as US diplomatic and consular officials, major race representatives including Frederick Douglass, John Mercer Langston, Mifflin

Wistar Gibbs, and John Stephens Durham helped promote an intense and reciprocal relationship between the protocols of international relations and New Negro strategies for interracial relations.

Offering a genealogy that is in some ways allied with Favor's, Barbara Foley has pointed toward the volkish tropes of region and soil as assuming special significance in the New Negro representational matrix. Foley describes New Negro writers as relying on metaphors of soil to evoke a *metonymic nationalism*, a nationalism asserting "that African Americans might 'stand for' the nation as ably as any other group—that they might figure metonymically to signify the whole" (ix). At one point, Foley illustrates metonymic nationalism's rootedness in the soil by quoting from James Weldon Johnson's poem "Fifty Years" (1913), which argues that

> This land is ours by right of birth,
> This land is ours by right of toil.
> We helped to turn its virgin earth
> Our sweat is in its fruitful soil.[3]

As Foley accurately points out, Johnson here relies on earth and soil to argue for black "inclusion within the inherited system of property ownership" (192). But what of the international and metonymically nationalistic performance that Johnson was engaging in as he wrote this poem? "Fifty Years" was composed, after all, while Johnson toiled far from US soil. He wrote it while working as a US consul in Nicaragua, where his dual status as a metonymic US representative and a metonymic race representative permitted international diplomacy to provisionally frame African Americans as representative of the nation.[4] This provisional framing, as chapter 2 discusses, equipped Johnson with a set of diplomatic methods he imported into the Harlem Renaissance.

In gesturing toward the diplomatic contexts of Favor's and Foley's narratives of New Negro representation, I am interested in drawing attention to the ways in which even the most seemingly domestic of representational mechanisms (i.e., folk and soil) have come into dialogue with and been undergirded by the internationalist formations produced by racial and literary representation's convergence with official diplomatic representation.[5] Examining the converging literary and diplomatic work of the black writer-diplomats opens new vistas in relation to what Henry Louis Gates, Jr., and Gene Andrew Jarrett have described as *New Negro politics*, a critical paradigm emphasizing the intense interdependencies of the politics of New Negro aesthetic representation and the culture of New Negro political representation (6–7). While Gates and Jarrett point specifically toward a New Negro political culture involving legislative and judicial efforts as well as Garveyism and left-wing radicalism (6, 8–9), their casual description of Alain Locke's "ambassadorial status" (8) is a reminder that the ambassadorial tradition in African American writing has remained uninterrogated in relation to one of the New Negro era's major arenas of political culture. This political culture operated on the planetary scale of official internationalism, and it became co-constitutive with the cultural politics of New Negro artistic ambassadorship.

1 / The Negro Beat: "Distinguished Colored Men" and Their Representative Characters

Frederick Douglass has been credited with many firsts, but when President Benjamin Harrison appointed him US minister to Haiti in July 1889, he was by no means the first black US diplomat. With African Americans' postbellum emergence as a voting constituency, US presidents and other officials looked for visible means of courting the so-called Negro vote, and appointing black diplomats functioned to curry favor with black voters while capitulating to the prejudices of white Americans who disliked seeing black citizens assume positions of prominence inside the United States. The first African American diplomat of this era was Ebenezer Don Carlos Basset, appointed minister to Haiti in 1869. Two years later, Basset was followed by John Milton Turner, who became the minister to Liberia. For decades thereafter, Haiti and Liberia remained the particular—and only—preserves of black US citizens working as diplomatic ministers. Meanwhile, African American consuls were sent to a wider variety of posts, but they nonetheless tended to find themselves working in regions of color.[1] These black nations and regions of color became known in State Department circles as the "Negro beat" or "Negro circuit."[2]

When in 1889 Douglass became a black appointee within the State Department's Negro beat, he was already well acquainted with the role of representative. Douglass had long been famous as African America's preeminent spokesperson and representative, with the successes of his life taken by many people as proof of the nobility and capacity of African Americans more generally. In many ways, his late-life appointment to represent the United States in Haiti seemed to affirm and cement the representative tenor of his life, but as this chapter later explains, his diplomatic work in the Caribbean produced a crisis of representation among many white US citizens, leading to his premature resignation in 1891.

Operating in the context of a much later crisis of representation, recent literary critics have also been concerned with Douglass's status as a representative. Bringing focus to the constructed and nonessential quality of Douglass's enduring position as a race representative, Deborah E. McDowell and Henry Louis Gates, Jr., have genealogized and critiqued an ingrained commonplace that situates Douglass as *the* representative head and father of the African American literary tradition. Clearly, argue McDowell and Gates, the representative persona that Douglass self-consciously constructed during his lifetime is too often taken as natural by today's literary-critical establishment, which leads toward a disproportionate emphasis on Douglass and an undue marginalization of many other early African American writers.[3] Though such observations arise specifically in response to the ways the African American literary tradition has been assessed, they nonetheless hold true for scholarly approaches to black participation in the United States' international diplomacy. Douglass was one of many figures participating in the State Department's Negro beat, but his diplomatic work has received more consideration in scholarly articles, book chapters, and other publications than that of any other black US diplomat. He stands alone as the only African American diplomat whose oeuvre of State Department dispatches has been collected and published in book form.[4]

To be sure, Douglass's work as a US minister must be regarded as a significant moment within the trajectory of African American participation in US diplomacy. His fame brought then (as it does now) heightened visibility to his work in Haiti, and his final autobiography, *Life and Times* (1893), was the first African American autobiography to address its author's work as a US diplomat. But informed by the literary-critical preoccupation with the limits of Douglass's representative capacity, I want to refrain from positioning his diplomatic and autobiographical work as a mythic and emblematic beginning for African American literature and culture's interactions with official internationalism. Rather, Douglass's ambassadorship must be regarded as one of many constitutive elements within a rich tradition that will remain far from finding adequate summary or representation in any one figure. Accessing this tradition requires Douglass's supplementation. Drawing increased attention toward writings by figures including John Mercer Langston,

Mifflin Wistar Gibbs, John Stephens Durham, Paul Laurence Dunbar, and Charles W. Chesnutt contributes to a view of an early New Negro political culture that framed diplomatic service as a singularly important means for African American men to attain or affirm their status as race representatives. As these writings reveal, however, status as an American representative abroad did not convert easily into status as a representative American at home.

From "Negro Representatives" to "Representative Negroes"

During a lecture given shortly after the Civil War, Douglass lamented that "great actions" by people of African descent "have not been sufficient to change the general estimate formed of the colored race." Explaining this insufficiency, he remarked that white Americans had denied any representational link between highly accomplished African Americans and the United States' larger black population: "the public . . . has sternly denied the representative character of our distinguished men. They are treated as exceptions, individual cases, and the like" (*Life and Writings* 4: 179). Douglass's postbellum lecture treads on the same ground as Richard Wright's later account of the New Negro era's "artistic ambassadors." Both writers describe a group of distinguished African Americans who perform for a predominantly white US public with the hope of changing the public's perception of the United States' larger black population. As these distinguished figures perform in the court of American public opinion, they are treated as what Douglass calls "exceptions, individual cases" or as what Wright calls "poodles who do clever tricks" ("Blueprint" 53). Yet in spite of Douglass's and Wright's analogous accounts of the black presence within the US public sphere, their narratives evince preoccupations that diverge from each other in ways that are structured by a contrast between retrospect and prospect. In reading the New Negro era retrospectively, Wright describes distinguished African Americans as "ambassadors," a term presupposing their representative capacity. Douglass, in contrast, speaks from a position of prospect, some years before the full emergence of the ambassadorial tradition that Wright disparages. Douglass does not have the luxury of assuming a representational link between African America's "distinguished men" and the nation's black masses. Hence, while Wright's retrospective account speaks condescendingly of the race representatives' decorum, recourse to Douglass's lecture reminds us that the question of representative character—or the very *ambassadorship* of Wright's New Negro ambassadors—has been a central point of struggle and contestation among the United States' black and white populations. This conflict over representation was a central concern of Douglass's life project, as he spent his career working to affirm his own representative character, without which, he knew, even his greatest successes must remain disconnected from the masses of African Americans.[5]

In ways that are less immediately evident than Wright's reliance on the trope of ambassadorship, Douglass's use of the term *representative character* draws on the conventions of international diplomacy in its description of African America's relations with the white US public. The theory of "representative character," in fact, has been foundational to—and to a large extent innovated by—the very notion of ambassadorship. As international law scholar Jeffrey K. Walker explains, "Very early in the history of the use of envoys, dating back at least to the Greeks, a general norm arose based on religious precepts that envoys of all kinds . . . stood in the shoes of—indeed were an extension of the *person* of—the sovereign who sent them" (244). By the eighteenth century, this "envoy-sovereign relationship" was "widely known as *representative character*," and while the Enlightenment largely purged the trope of its basis in religion, the notion of representative character persisted as the "legal fiction" that representationally bound diplomatic envoys to their sovereigns and states (252). According to this fiction, "the relationship of the ambassador to his principal was so close that an injury to the ambassador was deemed to have been inflicted upon his prince" (Ogdon 54).

The diplomatic theory of representative character maintained international and cultural currency throughout the nineteenth century and well into the twentieth—with the prince becoming, in the American context, the democratically elected president or more generally the sovereign nation itself. Mark Twain drew on this fiction in his short story "Diplomatic Pay and Clothes" (1899), in which the narrator asserts that diplomats must be adequately paid and appropriately dressed because "our representative is . . . the Republic. He is the United States of America" (402). James Weldon Johnson also alluded to this diplomatic fiction in his autobiography, which recounts an episode during which Johnson accidentally captures at gunpoint a delegate of the Nicaraguan president. The delegate charges Johnson "with having placed under arrest the President of Nicaragua," and Johnson concedes this point as "virtually true" (*Along* 280), or true via the fiction of representative character. Explaining the political ramifications of representative character, novelist and diplomat George Washington Ellis wrote to a friend that when a representative's "rank is that of ambassador he represents the person of the President and violence toward him is casus belli."[6] In this relationship of virtual oneness between the representative and the represented, the nation's wishes and ambitions theoretically determine the representative's speech during a diplomatic encounter; however, in what Jacques Derrida might describe as a perverse spirit of supplementarity, the fiction of representative character permits the representative's status virtually to determine the status of the nation.[7] Or—as highlighted in Twain's, Johnson's, and Ellis's writings—an impoverished, captive, or assaulted representative reconstitutes the nation itself as impoverished, captive, or assaulted.

When Douglass, in his lecture, implicitly argued for the "representative character" of the race's distinguished men, he was not directly gesturing toward questions of international relations. Instead, like Wright, he was deploying an internationally oriented metaphor to comment on the status of black race representation in the United States. Douglass was lamenting that African America's "distinguished men" were faced with the difficult task of certifying their representative capacity before they could suppose that their accomplishments would attain representational purchase in the court of American public opinion. Several studies of African American culture have examined the emergence of this representational capacity and the means of affixing it to the figures whom Wright described as African America's ambassadors. Scholars have pointed toward black prestige, racial uplift, black skin, black masculinity, and other signs as cultural markers that have been foundational to the economy of US race representation.[8] In a wider diasporic context, Paul Gilroy has suggested that work in aesthetic representation almost inevitably doubles as work in race representation. "The idea that artists are representative public figures," Gilroy observes, hinges on "the tension between the two quite different senses of a word [i.e., *representation*] which refers not just to depiction but to the idea of delegation or substitution" (*Small* 98).

Gilroy's attentiveness to intersecting modes of representation helps bring focus to a factor that usually has fallen outside the purview of humanities-based approaches to black race representation: if artistic representation melds readily into racial delegation, then racial delegation also has been forged out of official *political* delegation. Classic sociological studies of race leadership have acknowledged this point. In *Black Metropolis* (1945), St. Clair Drake and Horace R. Cayton frame "Race Leaders" as partially constituted by "elected and appointed politicians who 'represent The Race'" (392). Oliver C. Cox, in his essay "Leadership among Negroes in the United States" (1950), emphasizes the "emergence and political articulation of the black statesmen" as a significant facet of race leadership (235). Similarly, Ralph Bunche, in his 1940 study of "Negro leadership," remarks that "there is no single Negro leader in the country" (52) but lists the "Negro politician" as one of African America's leadership types (118). To such observations on the convergence of race leadership and political office-holding, I would add that Bunche's own dramatic rise within the ranks of race leadership (via his work as a politician within the US State Department and the United Nations during the 1940s) had its major precedent during the New Negro era of the late nineteenth and early twentieth centuries. During this earlier era, appointments to represent the United States internationally became especially powerful political signifiers of African American men's racially representative status. Because the postbellum State Department appointed African Americans to higher positions than did any other branch of the federal government, work in diplomacy afforded black men of the New Negro era with exceptionally significant opportunities to assert or affirm their status as race representatives.[9] New Negro diplomats were, in effect, drawing representative character from the original source, from the arena of official internationalism to which Douglass had referred metaphorically in his postbellum lecture.[10]

The writings of black diplomats, together with commentary by other black cultural and political figures of the era, attest to the ways in which diplomatic service assured or cemented African American men's status as race representatives. Douglass underscored the importance of his work in international representation by privileging it in the closing sentence of *Life and Times.* As if crowning his final autobiography, he described his "appointment by President Benjamin Harrison to the office of Minister Resident and Consul-General to represent the United States . . . [in] Haïti" as one of his "crowning honors" and "a fitting and happy close to [his] whole public life" (1045). It is indeed fitting that *Life and Times* positions Douglass's work in international representation as the crowning achievement of his life. Within the autobiography's narrative arc, Douglass's bill of sale attests to his status as a "freeman" (700), and his passport allows him to be "everywhere recognized as an American" (1014). Now, the closing sentence uses diplomatic representation to give an official stamp to the representative character he long worked to affirm.[11]

Similar to Douglass, John Mercer Langston, who was the second African American to detail his diplomatic service in an autobiography, lost no opportunity to remind readers of his representative work as the US minister to Haiti from 1877 to 1885. Published after a long career that also included work as an abolitionist and lawyer, *From the Virginia Plantation to the National Capitol* (1894) places a fine point on Langston's multiple representative roles in Haiti. Pivotally, Langston decided to narrate his autobiography from the third-person point of view, which heightens his ability to emphasize his representative capacity. Rather than referring to himself as "I," he repeatedly refers to himself as "the American minister" (359–95), "the United States consul-general" (380), and "the representative of the United States" (358, 395). Langston further foregrounds his status as a representative by emphasizing that in Haiti he held multiple representative roles. He was simultaneously "the diplomat, the consul-general, and the consul of his government" (378), and he occasionally served in a fourth representative role as the United States' "*chargé d'affaires* [to] . . . the government of Santo Domingo" (396). In fact, within the autobiography, Langston emerges as the representatives' representative. His earlier legal training permitted him to become the leader of the international diplomatic corps in Haiti—the "dean" of "the representatives of all the foreign governments residing at [that] time in the Republic of Haïti" (385, 388).

Following the diplomatic accounts of Douglass and Langston, Mifflin Wistar Gibbs's autobiography *Shadow and Light* (1902) quite directly links its writer's diplomatic work to his status as a race representative. Gibbs worked in Madagascar from 1898 to 1901, and during his "years abroad," "the thought occurred that [he] had had a varied career," the "portrayal [of which] might be of benefit to those who, eager for advancement, are willing to be laborious students to attain worthy ends" (xxi). Though he had been a prominent politician in Arkansas and the American West, it was apparently his consular work that convinced him his career could be taken as an improving model for the lives of others. He wrote much of his autobiography in Madagascar, and he devoted over a quarter of the volume to a four-year consulship that made up just a twentieth of his life to that point.[12] This disproportionate representation of his work in diplomacy reveals that, to Gibbs's mind, work as a US representative was exceptionally important to his identity as a representative of African Americans' potential for advancement.

Douglass, Langston, and Gibbs were not alone in implying that work in international representation certified one's work in race representation. In 1897, black writer Alphonso O. Stafford published a *Boston Evening Transcript* article detailing the history of African American work in US diplomacy. Titled "Negro Representatives," the article listed Douglass and Langston prominently among a score of other black US diplomats and concluded by observing that "their success has convinced the thinking world that the negro of character, learning and aptitude will reflect credit upon himself and his country in whatever field of effort his talents are engaged." Following Stafford in his willingness to position diplomacy's "Negro representatives" as representative Negroes, Paul Laurence Dunbar's 1903 essay "Representative American Negroes" devotes its most extensive coverage to the career of "the Hon. Richard Theodore Greener, our present Consul at Vladivostok" (200). Noting that the "Boxer uprising" had caused Vladivostok to become "one of the [Far East's] most important points of communication with the outside world," Dunbar highlighted Greener's frequent communications with the State Department and remarked that Greener "after years of patience and toil had come into his own" (204). Interestingly, Dunbar immediately thereafter mentions the "delightful autobiography" of "Judge [Mifflin Wistar] Gibbs, a man eighty years of age, but he, too, has kept abreast of the times . . . ; he is, in the race, perhaps, the best representative of what the old has brought to the new" (204–05). Undoubtedly, Gibbs's extended autobiographical account of his consulship played no small part in leading Dunbar to compare him to the US consul and representative Negro then residing in Vladivostok.

The importance of international representation to the project of race representation during the nascent New Negro era finds illustration in the 1883 chromolithograph "Distinguished Colored Men" (fig. 1), which visually distills the race's representative men down to what it presents as the eleven most distinguished. The illustration situates Douglass prominently among ten other African Americans, almost all of whom are listed as gaining their distinction through office-holding. The lithograph includes P. B. S. Pinchback as the ex-governor of Louisiana; it lists J. H. Rainey, Robert Brown Elliot, and Blanche K. Bruce as former senators and members of Congress. Henry Highland Garnet, Ebenezer Don Carlos Basset, and John Mercer Langston are showcased as gaining their distinction through work as US ministers to Haiti and Liberia. Meanwhile, Richard T. Greener and Frederick Douglass, here listed as dean of Howard University and "The Colored Champion of Freedom," before the turn of the century cemented their status as representative African Americans through what Douglass might call "crowning honors"—diplomatic work in Haiti and Vladivostok. "Distinguished Colored Men" condenses the greater part of African American distinction

FIGURE 1. "Distinguished Colored Men." (Courtesy of the Library of Congress)

into office-holding, and significantly, five of its eleven picks for African America's most distinguished men worked as diplomats. Of course, the preponderance of diplomats within "Distinguished Colored Men" is as much a reflection of the profession's high prestige as it is a reflection of the federal government's and US public's unwillingness to see black men assume positions of similar prestige within the United States. Cognizant of the diplomat's celebrated opportunity to stand as an "equal with the president of a [foreign] republic" (McFeely 353), one of the era's black diplomats explained that work as a US minister was "all [he could] hope for from politics in the way of . . . prominence"; seeking available positions in the United States would only cause him to "go backwards."[13]

Central to the interlocking arenas of international and racial representation are what Hazel V. Carby calls "the male-centered assumptions at work in . . . claims of representativeness" (5). We see a diplomatically driven naturalization of these masculinist assumptions in an 1894 letter written by John Stephens Durham. Just seven months after concluding his diplomatic work in the Caribbean, Durham sent a letter to the *New York Times* in which he criticized African American activist Ida B. Wells for her antilynching campaign in England.[14] Wells had reportedly told the British press that "in all these cases where negroes are summarily punished for outrages on white women it is the women themselves who have tempted the blacks, the latter being punished only when the men of the woman's family have discovered the scandal." Durham argued against Wells by using a diplomatically generated narrative regarding a person's capacity to speak on behalf of African America. Conspicuously drawing on the trope that had only recently permitted him to represent the United States in Haiti, Durham stated, "The person [Wells] who is reported as having made the charge against Southern women may safely be said to have no representative character." Instead, he suggested that he himself "represent[ed] the intelligent public sentiment of the colored people" when he denounced Wells's indictment of Southern white women (Mans and Durham). Durham was at the moment still famous for his service as a US minister, and his presumed capacity to speak for African Americans (and to deny the representative character of others) undoubtedly flowed from his work in international representation. Furthermore, Durham's description of Wells as lacking representative character underscores the gendered quality of the era's diplomatically generated narrative of race representation. Like Durham, Wells could travel and speak internationally, but unlike Durham, she could not base claims to representative character on the official nature of that speech and travel. Rather, because the State Department did not admit women to the Foreign Service until 1922, Wells's gender framed her as ontologically ineligible to draw on the source of representative character that created or cemented the representative status of such "distinguished colored men" as Douglass, Langston, Gibbs, and Greener.[15] Durham's letter to the *New York Times* is emblematic of black diplomats' journey from "Negro representative" abroad to "representative Negro" at home, and it offers a vivid reminder of the gendered exclusions written into the interlocking logics of racial and international representation.

Hybrid Representatives and American Myths

While black US diplomats were generally successful in converting international representation into credit in the arena of race representation, they always had their eyes on a horizon that was much more difficult to reach. They hoped that work as American representatives would permit them to emerge as representative Americans, a status that would certify their own entitlement (as well as the entitlement of their African American constituency) to the rights of full US citizenship. Diplomatic performance, in other words, was an effort at renarrating and reconstituting the nation they represented; it was, to borrow language from Homi K. Bhabha, an effort at changing the United States' narrative of itself so as to render it capable of "incorporating new 'people' in relation to the body politic," capable of forming "a chiasmatic 'figure'" in which black and white cultural differences merged and the "ambivalent nation-space [became] the crossroads to a new transnational culture" ("Introduction" 4). The obstacles to reconstituting the United States as a crossroads for its black and white national populations were formidable: lynching and the intransigent logic of the Jim Crow regime sought to keep black and white populations and institutions running along parallel and unequal lines. However, black work in official internationalism offered a theoretical means of throwing black and white populations off their parallel tracks and conducing toward an intersection. The notion of representative character—to the degree that the representative's status virtually determines the status of the represented nation—would suggest that black US diplomats' performances abroad could reconstitute the United States to include rather than to eschew the blackness of its population.

Among Douglass, Gibbs, and Langston, the latter was most aggressive in emphasizing the significance of his status as an *American* representative. Underscoring the diplomatic supplement's reconstitutive power in relation to the nation, Langston wrote that when he arrived in Port-au-Prince, he "found that the American Legation . . . was neither in appearance nor dignity what . . . it ought to be." Because the United States' "sovereignty, power and glory" were "housed in" (and hence contingent on) the legation, Langston exerted "special effort" to bring the building up to a fitting level of dignity (375). Even as he implicitly reminded readers that US sovereignty was contingent on the diplomatic performances of a black man, Langston emphasized that his performances were thoroughly American. He wrote of himself as "an intelligent American, patriotic and loyal," who was proud to represent a constituency of "sixty-five millions of people; the fairest, the richest, the most beautiful country of the earth" (357). Like a good American representative, he celebrated the Fourth of July, the "anniversary of American independence," with a reception and "dinner [that] was American in every feature" (376). He introduced "American blue denims" to the Haitian market, "driving out even English manufacturers" and leading a German merchant to complain "to the American consul-general, 'The Haytians have gone crazy on American blue denims'" (381). Within the economy of an autobiography written in the vein of what Sacvan Bercovitch famously described as the auto-American-biography, Langston's work as an American representative earns him the right to assert himself as a representative American.[16] As if taking a page from Ralph Waldo Emerson's definition of a *representative man* as someone from whom we can learn of ourselves (*Representative* 11), Langston self-positioned as a representative American by dedicating his autobiography "to the young, aspiring American, who . . . would," in imitation of Langston himself, gain "honors and *emoluments by his fellow-citizens*" (v). Similar to Langston's autobiography, though in less pronounced ways, Douglass's *Life and Times* also pushes toward reconstituting the United States as a space of black and white fellow-citizenship. Douglass's autobiography led readers such as Charles Chesnutt to celebrate the way in which Douglass emerges "as the representative of a nation which a few years before had denied him a passport" (*Frederick* 122).

Even as black diplomats hoped to create the United States as a crossroads for white and black populations, their work on the State Department's Negro circuit was implicated in the same segregationist logic that insisted on maintaining separate facilities, neighborhoods, and social institutions for the United States' white and black populations. And because this segregated diplomatic track reflected white US assumptions regarding black inferiority, it functioned to remind black diplomats that their own nation treated its black citizens in ways that resembled the oppressive regimes of empire and colonization that they witnessed in the locales to which they were sent. This promoted a sense of ambivalence regarding the exigencies of state-based patriotism versus a more transnational race-based loyalty. For instance, while Gibbs made his way to Madagascar, he glimpsed the American flag on the US consular residence at Port Said and felt a "baptism of patriotism . . . to see the national banner" (233). Yet of first seeing Africa's eastern coast, he wrote, "On that continent . . . lies the ashes [*sic*] of my forefathers. Peace abide with them, and may peace crowned with justice come to such of their descendants as are still the victims of dishonesty and inhumanity by enlightened and professedly Christian nations" (239). During subsequent comments, Gibbs made clear that he saw the very nation he represented as one of these oppressive and professedly Christian nations. Condemning colonialism, he stated that it was "the French in Madagascar, the English in Africa, and the Americans in the Antilles" (284). Remarking on the Spanish-American War, he drew analogies between "the colored American brother" and "the Cuban and Filipino colored brothers" (283).

Like Gibbs's *Shadow and Light*, Langston's and Douglass's autobiographies also mark black work in US diplomacy as promoting a tension between state-based US nationalism and race-based transnationalism. Through chiasmic descriptions of work in official internationalism, their autobiographies represent black US diplomacy as evocative of an international crossroads that complicates the project of creating the US nation-space as a site for the merging of black and white populations. Langston was elated to see for himself "an actual negro nationality" in Haiti (356). Although he was to represent the United States in "his official and semi-official consular and diplomatic duties," he arrived "in Hayti with open and undisguised sympathies for . . . a people whose national starting-point was so similar to his own as an individual" (400). Langston expressed this intersection of official duties and individual sympathies in the form of a chiasmus: "He was to represent the great Republic of the North, the matchless government of the Anglo-Saxon race, near that of the Black Republic of the South" (358). On the level of content, Langston was merely explaining that he represented the United States in Haiti, but his statement's inverted parallelism—as it intimates an equality between the United States and Haiti as well as between the Anglo-Saxon race and the Black race—gestures toward the competing racial and national exigencies and indices of identity he experienced as a black US diplomat in a black nation.

Suggestive of the ways that such ambivalences could fray into real or perceived reversals of loyalty, the conclusion of Douglass's *Life and Times* also brings Haiti and the United States into a chiasmic relationship. While representing the United States in Haiti, Douglass made an agreement with Haitian president Florvil Hyppolite to subsequently represent Haiti in the United States at the Columbian Exposition. Douglass wrote this reversal of national constituencies into his autobiography's closing sentence: "I have been the recipient of many honors, among which my . . . appointment . . . to *represent the United States* at the capital of *Haïti*, and my . . . appointment . . . to *represent Haïti* among all the civilized nations of the globe at the World's *Columbian* Exposition, are crowning honors to my long career and a fitting and happy close to my whole public life" (1045, emphasis added). The messy chiasmus with which Douglass closes his sprawling final autobiography is far from the neat chiasmus famously appearing in his compact first autobiography, but both sentences pivot on the chiasmic tropes of repetition and reversal—whether from man to slave and slave to man or from US representative in Haiti to Haitian representative in the United States.[17]

Douglass's portrayal of his reversal of national constituencies suggests the practical implications of the national and racial ambivalences expressed by figures such as Gibbs and Langston. In fact, historically speaking, Douglass's reversal of national constituencies fed into white US suspicions that black diplomats, because of their racial sympathies, might mix the interests of the nation they represented with the interests of the darker populations among whom they worked. This concern is illustrated in discussions surrounding Douglass's performance as the US minister. During his second year in Haiti, the State Department pressured Douglass to negotiate for military and economic concessions that Haitian leaders determined would impinge on their nation's sovereignty. When Douglass failed to obtain these concessions, leading US newspapers disparaged him, with a *New York Times* reporter asserting that "the interests of the United States are lagging in [Douglass's] hands and suffering accordingly." The reporter stated, "Mr. Douglass . . . is carried away by the ideal of a free and enlightened republic of his own race. His sympathies are naturally with these people, to the unconscious prejudice of the Nation he represents" ("Haiti's Broken").[18] Similarly, a well-placed US capitalist issued a damning statement against Douglass's performance as a national representative. Implying that Douglass was a national hybrid whose blackness signified a Haitianness stronger than his Americanness, the capitalist called Douglass "more a Haitian than an American" (qtd. in Himelhoch 168). Amid widespread disapproval, Douglass tendered his resignation on 30 July 1891.

Though allegations of race-based sympathy brought Douglass under fire, he was not unique among the United States' larger diplomatic corps in feeling and playing on a racial connection to the people of the nation to which he was sent. Race-based sympathy was a factor in the diplomatic performances of white diplomats as well. Henry Adams, in his autobiography, recollects living in London with his father, who in the 1860s was serving as the US minister to England. Adams remembers that his father had advantages over European diplomats because his background of "race" and "language" prompted the English to treat him as "one of themselves." Becoming "undistinguishable from a Londoner," his father had a "double personality and corresponding double weight" in his ambassadorial role (123). Three decades later, in the 1890s, at least one American hoped that Douglass's own double personality, like that of Adams, could be transformed into double weight as a US representative. A letter of recommendation in Douglass's State Department file observes that the Haitians "all desire . . . to have our Government represented by Mr. Fred. Douglas [*sic*]." The letter further contends that from the perspective of "the Haytian trade," "no greater good could be done and a friendlier feeling exist" than through Douglass's appointment.[19] For this letter writer, Douglass was to function, like Minister Adams, as a type of doubly native informant—with his American nativity tying him to the United States while his racial background beneficially ingratiated him to the putative natives among whom he worked.

Yet Douglass's double personality did not function like that of Minister Adams. The United States' naturalized race-based sympathy with England situated Adams's double personality as invisible or (when made visible) preferred. But a black diplomat's double personality was visible from the outset because the diplomat's identification with darker populations reminded the nation that its representative failed to conform to the myth of the United States as a white nation. This visible hybridity—as what W. E. B. Du Bois would call "an American, a Negro" (*Souls* 8)—is at odds with US discourse on the required purity of representative persons. A representative man, suggests Emerson, must embody "the quality pure" (*Representative* 12). A representative man must be "effective, generative" and "fertile": "A sound apple produces seed,—a hybrid does not" (*Representative* 13). Such assumptions regarding hybridity and representation, as they interfaced with racial ideologies, did not stop the United States from deploying African American diplomats to nations and regions of color. But these myths and assumptions help explain why the United States tended to send its black ministers and consuls to posts of lesser geostrategic importance and why the diplomats were generally unable to parlay their status as American representatives into status as representative Americans.

From Representative Character to Representative Characters

About a year after Douglass was appointed minister, Philadelphia editor and writer John Stephens Durham became the US consul in Santo Domingo, and when Douglass tendered his resignation in 1891, Durham was transferred to Haiti and promoted to the rank of US minister in Douglass's stead. In Port-au-Prince, Durham revealed an unwillingness to subject himself to the accusations of national disloyalty that Douglass had recently experienced. Whereas Douglass was "not ashamed" of his "sympathy for Haïti" (*Life and Times* 1029), Durham assured the State Department that his "sense of duty" to the United States trumped any "natural sympathy for members of [his] own race" (*PRFR* 371–72). To this end, whereas Douglass criticized the United States' gunboat diplomacy in Haiti (*Life and Times* 1039–40), Durham called for so many gunboats that the State Department began to feel he was overzealous (*PRFR* 370). Undoubtedly owing in part to this performed zeal for his "duty," Durham uncontroversially completed his assigned tasks in Haiti and left his post in September 1893, as was customary, at the conclusion of the administration of the president who appointed him.

After working as US minister to Haiti, Durham maintained a law practice in Philadelphia but also spent long periods in the Caribbean. In the 1890s, he worked for four years in the Dominican Republic as the manager of a sugarcane plantation. In 1902, after publishing a novel he wrote in the Dominican Republic, he moved to Cuba as an attorney with the Spanish Treaty Claims Commission, which adjudicated the claims of US citizens against Spain for losses occasioned by the Spanish-American War. After spending most of the decade in Cuba, Durham moved to Europe, where he lived in Munich from 1910 to 1913 and subsequently in London until his death in 1919.[20]

Though Durham's work for the State Department made up only three years of his peripatetic life, he was highly invested in redeploying the diplomatic fiction of representative character within nondiplomatic representational realms. In his eulogy on the death of Frederick Douglass, Durham drew on the deceased's official work in international representation, affirming Douglass's "representative character" as a racial spokesperson and calling him "the ambassador of the oppressed everywhere" whose "embassy" was "every heart that can respond to the thrill of human fellowship" ("Address" 219–21). This nondiplomatic redeployment of diplomacy's notion of representative character was consistent with the tack of Durham's letter addressing Ida B. Wells's transatlantic antilynching campaign. On one level, as I have emphasized, this letter highlights the male privilege inherent in asking work in diplomatic representation to double as work in racial representation. On another level, however, the letter is crucial to understanding Durham's work in *literary* representation. Even as it relies on representative character to validate race representation, it implicitly utilizes the literariness of the notion of *character* to delimit the cast of characters that may participate in the United States' national narrative. The letter projects the national narrative of an American "struggle to redeem the South from its state of semi-barbarism." But this struggle, the letter admonishes, "is entirely a family matter." Because "we are all Americans," the missive explains, the national narrative should not involve Wells and her work in England. Nor should it involve England, because "we can solve our problems without England's assistance." Instead, the letter asserts, this struggle should be the concern of "all thoughtful citizens, black and white" (Mans and Durham). Significantly, as Durham draws on a diplomatic trope to deny Wells's representative status, the trope of representative character permits him to emerge not merely as a spokesperson but as a character or agent (emblematic of the United States' thoughtful black citizens) within a familial allegory that engages the national effort to combat mob rule and to afford African Americans the full rights of US citizenship.

Understanding Durham's willingness to push the diplomatic trope of representative character into the narrative realm—and particularly into a narrative conceiving of the nation in familial terms—offers significant insight into his 1902 foray into literary representation with his novel *Diane, Priestess of Haiti*. From the standpoint of reception, Durham's work as a diplomat credentialed his work in fiction. After *Lippincott's Monthly Magazine* announced it would devote an issue to publishing the entirety of *Diane*, the *New York Times* reminded readers that "John S. Durham . . . was formerly Minister from the United States to the country of which he now writes" ("Items"). Following *Diane*'s publication, a reviewer observed that because Durham was "Ex-Minister to Hayti and Santo Domingo," the story was "drawn from sight" ("Literary"). From the standpoint of production, Durham's work in literary representation was more indebted to his work in international representation than these commentators were aware. His willingness to deploy the notion of representative character in nondiplomatic representational spheres, in conjunction with the transculturation arising from his longtime residence in the Caribbean, led him to write a novel in the mode of what Doris Sommer discusses as Latin America's romances of national consolidation, which are "stories of star-crossed lovers who represent particular regions, races, parties, economic interests, and the like" (5).[21] Representing disparate constituencies within a nation, these characters enter into "marriages that provide . . . a figure for apparently nonviolent [national] consolidation" (Sommer 6). National romances, like black US diplomatic performances, seek simultaneously to reflect and to reconstitute the nation. And in many ways, *Diane* is a continuation and literary instantiation of the nationally reconstitutive work that Langston, Douglass, Gibbs, and Durham attempted to perform as diplomats. *Diane* seeks to usher in national change, relying on *fictional representative characters* who reflect and reconstitute their constituencies as if via the *fiction of representative character.*[22]

Work in Haiti and the Dominican Republic brought Durham into dialogue with proponents of romances of national consolidation. One such proponent was Cuban patriot José Martí, whom Durham first met in Santo Domingo. While working as the US minister to Haiti, Durham also served as the United States' chargé d'affaires to the Dominican Republic, and in September 1892, his duties called him to the capital city to aid in a conflict surrounding a bridge. Martí was also visiting Santo Domingo, having just concluded his historic meeting with Máximo Gómez in Montecristi.[23] Recounting their overlapping stay at the Hotel Universo, Durham remembered, "We soon became acquainted, and finally, in a confidential way, [Martí] outlined to me his propaganda in order to learn what I thought would be the probable attitude of the United States." "It was so delightful in the evenings," Durham continued, "to . . . talk with this man, whose sole thought was the freedom of his fellow-countrymen." Concluding their "too short association in the Dominican hotel," Durham met this "dreamer" and "artist" "only two or three [more] times" but "knew some of his friends and . . . kept in touch with his work" ("Anecdotes" 479). Martí's work, of course, was both political and literary, and by the time Durham met him, the Cuban patriot had already defined his notion of literature's appropriate relation to politics: "In literary contests, the prize should not go to the best ode but to the best study of the factors of the country in which one lives" ("Nuestra" 18).[24] In keeping up with Martí's work, Durham also may have learned of the Cuban patriot's admiration for Manuel de Jesús Galván's *Enriquillo* (1882), a touchstone of Dominican fiction that uses a love story to forge and consolidate a Dominican national identity. Martí called this romance "the newest and most enchanting way of writing our American story/history."[25] Hence, by the late 1890s, as the former US minister drafted *Diane* while working on a sugarcane plantation in a nation having recently found reconstitution in *Enriquillo*, it is unsurprising that Durham wrote to his friend Charles Chesnutt, "I have a Haïtien story on the hook. . . . I purpose to make a complete study of the social and political life in Haïti soaked into a native love story."[26]

As a transculturated literary text, *Diane* appropriates the generic logic of a Latin American form while also selecting and inventing from this genre in ways specific to Durham's own aestheticopoliticial ambitions. If Durham wrote his novel in the Dominican Republic, then according to Martí, it ought to have focused on the Dominican scene rather than Haiti's social and political life. And if *Diane* is a "Haïtien story," then it ought to have been readily accessible to Haitians (i.e., written in French and perhaps published in Haiti) so as to unite Haiti's partisan minds by harnessing what Sommer calls the "passion for conjugal and sexual union" (5). Instead, *Diane* was written in English and offered to the predominantly white US public in a major American magazine.[27] Through its US publication venue and Haitian subject matter, Durham's novel worked to renarrate Haiti in the minds of a US audience as a legitimate national presence within the community of nations. This narrative project had implications not only for Haiti's place on the international stage but also for African Americans' place within the United States. If, as Randolph Bourne claimed in the early twentieth century, the United States' traditional model of assimilation had sought to Americanize "national clusters" of people who hailed from various "mother countr[ies]" (86, 88), then African Americans (who could not boast of hailing from any specific nation) were at a distinct disadvantage in their efforts at integration into the United States. Hence, *Diane*'s projection of Haiti as a Negro nationality seeks to reconstitute the United States by suggesting that African Americans, like other US populations, could point to an external site illustrating their racial facility with the national form. Demonstrating this racial-national capacity was an implicit petition for black citizens' full participation in the United States' national project.

Diane's nationalism (which is both black and state-oriented) projects the purification and union of two Haitian factions: first, a constituency of worldly Haitians who permit love of Europe to trump loyalty to Haiti;

and second, a constituency of volkish Haitians who use voodoo for purposes of demagoguery. These constituencies are, in Durham's words, "soaked into a native love story," a story involving two representative characters—Alcide and Diane. The cosmopolitan and polyglot Alcide hopes his employment with Germany's diplomatic minister will permit him to avoid service in the Haitian army (388). Alcide wants to attend school in Germany (461) and dreams of becoming "a distinguished black scholar . . . known in the European world" (413). But his love for Europe draws scorn from other Haitians. He is called "not Haïtien, but foreign" (390), "a black imitator of white men" (400), "a black German" (401), and "a mahogany-colored German" (425). In contrast, Diane's skin is "very black" (389). She is a woman of "uncivilized directness and simplicity" (440) who dresses in "the loose gown of the country" (388). She can "barely read and write" (440) but is the apprentice of Haiti's most powerful voodoo priest, and her "most cherished dreams" involve using voodoo to "control the crowd" (408). In spite of Diane and Alcide's differences, the novel's opening chapters reveal that they love each other. Alcide, however, wants Diane to give up the "quackery" of voodoo (390), and Diane feels "so pained" by Alcide's lack of national consciousness (448).

Diane and Alcide are separated when they become pawns in a political and military plot aimed at overthrowing the president. As the would-be lovers wend their way back into each other's arms, each determines to reform. Alcide disregards the legation protection offered by Germany (445) and joins the Haitian army, determining that "his place [is] at the front to defend the national government" (447). Then, as a token that "he [is] a true Haïtien" (447), he declines the opportunity to attend school in Germany: rather than "fleeing from home to a strange country," he stays in Haiti to be reunited with Diane (461). Meanwhile, Diane decides that "Alcide was right" and the voodoo "'cures' [are] no good" (439). She begins dispensing "little white pill[s]" and refusing payment "until [her patients] tell her that her cure is good" (462). After the lovers are reunited, the Haitian president requests Alcide's services as an adviser (465).

Clearly, this love is nationally significant. Diane and Alcide's passion for each other is particular to themselves, yet it floats on the supposedly "universal" (391) forms of Alcide's "husband-love" (391, 463) and Diane's status as a true "woman" (441). This conjugal love—both particular and universal—is emblematic of Haiti's nationality. Tellingly, Diane and Alcide are reunited during a scene in which Haitian peasants form an "audience [on] the street" to listen to the German national anthem, "Heil dir im Siegerkranz," which the narrator observes has a "choral which the patriotic hymns of three nations [Great Britain, the United States, and Germany] have made familiar around the world" (455).[28] Undoubtedly, *Diane*'s contextualization of the lovers' reunion with this scene speaks to Haiti's situation within the international world. If a national anthem permits "people wholly unknown to each other" the feeling of "unisonance" as they "utter the same verses to the same melody" (Anderson 145), then *Diane*—underscoring the *same* melody as the vehicle for *different* verses—inducts Haiti into the international community of specific cultural traditions that have taken upon themselves the common form of the nation-state. In thus renarrating Haiti for his US readers, Durham also seeks to reconstitute the United States by emphasizing that African Americans are not people whose origins in colonized Africa have created them as the United States' internal colonials. Instead, African Americans, like Anglo-Americans or German Americans, can point to a nation-state, illustrating their racial capacity to operate within the national form and thus to participate fully in the United States' national project. This image of black people as fully nationalized resonates with what Durham's friend Booker T. Washington described as the New Negro for the new century.[29]

Durham's use of Haiti as a site at which to racially renarrate the United States is consistent with the practices of other black US diplomats, who also tended to frame conditions at their posts as indicative of African Americans' constitutional fitness for integration into the US body politic. More common than writing romances of national consolidation, however, was the method of representing black officeholders of other nations as reflective of African Americans' fitness for holding high offices within the United States. Gibbs observed that in Madagascar, "there are colored men occupying places of prominence as officials." Such men were present at "social occasions, . . . and, strangest of it all, on the following day the sun and other heavenly bodies seem to stand or revolve in their accustomed orbits" (246). Similarly, Langston recounted seeing "extremely back men . . . appearing in uniforms of official character" (359). Making much of seeing "men of their complexion holding such positions," Langston represented Haiti so as to reveal African Americans' fitness for high office within the United States: "He had hitherto only seen the negro" in America, living "in nominal freedom and dependence. Now he beholds him the owner of a great country, the founder and builder of a great government, with a national sovereignty" (360). Also framing the black presence within high governmental offices abroad as indicative of

African Americans' capacity at home, James Weldon Johnson described how he, as a US consul, attended a ball in honor of the Venezuelan president. Johnson remarked, "I could not help but note that one of . . . [the] generals present at the ball was a gigantic, full-blooded Negro; and I was mildly surprised, because there were, comparatively, only a few Negroes in Venezuela" (*Along* 243).

Similarly, Durham's *Diane* asks readers to see black officials in Haiti as metaphors for actual and potential black officeholders in the United States. Durham himself suspected that certain elite figures in US political history might have been of African descent, but the alleged blackness of high-ranking US officials was not something he felt he could address directly. Writing to a friend regarding the rumor that US founding father Alexander Hamilton may have had African ancestry, Durham remarked, "The question as to Hamilton's descent is one of the most delicate things to students of our history. . . . My attitude is that if he did have a negro somewhere among his ancestors, it is not a matter which a colored man in this country could discuss with propriety."[30] But Durham could with propriety discuss the blackness of high-ranking Haitian officials in his literary writing. In *Diane*, the president of Haiti is "comely and distinguished. . . . The [president's] eyes . . . bespoke the character of the man—wide open, alert, the cornea as clear as that of a baby" (394). Hence, rather than chasing rumors regarding the alleged African descent of important US leaders, Durham used *Diane*'s Haitian setting to affirm that African-descended people indeed possessed the attributes necessary to occupy the highest positions offered by a sovereign republic, whether that republic was Haiti or the United States.

A particularly self-reflexive facet of this tack emerges from the novel's depictions of the chief "Haïtien diplomat" (432), Minister of Foreign Affairs Jules Pirot. Within *Diane*, Pirot is not merely the Haitian diplomat but also a metaphor for black diplomats more generally. Contravening the image of black diplomats as letting personal convictions interfere with their official instructions, Pirot tells the Haitian president, "I don't agree with your politics" (421), but he assures the president of his intentions, in spite of any disagreement: "As part of your government [I will] do all in my power to support you to the point of dying at your side if need be" (421–22). Although readers know Pirot is sincere, the president begins to suspect the diplomat of plotting to overthrow the government. Consequently, the president places him "under close surveillance" (432) and is ready to "execute him at once" based on counterfeit evidence (429).

As readers begin contemplating in advance the unjust image of the black diplomat "filled with gaping wounds" (433), *Diane* shifts to a scene that borrows energy from the novel's operation within a genre advancing political content through romantic and sexual allegory. The scene is set inside the home of Minister Hauffman, the chief German diplomat in Haiti. Hauffman is in his parlor when "an ordinary public 'bus'" arrives at his residence. Out of the taxi steps "a lady decently dressed." The woman pays the driver and tells him "that he need not return" (434). At the front door of the home, she asks for the German minister, and although he does not recognize her, Hauffman invites her in. She enters with "a pretty, mincing step" and after some pleasantries throws "back her veil . . . and look[s] . . . straight at" her host. "'Don't you remember me?' she ask[s] sweetly." Hauffman is "plainly embarrassed that he [can]not recognize her" (435). By now, the woman's appearance at Hauffman's home may have begun to raise readers' suspicions. Why does the woman not need the taxi to return? How long does she plan on staying with Hauffman, and what are her plans for this stay? Hauffman to this point has been depicted as a character of great probity, so readers may anticipate a scandalous revelation regarding Hauffman's present or past dalliances. Readers might wonder if the novel is poised to reveal that Hauffman was once unfaithful to his German wife and had an affair with a Haitian woman. What's more, Hauffman does not even recognize her—perhaps the woman in his parlor is one of many mistresses he has had during his several years in Haiti. Readers pursuing this vein of speculation might recall that once, desperately seeking to protect Alcide from service in the Haitian army, Hauffman declared, "He deserves all I can do for him. He is my son" (418). Earlier, it was easiest to dismiss Hauffman's assertion of paternity as metaphorical, but now readers may wonder if Alcide truly *is* Hauffman's son—and if the description of Alcide as a "black German" is more than an epithet. Alcide's childhood, after all, has been referenced repeatedly (390, 399), but his parents have never been mentioned. Perhaps the woman in the parlor is Alcide's mother, seeking out the father of her child after many years away. Or perhaps she is *not* Alcide's mother but a different woman, who has arrived to make the minister aware of another of his children. As Hauffman stammers awkwardly, he is "interrupted by uproarious laughter from the dainty one with the mincing steps" (435). The "woman," it turns out, is a man in women's clothes, and the man is Pirot, Haiti's chief diplomat, fleeing unjust execution by seeking asylum in the German minister's home.

The meeting of two diplomats is always a semiotically charged occasion, as the two officers stand as signs of their respective nations. But the present scene's delayed gender decoding redoubles this diplomatic encounter's semiotic richness, as the delay affords readers a rare opportunity to hypothesize that two men, namely, the Haitian and German diplomats, have together conceived a child. Especially in light of the novel's indebtedness to a genre asking readers to see political allegory in conjugal and sexual union, we should pay special attention to the political implications of this suggested yet absent conception of a nationally ambivalent child. As Durham witnessed during Douglass's famous and controversial diplomatic work in Haiti, white US citizens were concerned that black US diplomats would metaphorically sleep with those from whom they were tasked to extract political concessions. A predominantly white United States feared national betrayal and approached black diplomats with a hermeneutics of suspicion. Implying the naivety of this suspicion-driven interpretive approach, *Diane* presents Pirot's quick conversion from woman to man so as to suggest that cagey spectators ought to regard as superficial and illusory the appearances pointing toward a black diplomat's sympathy with other nations. Indeed, Pirot's physiological incapacity to conceive the previously suspected child with Hauffman projects a view of black diplomats as somehow ontologically incapable of engaging in disloyal transnational liaisons with those among whom they are sent to negotiate. Through this scene, the novel seems to say to a predominantly white United States: when a black diplomat walks into a diplomatic encounter, you immediately anticipate a nationally hybrid product; you anticipate that the treaty he negotiates will be, figuratively, a nationally ambivalent child—but if you wait, you will see that this eventuality was precluded from the start.

The scene also is suggestive in relation to the effects of suspicion on black US diplomats and the nation they represent. The president's suspicions regarding Pirot are unwarranted, and they have the effect of feminizing Haiti's chief diplomat. The allegorical implications of this feminization are both sophisticated and unsettling in their gender biases. On one hand, because diplomacy of the day did not brook international representation by women, the president's suspicions regarding Pirot's loyalty (inasmuch as they prompt the diplomat to dress in women's clothing) seem to remove Pirot from the masculinist ontological category of national representative. In other words, publicly expressed suspicions regarding the loyalty of black diplomats tend to undermine the diplomats' authority to speak on behalf of the nation. On the other hand,

Pirot's revelation that his womanhood is a façade suggests that any claim regarding a black diplomat's lack of representative character is superficial and far from theoretically accurate. Regardless of accusations launched against him by his fellow citizens, he is commissioned to represent the nation. And the supplementary quality of his representative character makes it so that changes in his own status function to reconstitute the nation he represents. Hence, his appearance in women's clothing—allegorizing the effects of national suspicions regarding his loyalty—has the upshot of feminizing the nation. To be sure, nations in general and the United States in particular often conceive of themselves as feminine entities. But as Amy Kaplan observes, this feminine self-conception is implicated in an ideology of separate geopolitical spheres, in which the nation's domestic life is a "feminine counterbalance" (*Anarchy* 25) to the manliness of the nation's engagements beyond its own borders (95).[31] In this context, Durham's novel suggests that the US public, when accusing black diplomats of disloyalty, not only undercuts the authority of its diplomats but also harms itself by negating the nation's manly vitality on the international stage.

Compromise and the Lion's Mouth

As a novel with political aims, *Diane* had certain liabilities. On one hand, in depicting Haitian officials as metaphors for high-ranking black US officials, and in depicting Haitian nationality as an argument for full African American citizenship, the novel's allegorical work hinges on the common blackness of two diasporan populations, Haitians and US citizens of African descent. Offered to a white US reading public, such an argument flirted with dangers similar to those inherent in black US diplomats' work on the so-called Negro circuit: the novel risked cross-pollinating American race prejudice with American xenophobia by reanimating the suspicions of those who worried that African Americans' race-based affinities with other diasporan subjects were stronger than their US patriotism. Another of *Diane*'s liabilities involves its subtletly. Subtle allegories and indirect arguments often go unnoticed by readers who are unprepared or disinclined to look for them. In 1903, H. Harrison Wayman of the *Colored American Magazine* described *Diane* as "a very popular novel" (889), and John E. Bruce elsewhere described it as "perhaps the most ambitious effort ever made by a man of color in the realm of fiction" (4); but the public's recorded response to the novel offers little indication that it was read as an allegory for racial progress within the United States. Durham probably saw this lack of acknowledgment as a triumph, considering that he believed "the less fuss we make about 'the progress of the race,' the more progress" (*BTWP* 6: 328).

Diane's Haitian narrative may have exerted some type of domestically progressive yet uncommented influence on readers of *Lippincott's Magazine*, but among literary critics, the novel's Haitian subject matter eclipsed its domestic aims for most of the twentieth century. Probably voicing a stance indicative of the rationale for *Diane*'s traditional exclusion from discussions of African American literature, Hugh M. Gloster in his 1948 study *Negro Voices in American Fiction* declined to comment on Durham's novel because it "does not deal with Negro life and thought" in the United States (260). Though the amount of critical attention given to *Diane* remains limited, recent scholars have been less inclined to overlook the ways in which Durham's novel reflects on and allegorically addresses US racial conditions. J. Michael Dash places *Diane* within a tradition of African American admiration for Haiti's nationality (48–49), and Dickson D. Bruce remarks on Durham's use of a Haitian setting to comment, "however subtly," on racial dynamics in the United States (*Black* 134).

Contemplating *Diane*'s subtlety is important to assessing both Durham's approach to literary representation and the approaches taken by black US diplomats within the realms of racial and international representation. *Diane* is a novel of strategic compromise and indirection; to avoid the controversy attendant to directly pointing out racial injustices within the United States, the novel resorts to a Haitian setting and thereby risks becoming illegible as a text addressing the United States' domestic racial conditions. Like *Diane*, black US diplomats also made strategic compromises. In turning toward international diplomacy to pursue domestic race leadership during the New Negro era, black US ministers and consuls agreed to spend years away from the black US constituency they sought to represent. And in drawing on the diplomatic and masculinist trope of representative character, they implicitly detracted from the activisms of black women, who could not draw on official representative character. Moreover, as New Negro diplomats sought to become representative Americans and thus to erase the color line in the United States, they acquiesced to working for a State Department that maintained a segregated "Negro circuit." Such compromises were dangerous and might be thought of as international iterations of what, in Ralph Ellison's *Invisible Man*, the grandfather describes as "overcom[ing] 'em with yeses," living "with your head in the lion's mouth" (16). The ethics and efficacy of this approach to racial progress have never been uncontroversial, but the approach came under increased scrutiny during the early twentieth-century methodological conflict that is heuristically described as the Booker T. Washington–W. E. B. Du Bois debate. Pitting a Washingtonian tendency toward equivocation against an uncompromising Du Boisean directness, this debate asked what methods were legitimately available to African American race representatives. Fittingly, as the subsequent chapter explores, black America's intertwined diplomatic and literary traditions weighed in on the methodological questions faced by the New Negro race leaders who took up the mantle of ambassador as they entered the court of American public opinion.

2 / Passing into Diplomacy: US Consul James Weldon Johnson and *The Autobiography of an Ex-Colored Man*

When Richard Wright dismissed the African American writers who preceded him as "prim and decorous ambassadors" who "curts[ied] to show that the Negro was . . . human" ("Blueprint" 53), he took aim at the African American middle class (the college bred, the bourgeoisie, the talented tenth) who had worked, especially during the first three decades of the twentieth century, as apparently self-appointed spokespersons for the nation's black masses. Yet Wright's objections to African America's artistic ambassadors went beyond mere misgivings regarding the representation of the masses by the elite few. Wright's concern was also methodological. He resented the indirect aesthetic argument (i.e., the "curtsying") that the ambassadors advanced as they "went a-begging" for the humanity they supposed would warrant civil rights for black US citizens. He objected to the type of aesthetic indirection that culminated in what David Levering Lewis has called the Harlem Renaissance's operative principle of "civil rights by copyright" (*When* xxiii, xxviii). Or, to put it in terms of Wright's own ambassadorial metaphor, Wright resented that the New Negro race representatives employed the ambassador's signature method: diplomacy, the effort toward advancement through strategic indirection.

Prominent among the early twentieth century's artistic ambassadors was James Weldon Johnson, whose oblique aesthetic methods might be taken as emblematic of the indirection that Wright criticized. For instance, rather than calling for direct protest in his 1922 preface to *The Book of American Negro Poetry*, Johnson suggested that African

Americans could best change the "status of the Negro in the United States" through "a demonstration of intellectual parity by the Negro through the production of literature and art" (vii). Clearly, the aesthetic performance of individual African Americans was to function as an indirect argument for African American civil rights more generally. One might ask how such obliqueness was sustained as a modus operandi during the first decades of the twentieth century, especially when W. E. B. Du Bois had rung in the new century by calling for a new directness, for an end to equivocation (*Souls* 42). To provide at least a partial answer to this question, we do well to turn toward the geopolitical routes of one of the era's touchstone novels, James Weldon Johnson's *The Autobiography of an Ex-Colored Man*. In 1927, Johnson affixed his name to the second edition of this novel, which had before only appeared anonymously in 1912. Whereas the 1927 publication found Johnson acting as a Renaissance-era artistic ambassador, *The Autobiography*'s previous publication found him working in international diplomacy as a US consul in Puerto Cabello, Venezuela (1906–1909), and Corinto, Nicaragua (1909–1913).[1] Out of this earlier diplomatic milieu, the novel emerged not only as a treatment of the phenomenon of racial passing, as it has traditionally been read, but also as a geopolitically inspired literary exploration of the type of strategic indirection Johnson later influentially imported into the Harlem Renaissance.

The Poetics of Revolution

With the aid of Booker T. Washington, Johnson in 1906 received a consular appointment that transformed his image from that of a bohemian songwriter-musician to a "race man of merit" (Goldsby, "Keeping" 254). Working as a consul situated Johnson as a participant in the United States' interventionist program for Latin America, and this was especially true during his time in Corinto. His consular notebooks reveal that as the United States plotted to overthrow the Nicaraguan president, Johnson surveilled the activities of Nicaraguan gunboats, wrote reports for the State Department on these activities, and used a secret code to convey the intelligence to the captain of a US gunboat that visited Corinto repeatedly.[2] After a US-supported revolution successfully overthrew the Nicaraguan president, Johnson spent time evaluating counterrevolutionary sentiment among Nicaraguans, thereby supporting the United States' efforts to arrange for the rise of a US-friendly Nicaraguan leader. In November 1910, for example, Johnson sent the State Department a translation of one of many newspaper "articles of an incendiary nature regarding what [anti-US Nicaraguans] term 'The American Intervention.'" This article quoted a "young man" who declared, "Gentlemen, here is my hand, it is ready to do justice, with it I shall bury my dagger . . . into the heart of that yankee, who comes to give our country over to those infamous [US-backed Nicaraguan] traitors. . . . I shall kill him as I would a sick dog, in order to make a warning so that the yankees may know how a weak people answers the brutal impositions of force." Johnson explained to the State Department, "Such articles are being published daily, and are well calculated to inflame and incite certain elements in the population." He believed articles of this ilk were responsible for occurrences such as a recent anti-US riot in the nearby city of Leon.[3] In spite of these riots, the United States successfully arranged for the former clerk of a US company to assume the Nicaraguan presidency. This move further incensed many Nicaraguans and prompted a revolt that was poised to overtake the town of Corinto, where Johnson worked as the chief US representative. Under intense pressure, Johnson's facility with rhetorical posturing allowed him successfully to stall the insurgency and thereby to buy time for the landing of twenty-six hundred US Marines for the new president's protection.[4] Johnson later recalled that while in Latin America, he knew the United States should never have intervened in Nicaraguan affairs (*Along* 283), but he also felt at the time that diplomatic service honed his "intellect and character"[5] while constituting a form of racial "missionary work" that facilitated African Americans' advancement toward equality (qtd. in Jackson 187).

We gain perspective on the tumultuous incidents surrounding Johnson's diplomatic service in Latin America as we contextualize this work with the geopolitical nuances of Charles Chesnutt's novel *The Marrow of Tradition*, published only a few years before Johnson's first consular appointment. In 1901, Chesnutt's novel had powerfully positioned US intervention abroad as antithetical to African American interests at home. In fact, one of the novel's archvillains—as a former US diplomat in Nicaragua—bears what might be taken as an instructive occupational resemblance to Consul James Weldon Johnson himself. Set in the city of Wellington, *Marrow* is a fictionalization of Wilmington, North Carolina's 1898 race riot. The novel traces the efforts of three white-supremacist conspirators—called the "Big Three" (80)—to organize a race "revolution" (253) that will put an end to what they term "negro domination" (33). Particularly useful in orchestrating this riot is General Belmont, a member of the Big Three and formerly the US ambassador to Nicaragua.

As represented in the novel, Belmont's diplomatic work in Nicaragua deeply informs the logic of Wellington's race riot. "Down in the American tropics," Belmont explains, "they have a way of doing things. I was in Nicaragua, ten years ago, when Paterno's revolution drove out Igorroto's government. . . . Igorroto was not looking for trouble, and the guns were at his breast before he knew it. [Here in Wellington,] we have the guns" (249–50). Commenting on the novel's portrayal of US intervention abroad as providing a template for the Big Three's conspiracy to end "negro domination," Susan Gillman observes that *Marrow* "implicitly [links] racial revolution at home with the frontiers of empire abroad, or at least [suggests] that the latter serve as a model for the former" (99). Even as the novel links racism at home to imperialism abroad, it is particularly attentive to the ways in which rationalizations of revolution (whether in the context of the United States' imperial endeavors or its racial struggles) sought to sanitize the seizure of power by aestheticizing it. In describing a Wellington race revolution that is to be modeled after a Latin American revolution, General Belmont eloquently speaks of "the purity of our motives" (Chesnutt, *Marrow* 81) in "cleansing the Augean stables" (250). In response to this lofty description of revolution, one of Belmont's less eloquent co-conspirators calls for more directness: the co-conspirator asks, "Why waste our time in mere pretense? . . . If I want a thing I take it, provided I'm strong enough." Belmont answers that his florid framing of events is necessary "diplomacy" (81), and the narrator portrays Belmont as intent on preventing his co-conspirator from "robb[ing] the enterprise of all its poetry" by putting "a solemn act of revolution upon the plane of a mere vulgar theft of power" (253).

Johnson, of course, differed radically from Belmont with regard to his ambitions for the rights of African-descended people in the United States, but Johnson, like Belmont, also found in "poetry" (and aesthetic expression more generally) a means of rationalizing his participation in the "vulgar theft of power." Drawing on his earlier work in musical theater, he now tended to think of Latin American revolutions in terms of "comic operas."[6] This perspective is reflected in his songlike poem "Down by the Carib Sea," written while he worked as a US diplomat. The poem describes a "land of the dark-eyed *gente* [people]" dreaming "away / Both night and day" (1, 3) in a cloud of "redolent smoke" that "lazily curls" from their cigarettes (6–11). Having represented the *gente*, or Latin American people, as complacent in a lazy haze of smoke, the poem continues in lines 15–19:

Tropical constitutions
Call for occasional revolutions;
But after that's through,
Why there's nothing to do
But smoke—smoke.[7]

In constructing "Down by the Carib Sea," Johnson was apparently neither critical of the United States' revolutionary program for Latin America nor critical of his participation in that program. Rather, his lilting rhyme "Tropical constitutions / Call for occasional revolutions" functions as a type of smokescreen for US power plays in Latin America. Here, the "Tropical constitutions" (a double entendre referring both to Latin Americans' governing systems and their ostensibly inherent nature) call out for their own revolutions, and the United States' role—as an agent or otherwise—in these revolutions is elided. Alluding to "Down by the Carib Sea" shortly after its publication, poet and literary critic William Stanley Braithwaite positioned this poem as one that "strike[s] a universal note" rather than dwelling on African Americans' particular "web of racial life" (9). Whatever else Braithwaite meant to communicate with such comments, it is clear that wrapped up in Braithwaite's observation is a sense that Johnson's poetic rendering of Latin American revolutions is resonant with the era's universal (i.e., white American) geopolitical complacency regarding the United States' role in Latin American revolutions. In part, then, it was Johnson's poetic obfuscation of US power motives in Latin America that prompted Braithwaite to describe him as unconfined to a "racial attitude" but taking "inspiration in the human scale" (9).

Especially when contextualized with Chesnutt's eloquent and devious ex-diplomat General Belmont, Johnson's work as both a race man and a consul appears curious and perhaps hypocritical. Indeed, in light of *Marrow*'s link between antiracism and anti-imperialism, Johnson's performance in Latin America attests to the accuracy of William Andrews's observation that Johnson was "a reconciler of differences among those whose ideological agendas seemed to preclude . . . cooperative action" (xii). Johnson spent six years as a consul attempting to meld US intervention abroad with ambitions toward racial equality at home. As he did so, he hoped not only that his consular service would function as an indirect argument for racial advancement but also that the novel he wrote as a consul would engage the question of indirection as a method. Specifically, *The Autobiography* deploys and interrogates categories of ambassadorship and compromise in ways that seek to reenvision and to racially remap the implications of seeking advancement through oblique methods.

Black Hypocrisy, White Diplomacy

Unsurprisingly, the question of ambassadorship or representative capacity makes its first prominent appearance in *The Autobiography*'s third chapter, which Johnson wrote only after his arrival as a diplomat in Venezuela (Andrews xi). In this chapter, Shiny, the narrator's African American schoolmate, presents Wendell Phillips's lecture "Toussaint L'Ouverture" at a graduation ceremony. Speculating on Shiny's thoughts as he "looked into that crowd of [white] faces," the Ex-Colored Man remarks, "I think that solitary little black figure standing there felt that for the particular time and place he bore the weight and responsibility of his race; that for him to fail meant general defeat" (Johnson, *Autobiography* 31). Furthermore, according to the Ex-Colored Man, Shiny's very representative mantle is representative of the mantles worn by elite African American men in the public eye. The narrator explains, "I have since known of colored men who have been chosen as class orators in our leading universities, of others who have played on the varsity football and baseball teams, of colored speakers who have addressed great white audiences. In each of these instances I believe the men were stirred by the same emotions which actuated 'Shiny' on the day of his graduation" (31). As a representative of elite African American representativeness, Shiny inspires the narrator's desire for his own ambassadorial relationship with people of African descent. Of listening to Shiny's speech, the Ex-Colored Man remembers, "I felt leap within me pride that I was colored; and I began to form wild dreams of bringing glory and honor to the Negro race. For days I could talk of nothing else with my mother except my ambition to be . . . a great colored man, to reflect credit on the race and gain fame for myself." The narrator adds, "It was not until years after that I formulated a definite and feasible plan for realizing my dreams" (32). This statement reveals Shiny's pivotal role in the novel. It is Shiny's speech, after all, that lays the groundwork for the Ex-Colored Man to eventually decide he will represent the race well (by translating ragtime into a classical musical register). And this decision influentially draws him into the US South, where he witnesses a lynching that motivates him to pass into white society.

Several scholars have noted Shiny's function in inspiring the narrator's aspirations toward racial ambassadorship,[8] and Harilaos Stecopoulos has importantly pointed toward "Shiny's passionate articulation of the great Haitian's accomplishments" as causing the Ex-Colored Man to identify Toussaint L'Ouverture "as a model of black social and political action" (62). I would extend these observations on race representation by further focusing on the significance and content of Shiny's speech, Phillips's "Toussaint L'Ouverture." The speech's title might at first lead us to reflect on the nineteenth-century tradition of black revolution that imagined Haiti as "the fearful precursor of black rebellion throughout the New World" (Sundquist, *To Wake* 32). However, *The Autobiography* emerges from—and participates in—an early twentieth-century modernity that ushered in a hemispheric shift in the cultural semiotics of revolution. This shift unsettled Caribbean revolution's previously naturalized bond with Haiti (and blackness more generally) and reconscripted it for use in the US military-diplomatic program for Latin America. This was a program, as historian Walter LaFeber explains, that first justified US intervention by citing the hemispheric chaos resulting from Latin America's frequent coups d'etat and subsequently perpetuated a new revolutionary tradition by consistently supporting and inciting pro-US revolutionary factions in Latin America (*Inevitable* 39).

An awareness of the fundamental shift in the hemispheric signification of revolution, as well as a heightened attentiveness to the Ex-Colored Man's points of emphasis, ought to guide us in further exploring *The Autobiography*'s engagement with the question of racial ambassadorship at this pivotal juncture in the novel. The only section of the speech to which the Ex-Colored Man directly refers is "the famous peroration," which when spoken by Shiny draws the audience into a standing ovation (Johnson, *Autobiography* 31). Though not quoted in *The Autobiography*, the peroration declares that the audience ought to rank Toussaint above the great soldier-statesmen of the Western tradition. The peroration concludes by referring to Haiti's patriot as "the soldier, the statesman, the martyr, Toussaint L'Ouverture" (Phillips 494). The name *Toussaint*, here spoken within an imperialist system that had resignified revolution for its own uses, emerges not as the epitome of black, anticolonial insurgency but as a black embodiment of the very apparatuses the United States was coming to rely on in its geopolitical ambitions for Latin America—namely, statesmanship and military might. The peroration suggests that Toussaint, and hence members of the race he represented, would have been, like Johnson himself, more than capable of excelling within an institution such as the US military-diplomatic establishment.

Another section of Phillips's lecture, which compares Toussaint to Napoleon Bonaparte, moves us further from the novel's depiction of Shiny's commencement address yet provides a remarkable entrance to *The Autobiography*'s preoccupation with indirection as a method of advancement. Within the novel, Shiny's recitation of "Toussaint L'Ouverture" would have reminded his audience that the leaders of both Haiti and France employed strategic indirection to conceal their intentions. "Like Napoleon," Shiny would have emphasized, "no man ever divined [Toussaint's] purpose or penetrated his plan." However, the leaders' shared indirect technique and resulting inscrutability elicited a set of disparate, race-based interpretations: "[Toussaint] was only a negro, and so, in him, they called it *hypocrisy*. In Bonaparte we style it *diplomacy*" (Phillips 483, emphasis added). Shiny's speech, in other words, would have reminded his audience of the Western tradition that interprets strategic indirection when coded white as diplomacy but the same behavior, when coded black, as hypocrisy.

Electing not to reference this section of the speech in the novel, Johnson did not offer such a reminder to *The Autobiography*'s readers. Yet I draw on Phillips's explanation because it vividly summarizes a discursive tradition within which Johnson's novel implicitly operates. Few could match Phillips's flair in describing the conventions that interpret strategic indirection as (black) hypocrisy or (white) diplomacy, but the racial architecture of this tradition becomes apparent in a glance at American interpretive strategies regarding dissimulation and inscrutability. If (as forays into deconstruction have reminded us) every position is fraught with some degree of pretense and inconsistency, then it becomes especially clear that an accusation of hypocrisy is, generally speaking, less an appeal to ethics and more an ad hominem attack selectively underscoring the particular inconsistencies of people already held in disdain by the accuser. Hence, it should come as no surprise that race prejudice within the United States (and the West more generally) has long placed people of African descent on the receiving end of the racial ad hominem (i.e., hypocrisy) referenced by Phillips. Indeed, blackness has emerged as one of hypocrisy's prominent signs. During the early days of the United States, for instance, Thomas Jefferson preferred the white face over the black, implying in *Notes on the State of Virginia* (1784) that the white face can be a gauge of sincerity, as "the expressions of every passion" appear in "greater or lesser suffusions of [blushing] colour." In contrast, he observed, the black face possesses an "immoveable veil of black which covers all the emotions" (138). Racially deleterious, Jefferson's observation on this point was not an accusation of hypocrisy per se but instead an intimation that, because black people allegedly did not verify their inner emotions through their surface features, onlookers were left to guess at the (possible) insincerity concealed beneath their black "veils." By the early nineteenth century, the physiognomic underpinnings of Jefferson's remarks were codified into what Karen Halttunen has called the "cult of sincerity" that dominated the Victorian United States (34). This moral economy positioned hypocrisy as the greatest sin and maintained that "all aspects of manner and appearance"—but especially aspects relating to the face—"were visible outward signs of inner moral qualities" (40). Of course, as facial physiognomy resonated with racial physiognomy in hackneyed phrases such as "black hypocrisy" and "painted hypocrite," people of African descent endured unflattering interpretations of their indirection and inconsistencies.

This interpretive tradition is crassly embodied by the Southern plantation dictum "niggers will lie"[9] but is more delicately expressed in discussions of black hypocrisy. From the colonial days, field slaves were regarded as "liars, parasites, hypocrites, and thieves" (Reiss 57), while an antebellum planter memorably explained that "the most general defect in the character of the negro is hypocrisy," manifest in a tendency to strategically deceive in order to avoid work (Breeden 34). Prejudice and physiognomy combined with such force that even commentators who opposed slavery negatively interpreted black indirection, with one writer discussing "craft and cunning" as "the sole resource of a slave" and framing such behavior as "hypocrisy" (Hildreth 117) and another explaining that the slaves' "hypocrisy" arose in response to "the caprices of the masters, and the cruel supervision of the overseers" (Weiss 302).[10]

In the twentieth century, the tradition of describing black strategic indirection as hypocrisy continued among white commentators ostensibly sympathetic to African American culture. For instance, Newbell Niles Puckett, in his *Folk Beliefs of the Southern Negro* (1926), took African American hypocrisy as a matter of course, speculating that "the organized hypocrisy of the Southern Negro [may] be an adaptation forced upon him by conditions of life" (9–10). Puckett's continued willingness to interpret African Americans' strategic indirection as hypocrisy was not directly taken to task in white discourse until 1941, when Melville Herskovits observed in Puckett's query a fundamental "misinterpretation" arising out of the force of tradition. "Diplomacy, tact, and mature reserve," Herskovits responded, "are not necessarily hypocrisy" (158). Herskovits's salutary reinterpretation of black indirection employed the same rhetorical flourish that white Americans had used for decades in speaking of their own strategic pretenses and contradictory stances. For occasions when white pretense is not easily ignored, Walt Whitman and Ralph Waldo Emerson have provided sage dictums validating self-contradiction and inconsistency,[11] but a more quotidian papering over of indirection has involved recourse to the notion of diplomacy. Charles Chesnutt saw this interpretive tendency clearly, as *The Marrow of Tradition* showcases ex-ambassador Belmont rejecting the label of "hypocrite" (81) and insisting on his stratagem—not to mention his "gift of eloquence" (34)—as "diplomacy" (81), a rhetorical move that tropes international diplomacy (itself riddled with pretense) to describe indirect methods more generally. Meanwhile, as Herskovits's observation suggests, the "force of traditional sanctions" had not made the comparatively anodyne term *diplomacy* readily available to descriptions of African American behavior (158). Of course, the many African American students and alumni who had, like Shiny and the Ex-Colored Man, heard and memorized Wendell Phillips's "Toussaint L'Ouverture" would not have needed Herskovits to remind them of these separate and unequal interpretive traditions. Frequent repetition of Phillips's speech undoubtedly underlined *hypocrisy* and *diplomacy* as value-laden terms that could be used polemically to underscore or ameliorate indirect methods.[12]

In fact, among prominent African Americans—and particularly among the New Negro era's race leaders—the hypocrisy-diplomacy dichotomy was both echoed and complicated by a methodological dispute regarding racial advancement. Here again, assertions of hypocrisy and diplomacy became value judgments, as people friendly to Booker T. Washington described his trademark approach as diplomacy, while those discontent with the Washingtonian status quo reviled his indirect methods as hypocrisy. For instance, in a departure from the white American trend interpreting strategic indirection by black people as hypocrisy, friends of Washington framed oblique methods as "diplomacy" and "tact" (*BTWP* 12: 333), noting the "diplomacy" of Washington's attempt to "get the wooden horse inside the walls of Troy" (Harlan 76).[13] Paul Laurence Dunbar put it concisely when he observed that "the race has produced no more adroit diplomatist than [Washington]" (195). In framing African American strategic indirection as diplomacy, those who were in Washington's camp ineluctably pushed against a centuries-old tradition that would have racially read such behavior as hypocrisy; yet Bookerites were also—and more immediately—responding to an emergent discourse surrounding Du Bois's rising star. In disagreeing with Washington's methods, Du Bois prominently read black strategic indirection as hypocrisy. In *The Souls of Black Folk*, he explained that the "double life" of African Americans "must give rise to double words and double ideals, and tempt the mind . . . to hypocrisy or to radicalism" (136). The black mind tending toward "hypocrisy," according to Du Bois, "sees in the very strength of the anti-Negro movement its patent weaknesses, and . . . is deterred by no ethical considerations in the endeavor to turn this weakness to the black man's strength." Observing that this "type of Negro . . . is too often found a traitor to right," Du Bois remarked that African Americans tending toward "hypocritical compromise" (137) employ "the same defence which the Jews of the Middle Ages used and which left its stamp on their character for centuries" (138). While he damned African American (and Jewish) compromise as "hypocrisy," Du Bois revealed that he had not been immune to the impress of the older tradition regarding strategic indirection; he himself afforded at least a modicum of dignity to the North's post-Reconstruction willingness to compromise with the US South when he described this implicitly white compromise as ineffectual but nonetheless framed it as "diplomacy and suaveness" (44).

Passing and the Impassable Gulf

As is clear from the foregoing discussion, by *The Autobiography*'s 1912 publication, there existed on both sides of the color line certain discursive trends that were racially and (in Du Bois's case) ethically motivated to interpret African American strategic indirection as hypocrisy. Yet such a conception would render black ambassadorial figures incapable of legitimately using the ambassador's signature diplomatic methods. Furthermore, this conception was doubly disempowering to someone like Johnson, who had assumed the role of national diplomat and in so doing had fashioned himself a racial diplomat. Hence, it is unsurprising to find within Johnson's novel an interrogation of what it means for an African American to seek advancement through strategic indirection. Specifically, *The Autobiography* addresses the indirect methods of a string of "representative" black figures, including Shiny, Booker T. Washington, the Ex-Colored Man, and James Weldon Johnson himself. Whereas the Western interpretive tradition or a Du Boisean approach might suggest we read these figures as hypocrites, *The Autobiography* destabilizes this interpretive strategy, instead framing strategic black indirection as diplomacy and extending validation to such performance by suggesting that it conduces ultimately toward "truth."

The novel is built around depictions of indirection, but *The Autobiography*'s most direct description of indirection as a strategy emerges as the Ex-Colored Man recounts one leg of his journey through the US South. While on a train from Atlanta to Macon, he overhears a conversation among a half dozen men, including a Union Civil War veteran, a Texas cotton planter, and a Jewish cigar manufacturer. Noting the cigar manufacturer's position on "the Negro question," the Ex-Colored Man remarks,

> In the discussion of the race question the *diplomacy* of the Jew was something to be admired; he had the faculty of agreeing with everybody without losing his allegiance to any side. He knew that to sanction Negro oppression would be to sanction Jewish oppression and would expose him to a shot along that line from the old soldier, who stood firmly on the ground of equal rights and opportunity to all men; [meanwhile,] long traditions and business instincts told him when in Rome to act as a Roman. Altogether his position was a delicate one, and I gave him credit for the skill he displayed in maintaining it. (116, emphasis added)

Here, the narrator's praise for the "skill displayed" in "the diplomacy of the Jew" resonates with official international diplomacy's regard for strategic "ambiguity" as a "constructive and creative" hallmark of "diplomatic communication" (Jönsson and Aggestam 151). Yet, racially speaking, the narrator's praise for "the diplomacy of the Jew" carries even more significance. In light of Du Bois's earlier reading of African American compromise as analogous to so-called Jewish hypocrisy, and also in light of the Ex-Colored Man's own comments regarding Jews' and African Americans' similar status vis-à-vis "the race problem" (Johnson, *Autobiography* 111), the novel's portrayal of the cigar manufacturer's posturing as admirable "diplomacy" represents a significant intervention in a performance category that many white people held as whiteness's perquisite. Quite clearly, the Jewish cigar manufacturer uses indirect language as he agrees "with everybody without losing allegiance to any side." Less perceptibly (and hence more indirectly), the Ex-Colored Man also compromises, as he validates as "diplomacy" the behavior of a man who equivocates regarding the issue of "equal rights and opportunity to all men." As the Ex-Colored Man's willingness to equivocate mirrors that of the cigar manufacturer, the narrator subtly opens the door for his own behavior, as well as that of his fellow passenger, to pass into diplomacy.

The Autobiography facilitates this passing and further validates the black ambassadorial figure's methods by providing for a reappearance of Shiny, the novel's early representative of black representativeness, whose own indirection is presently depicted as diplomacy. One day, after the narrator has decided to pass as a white man, he has a chance meeting with the white woman in whom he is romantically interested. They decide to spend half an hour at a museum (147). At the museum, however, the Ex-Colored Man is mortified when he and his love interest cross paths with Shiny, an old acquaintance who of course knows of the narrator's African descent. Seconds into their conversation, the Ex-Colored Man recollects, "Whatever fears I had felt were quickly banished, for [Shiny] seemed, at a glance, to divine my situation, and let drop no word that would have aroused suspicion as to the truth." During the subsequent fifteen-minute conversation, the narrator remembers, Shiny "asked me about myself . . . in so *diplomatic* a way that I found no difficulty in answering him." By the time the conversation ends, furthermore, Shiny's refined demeanor has impressed the narrator's love interest to such a degree that "the 'Shiny' incident [gives the Ex-Colored Man] encouragement and confidence" to finally reveal to her his racial background (148, emphasis added).

Here, the Ex-Colored Man has felt self-conscious regarding the ethics of his decision to "raise a mustache, and let the world take [him] for what it would" (139), an act he later terms "indirect deception" (146) inasmuch as it permits his racially ambiguous features to invite an interpretation of whiteness without directly asserting whiteness as the only interpretation. Yet when Shiny appears as a deus ex machina, the novel's first black ambassadorial figure does not reveal the narrator's racial descent but instead abets the continued indirect deception, adding his own indirection to that of the narrator. Indeed, the ambiguity of Shiny's "diplomatic" questions concerning the narrator's racial past mirrors the ambiguity of the narrator's racial features. Beyond merely using the term *diplomacy* to validate black strategic indirection, however, this scene reminds readers that "indirect deception" becomes strategic indirection when the behavior drives toward a salutary end, when it compromises temporarily for a gain in the future. Here, of course, Shiny's diplomacy leads the Ex-Colored Man to tell his love interest "the truth" regarding his racial descent (149), which permits the narrator to marry her in good conscience. If we acknowledge Shiny's diplomacy as paving the way for the narrator ultimately to marry in good conscience, then we must also remember that it was the narrator's indirection that provided for the marriage's preconditions—the narrative makes clear that she would not have married him had she not grown to love him before she knew of "the drops of African blood in [his] veins" (149).

While "the 'Shiny' incident" clearly situates African American pretense as results-driven diplomacy, a second African American ambassadorial figure prompts the Ex-Colored Man to write his autobiography, a text resulting in an even greater disclosure of truth than that elicited by Shiny. The novel's penultimate paragraph describes the Ex-Colored Man's attendance at a meeting held in Carnegie Hall for the benefit of Hampton Institute. Among the event's speakers were R. C. Ogden, ex-ambassador Choate, and Mark Twain, but the greatest interest of the audience "was centered in Booker T. Washington . . . because of what he represented with so much earnestness and faith." The narrator further explains, "And it is this that all of that small but gallant band of colored men who are publicly fighting the cause of their race have behind them": "the eternal principles of right." The Ex-Colored Man muses, "I, too, might have taken part in a work so glorious." He then embarks on his closing paragraph, suggesting that in passing he may have "sold [his] birthright for a mess of pottage" (154).

The penultimate paragraph lionizes Booker T. Washington, who needs no one to highlight his status as ambassador of his race. Yet *The Autobiography* calls attention to Washington the race representative as it reminds readers of "what he represented" and showcases Washington's public appearance with Joseph Hodges Choate, who from 1899 to 1905 famously served as the US ambassador to England. Readers familiar with *Up from Slavery* will remember that during Washington's European tour, it was Ambassador Choate who introduced Washington to his audience and then presided over the meeting while Washington represented African America to the "distinguished persons" gathered in Essex Hall (166). Thus, as Washington and Choate appear publicly in a second African American literary text, Washington's status as an ambassador is heightened allusively and metonymically. His underscored ambassadorial role is then coupled with the novel's positive assessment of his famously indirect methods. Washington's appearance within the novel cannot help but recall the famous Atlanta Compromise, and Du Bois had only recently implied that Washington's methods employed a strategy of "dangerous half-truth" (*Souls* 43). Yet *The Autobiography* suggests that

Washington, like Shiny, only temporarily compromises on the issue of truth—in fact, Washington himself may "go down in defeat," but his course will ultimately be justified by the "eternal principles of right" he has on his side (Johnson, *Autobiography* 154).

These eternal principles of right, the novel's structure asserts, conduce toward a truth more expansive than the truth facilitated by Shiny's diplomacy. In the novel's opening paragraphs, the narrator refers to the end of his autobiography, remarking on why he writes: "I suffer a vague feeling . . . of regret . . . from which I am seeking relief, and of which I shall speak in the last paragraph of this account" (1–2). Clearly, this is a regret specifically inspired by Washington's success in causing the narrator to reflect that he "might have taken part in a work so glorious" (154), that he might, like Washington and Shiny, have been a racial ambassador if he had not decided to pass. Yet the Ex-Colored Man has not foregone all opportunity to represent the race. Washington's speech inspires him to write his autobiography, which demonstrates to a skeptical white public that possessing "Negro blood" does not "render . . . a man unfit" (144). It is an autobiography whose American success story argues that when a so-called colored man is treated as a so-called white man, the man in question may become "remarkably successful" (143). In other words, *The Autobiography* suggests that Washington may, as Du Bois asserted, truck in "half-truth," but Washington's methods lead ultimately toward greater truths. We now see that the influence of Washington's indirection has transformed the Ex-Colored Man's act of passing from an act of hypocritical cowardice to a tactical move ultimately permitting the narrator, who becomes a successful New York real estate investor, to illustrate an African American capacity for success on a level economic playing field. Undoubtedly, the costs inherent in this compromise—even when framed as diplomacy—have made it a melancholy triumph. The narrator's conflicted position—"glad" (154) yet "feeling . . . unsatisfaction" (1)—is reminiscent of the etymology of the term he has used to describe indirection on the part of Shiny and the Jewish cigar manufacturer. *Diplomacy* recalls the diplomatic credential (or diploma), which, while certifying speech, is a document literally folded against itself, betokening "doubling" and "bend[ing]" from the start.[14]

The Autobiography does not stop at sympathetically treating indirection on the part of Shiny, Booker T. Washington, and the Ex-Colored Man. It also seeks to ameliorate—and indeed to perpetuate—Johnson's own overlapping work in racial and international diplomacy. We see an effort at validating international diplomatic work in the narrator's comments regarding his occupation as an agent in the South American department of a US wholesale house. Upon earning his first thousand dollars at this job, the narrator refers to his feat as the culmination of "honest and patient work" (143). An understanding of the milieu out of which the novel emerged must lead us to view the Ex-Colored Man's "honest and patient work" as a glimpse at the work that Johnson himself facilitated as he provided business-contact information and reports on Latin American markets to the scores of wholesale-house agents that contacted him during his consulships.[15] But a brief allusion to Johnson's consular work is small in comparison to the larger impress that his consulship apparently left on his book and its legacy. Scholarly discussions of the motives for—and ramifications of—the novel's original anonymous publication are varied, usually speculating on anonymity's link to subversive potential or remarking that Johnson published anonymously in order to spur sales.[16] Yet Johnson's decision to publish anonymously may have been more indebted to diplomacy (both as tact and geopolitics) than these astute readings are apt to acknowledge. Ellen Tarry, who gathered material on Johnson through years of informal conversation with his wife, Grace Nail Johnson, once offered a pithy yet instructive explanation of the novel's original anonymous publication: "In 1912 the first edition of *The Autobiography of an Ex-Colored Man* was published anonymously; the writer felt a diplomat should not affix his name to so controversial a book" (215).[17] Since Tarry's explanation was offered in 1967, it has gone unremarked, but the proposal that Johnson chose anonymity because of his consulship repays critical attention. In fact, I would argue, *The Autobiography*'s anonymous publication ought to be framed as the novel's tour de force in its work to validate strategic indirection when practiced by African Americans, since, as I explain later, Johnson's maintenance of anonymity was no doubt partially inspired by his desire to continue in what was for him the compromising role of US diplomat.

As a consul who claimed he was aspiring to become the "American Minister to somewhere" (qtd. in Jackson 184), Johnson was subject to constraints—both de jure and de facto—regarding the pronouncements he could comfortably make. The then-current handbook for US consuls offered much in the way of curtailing speech. Under the headings "Public Speeches" and "Correspondence with the Press," Johnson would have read that he was forbidden to remark on "any matters in dispute between the United States and any other government" (*Regulations* 171) and that he was not to correspond "in regard to the public affairs of any foreign government . . . [except] with the proper officers of the United States" (172).[18] Referring to this set of regulations during the year of Johnson's first consular appointment, former secretary of state John W. Foster expressed the following rule of thumb: the State Department's "official prohibitions and injunctions support the view that the less a diplomatic representative speaks in public, the better for his own reputation" (119–20). Evidently, Johnson lived by such a rule of thumb, carefully guarding his words even when they would not come into direct conflict with State Department regulations. For example, during a 1906 stop through Puerto Rico en route to Venezuela, he was curious about the "exact status of the pure blacks" under the US occupation but refrained from inquiring because "there was no one whom [he] could question confidentially" (*BTWP* 9: 27).

If merely inquiring after the status of "pure blacks" in Puerto Rico gave Johnson pause, *The Autobiography*'s frank treatment of lynching and racial mixture within the United States must have seemed as though it could become an egregious impediment to his good standing with the State Department. *The Autobiography* does not avoid "matters in dispute" between the United States and other governments, as is evident when the Ex-Colored Man situates lynching as a trend that cuts to the heart of the United States' international status and its relations with other states. The Ex-Colored Man seethes, "[I feel] shame for my country, that it, the great example of democracy to the world, should be the only civilized, if not the only state on earth, where a *human being* would be burned alive" (Johnson, *Autobiography* 137, emphasis added). By 1912, lynching had long been an issue of open dispute between the United States and other nations, and the narrator's discussion of "human beings" being burned alive could do more than remind readers of African American humanity. It could also remind an international audience that any human, regardless of race or nationality, might be lynched. This point had been driven home repeatedly, as in 1891, 1896, and 1907 the United States paid reparations to Italy during diplomatic crises fueled by repeated incidents in which white Southerners lynched people of Italian descent (Rimanelli, "New" 144; Rimanelli, "1891–92" 256). Less international in scope but no less dangerous to Johnson's diplomatic career could have been *The Autobiography*'s depiction of the Ex-Colored Man's marriage to a white woman who knows of her husband's African descent. Newspaper articles treating interracial sexual liaisons had famously led to threats of lynching and provided the pretext for race riots in the US South.[19] Of course, Johnson's posts in Latin America kept him geographically removed (for the most part) from US-based white supremacists, but, even from a distance, popular white outrage over the novel's portrayal of interracial relations might have easily become a pretext for Johnson's removal from office.[20]

In writing a novel whose anonymity sought to maintain his position as a conflicted US diplomat, and whose text framed African American indirection as diplomacy rather than hypocrisy, Johnson was undoubtedly interested in provisionally legitimizing methods (and careers) that were traditionally seen as unavailable to African Americans. Certainly, Johnson's status as a racial and national diplomat would benefit from such a legitimization. Yet more ambitiously, the novel seeks to disrupt the essentialist interpretive approaches that have influenced racialized readings of strategic indirection as either hypocrisy or diplomacy. To observe this latter aim is consistent with recent critical approaches to *The Autobiography*, which have adeptly underscored the novel's efforts to expose and thus to debilitate the racial fictions by which the United States was divided.[21] Permitting such antiessentialist approaches to inform our assessment of issues of diplomacy within Johnson's novel, we can see that if, in the short view, *The Autobiography* sends black figures passing into diplomacy, then in a long view, the novel works toward a moment when "passing" (into whiteness and/or diplomacy) would have no meaning. On this point, the novel's penultimate chapter is instructive. Explaining the overarching logic of racial segregation within the United States, the narrator observes that "Southern opinion" has foisted on the nation an image of a "'great and impassable gulf' between the races 'fixed by the Creator at the foundation of the world'" (137). Responding to this metaphor, the Ex-Colored Man explains that "reference to the 'great gulf' loses force in face of the fact that there are in this country perhaps three or four million people with the blood of both races in their veins" (137–38). As the Ex-Colored Man is ranked among this four million himself, he vividly illustrates a lack of racial fixity: his autobiography reveals that he has arisen from an interracial relationship, he has entered into such a relationship, and he has fathered children that promise a continuation of relationships that will attest to the fictionality of an impassable racial gulf. Certainly, Johnson's depiction of pervasive yet unacknowledged racial mixture within the United States is only a reminder of what any student of geopolitics must always remember—that two points separated by a gulf need no bridging, that a gulf's division is coeval with its connection, which is easily forgotten but always found along the oblique path of the coastline. The degree to which *The Autobiography* is successful in driving home this racially destabilizing point is also the degree to which the novel ultimately succeeds in undercutting the gulf between (black) hypocrisy and (white) diplomacy. In absence of an "impassable [racial] gulf," of course, the racialized interpretive gulf between hypocrisy and diplomacy also becomes moot, with the connection between these interpretations found to have always existed along the indirect path of indirection itself.

Importing Artistic Ambassadorship

Although it had been Johnson's "earnest wish to remain in the Service,"[22] he resigned his consulship in 1913, when Woodrow Wilson's Democratic State Department confronted the Republican consul with party "politics plus race prejudice" (Johnson, *Along* 293). After his resignation, Johnson took a job as a contributing editor at the *New York Age*, a paper with traditional ties to Booker T. Washington. From this position, he wrote scathing critiques of the administration that had strong-armed him out of the State Department (Oliver 212), but, still hoping for another diplomatic post during a later Republican administration (W. Gibbs 336), Johnson demonstrated a marked reluctance to criticize the geopolitical principles the United States used to rationalize intervention in the Western Hemisphere. His ability to walk a rhetorical tightrope was something that interested the leaders of the NAACP, who were by 1916 looking to generate new unity among a black US population that had long been divided by a line between Booker T. Washington's Tuskegee and the NAACP's own more confrontational politics (Levy 180). To this end, the NAACP recruited Johnson to its ranks, noting that he was "a good talker, and would offend no group or audience." Given that Booker T. Washington had aided Johnson in attaining his consulship, and given that the ex-consul presently worked for the *New York Age*, it is understandable that NAACP chairman Joel Spingarn characterized Johnson's recruitment as "a coup d'état."[23] However, if Spingarn was correct in affording a geopolitical spin to the NAACP's acquisition of Johnson, Spingarn nonetheless might have been more accurate had he shied away from bellicose imagery and instead characterized the recruitment as shrewd diplomacy on both sides. After all, in order to benefit from Johnson's ability to "offend no group or audience," the NAACP was willing to recruit a man seen by some people as too conservative. Meanwhile, Johnson had written a novel (which he had by now publicly claimed) that made sure to leave its writer open to the prospect of such a recruitment. Like the Jewish cigar manufacturer, the novel itself worked to agree with everybody without losing its allegiance to any side: as the Ex-Colored Man admired Atlanta University (with which Du Bois was affiliated), he placated readers of the Washingtonian persuasion by noting that he was "especially interested in the [university's] industrial building" (Johnson, *Autobiography* 44). And while the novel purported to owe its very existence to feelings stirred by Washington's speech, it praised "that remarkable book by Dr. Du Bois, *The Souls of Black Folk*," as a model for "the future Negro novelist and poet" (123). Indeed, as it turned out, Johnson's facility with indirection not only left him open to recruitment by the NAACP but also became an important selling point. The NAACP's acquiescence to the utility of rhetorical tact and diplomacy, and its deployment of a former US diplomat for these specific rhetorical purposes, helped set the methodological tenor for the New Negro race representatives who greeted *The Autobiography*'s 1927 republication. These were the artistic ambassadors who, according to Wright's "Blueprint for Negro Writing," compromised the Harlem Renaissance.

Yet even as Johnson brought a racial remapping of the notion of strategic indirection to the Harlem Renaissance, involvement with the NAACP functioned to bring a new confrontationalism to his perspectives on international politics. Before joining forces with the NAACP, he continued to support the US policies undergirding his earlier actions in Latin America. In August 1915, he published two editorials that defended the US invasion of Haiti. Explaining that Haiti lacked a "stable government," he implied that the invasion was justified because the nation shared a "political heritage" with "Mexico, Guatemala, Honduras, Nicaragua and some of the South American countries" (Johnson, "Haiti"). The following week, he clarified the nature of this "political heritage" as he more explicitly justified the United States' Haitian intervention by recourse to principles outlined in the Monroe Doctrine and Roosevelt Corollary. "The United States," he explained, "has before now taken similar action in various Latin-American countries; in fact, the international status of these countries as between the United States and Europe compels this Government, under certain conditions, to take action whether it wishes to do so or not" (Johnson, "Haitian"). To be sure, in making these arguments Johnson was jockeying for another diplomatic post, but his arguments also had something else behind them. In deemphasizing the "racial" heritage shared between Haitians and African Americans, Johnson pointed to Haiti's Latin American heritage so as to invalidate the notion that "the state of affairs in the Island Republic is due to the innate incapacity of the

Negro for self-government" (Johnson, "Once"). It becomes clear, then, that in the days before his involvement with the NAACP, Johnson's continued endorsement of US policy in the Western Hemisphere was a tactic aimed at disrupting Haiti's capacity to reflect and represent some type of innate shortcoming on the part of African-descended peoples.

Yet after being recruited by the NAACP, Johnson began condemning the Monroe Doctrine he had once upheld, now decrying it as "the recognized right of the United States to exercise a suzerainty over the whole American continent" (Johnson, "Monroe"). This revised stance led him eventually to go before the Senate Foreign Relations Committee to impugn the Nicaraguan intervention in which he had participated as consul ("Would Curb"). Johnson also began using his *Age* editorials to imply that the US government's invasion and occupation of Haiti arose not because of Haiti's Latin American political heritage but because of the United States' heritage of race prejudice.[24] Such observations culminated (after his NAACP-sponsored trip to Haiti) with his famous essay "Self-Determining Haiti" (1920), which lambasted the continuing US occupation of the republic. Furthermore, instead of attempting to disrupt the view of Haiti as representationally bound to African America, Johnson now reinforced the representational relationship. He explained, "The colored people of the United States should be interested in [Haitian independence and sovereignty], for Haiti is the best chance that the Negro has in the world to prove that he is capable of the highest self-government" (Johnson, "Truth" 252). As he affirmed African American interest in seeing African-descended peoples prosper via the vehicle of the nation-state, Johnson redeployed his diplomatic skills to participate in what has been discussed as an African American tradition of protecting and promoting black nation-states so that the progress of black governments can demonstrate "the capabilities of the black race . . . , thereby securing the worldwide emancipation of people of African descent from slavery, subjugation, and scorn" (Skinner 14). Certainly, Johnson continued to vividly exhibit this interest when, after the First World War, he wrote an editorial advocating self-rule for the African colonies formerly held by Germany. "Internationalization of the former German colonies," he explained, "should eventually lead to the whole of Central Africa being ruled by native Africans, and that in turn should lead to . . . a great change for the better in the status of people of Negro blood all over the world" (Johnson, "Internationalization").

As Johnson spoke in the interest of African self-rule, he was envisioning a reciprocal representational relationship between African

Americans and a black world poised to exhibit success in employing a nation-state model. This vision asserts that insofar as possible, African Americans should act as spokespersons representing the interests of black nation-states; in turn, the advancing black nation-states should represent black national capacity to the world, thus improving conditions for all peoples of African descent, including African Americans. Of course, Johnson's diplomatic work in Latin America as a governmental and racial representative made him well qualified to appreciate the strategic value of such a representational and coalitional relationship, but other US representatives of African descent, whose lessons in international representation had occurred during official service in Africa, were in many ways uniquely qualified to use literary writing to theorize and interrogate the tropes structuring relations between African Americans and broader populations of African descent.

PART II

Lost Theaters

Black Transnationalism and a New Negro Politics of Immanence

Although scholarship on the New Negro era traditionally has focused on the spaces of Harlem and the United States more generally, several recent studies in black transnationalism have brought attention to the New Negro movement's intersections with spaces beyond the United States' borders. Fittingly, scholars oriented toward the New Negro's transnational circuits have found a sort of favorite son in Jamaican American writer Claude McKay and a touchstone text in McKay's 1929 novel *Banjo*, which has a French Mediterranean setting and focuses on a heterogeneous community of black men living on the Marseilles waterfront.[1] According to Brent Hayes Edwards, *Banjo*'s portrayal of a transnational community of black tramps evokes a "vagabond internationalism" marked by radical doubt "that blacks can 'fit' into the logics of modern civilization" (198). This is an internationalism of "the unregistered, the undocumented, the untracked." As such, it "laughs at the logic of consulates" (239). Edwards's denationalized reading of *Banjo* finds a counterpoint in Michelle Ann Stephens's *Black Empire* (2005), which situates McKay's novel in relation to a tradition of Caribbean intellectuals who drew on particular and key "element[s] of imperial and national discourse" (14) to arrive at "a transnational form of black nationality" (4). In *Banjo*, Stephens remarks, the privilege generated by African Americans' US citizenship creates the novel as both a transnational story and a "story of imperial American nationhood" (183).[2]

The black transnational formations described respectively by Edwards and Stephens may be conceptualized through two political modes discussed by Paul Gilroy: the politics of transfiguration and the politics of fulfillment. The politics of transfiguration, says Gilroy, "strives in pursuit of the sublime" (*Black* 38), in pursuit of "qualitatively new . . . social relations . . . and modes of association" (37). The politics of fulfillment, meanwhile, "is mostly content to play occidental rationality at its own game" (38). It "demands . . . that bourgeois civil society live up to the promises of its own rhetoric" (37). Edwards's vagabond internationalism laughs at the logics of modern civilization and hence allies itself with transfiguration, while Stephens's black empire resembles fulfillment as it draws on imperial and national discourse. In bringing focus to New Negro participation in official international diplomacy, *Artistic Ambassadors* limns a third political mode. This is a politics of immanence. Immanence neither laughs derisively nor makes demands but rather, in resonance with the diplomatic construct of representative character, recognizes itself as partially constitutive of the West and hence partially empowered in constituting its present and its destiny.[3]

Like fulfillment and transfiguration, the politics of immanence makes its appearance in *Banjo*'s heteroglossia of black internationalisms. During the novel's third section, the African American character Goosey leaves his vagabond life in Marseilles and travels to "a town near Lyon," where he learns he will not be permitted to work "unless he [can] obtain French papers." Goosey asks for aid from the town's resident American consul, who cannot offer any help. Discouraged, Goosey returns to Marseilles, where a friend tells him "that the consul was Negroid, for he had read about him and seen his photograph in an American Negro publication." The consul had been "so near white" that Goosey had not realized he "was a colored man" (253). *Banjo*'s Negroid consul is an unadorned representation of William Henry Hunt, who worked near Lyon at the consulate in Saint-Étienne from 1907 until the consulate's closing in 1927.[4] As *Banjo* offers a literary representation of Hunt's light skin and distinguished appearances in such New Negro periodicals as the *Crisis*,[5] it conveys the image of an elite New Negro movement that stakes its internationalism not to transfiguration or fulfillment but rather to a politics of immanence permitting diplomatic protocol to obviate New Negro internationalists' race-based allegiances: the Negroid consul is unidentifiable as black, he does not identify himself as such, and he will not be influenced by racial concerns in performing his official duties. While *Banjo*'s larger cast of undocumented vagabonds may be conceptualized through what Ifeoma

Kiddoe Nwankwo has termed black "cosmopolitanism from below" (14), the novel's treatment of Consul Hunt frames the internationalism of the New Negro establishment as a racially ineffectual cosmopolitanism from above. In this vein of New Negro internationalism, color becomes incidental, and insider status (within the nation and the international community) becomes paramount. As depicted in *Banjo*, this is an elite internationalism cultivated by black diplomats and tacitly endorsed by the US-based New Negro periodicals that lionize them.

In tracing New Negro internationalism's politics of immanence, I am interested in presenting a view that resonates with—even as it strives for greater complexity than—the view that *Banjo* offers. Undoubtedly, as McKay's novel intimates, diplomacy's strictures could function to stymie racially interested black speech and activism: New Negro diplomats were hindered by the diplomatic scripts that they relied on as they performed their immanence to an occidental internationalism of nation-states and subordinate colonies. Yet performances of immanence were inevitably imperfect and incomplete, as is illustrated in the literary and diplomatic writings of George Washington Ellis and Henry Francis Downing in chapter 3 and of Angelina and Archibald Grimké in chapter 4. These imperfect and incomplete performances contributed to several theaters of black internationalism that generally have been lost to historians as well as to literary and cultural critics. Ellis's and Downing's work offers a window into the ambivalences held by the State Department and the black diplomats themselves regarding the prospect of black immanence within official US diplomacy. Such ambivalences resulted in structural convergences and divergences between New Negro speech on behalf of the United States and New Negro speech on behalf of the black diaspora. Archibald Grimké's difficulties become emblematic of the fights and sacrifices made by New Negro race men to assume roles permitting them to perform a black politics of immanence. And Angelina Grimké's writings help draw attention to the racial activism and broader black womanist internationalism imperfectly occluded by the performance imperatives of official diplomacy's international matrices.

3 / Diplomatic and Modern Representations: George Washington Ellis, Henry Francis Downing, and the Myth of Africa

In 1913, the year James Weldon Johnson resigned his Nicaraguan consulship, ex-diplomat George Washington Ellis responded to a friend's request for a letter treating the topic of "the Negro in the American Foreign Service." Ellis pointed to Johnson and others to suggest that "the Negro official . . . holds a number of dignified and desirable consulships." He further recalled the international work performed by "some of the greatest names in the race," mentioning the "race's most famous orator and leader," Frederick Douglass, and noting that John Stephens Durham and John Mercer Langston had "time and again . . . distinguished themselves in the diplomatic history of the United States." Ellis observed that "the Negro in the diplomatic service" had performed "with credit to the race and entire satisfaction to the American Government."[1] His latter statement—emphasizing "credit to the race" and "satisfaction to the American Government"—is a reminder that for many figures of the New Negro era, entrance into the arena of international representation functioned to shore up the ongoing project of positive race representation.

However, with good reason, some in the black community voiced cynicism regarding the prestige and salubrity of the posts to which the United States deployed its black diplomats. Paul Laurence Dunbar recounted that when Richard T. Greener was sent to an "out of the way" post, his friends called it "exile" and sarcastically asked, "Why didn't the Government make it a sentence instead of veiling it in the guise of an appointment?" (202–03). Similarly, one of James Weldon Johnson's friends referred to the post in Nicaragua as a "hot and unsanitary hole" (*BTWP* 10: 495), and Langston Hughes spoke sardonically of the United

States' practice of sending black consuls "to any little old colored country" ("See-Saw" 32). Clearly, these relatively minor diplomatic appointments were grounded in the project of political representation—but the appointments functioned more as the domestic representation of a US president's acknowledgment of black support during an election and less as an indication of the United States' concern with political representation in out-of-the-way locales. Unsurprisingly, then, African American men sometimes "decline[d] posts offered them," believing that such "assignments were more likely the end than the beginning of a career" (Blakely, "Black" 9).

In spite of career risks, health conditions, and comparative lack of representational significance abroad, many black men of the New Negro era accepted minor consulships and other less prestigious appointments. These appointments could (the cynics not withstanding) increase one's status domestically. After all, as Ellis's letter demonstrates, employment with the State Department offered the chance to introduce one's name to a select list of race men that included Douglass and Langston. And assignments specifically to Africa came with the added fascination of living on a continent to which many black diplomats felt ancestral ties. On one hand, the weight of these ties is reflected in Elliot P. Skinner's important discussions of African American diplomats' contentions with the State Department for policies that would benefit black populations in Africa.[2] A second and as yet uninterrogated reflection of these ties' importance emerged as several New Negro diplomats who served in Africa later wrote books, articles, and speeches that contemplated the task of representing Africa accurately.[3]

If contemplating and developing accurate representations of Africa frequently has been a difficult and ethically fraught task, it was uniquely so during the late nineteenth- and early twentieth-century phase of what has been described as "colonial modernity," a term acknowledging the global effects of "a capitalism emanating from Euro-America" on "the contemporaneity and the complicity of the modern and the colonial" (Dirlik 18, 20).[4] The interrelation of the colonial and the modern—epitomized by transnational circuits of capital, diaspora, aesthetics, and scientific theory—placed Africa (and people of African descent) behind what Ellis termed a "veil of misrepresentation" ("Psychology" 314). The effects of this misrepresentative veil were pervasive. In the United States, Du Bois recognized that white populations fortified the white-supremacist regime via a scientific and historical tradition that "unconsciously distorted" the truth about Africa (*Black Folk* vii). In London, a black and Asian collective observed that Britain's colonially interested media engaged in "systematic injustice and misrepresentation" of the empire's dark populations ("Foreword" iii). Concomitantly, on a transnational artistic front, aesthetic modernism's primitivist streak saw modernists (among them Ezra Pound and Pablo Picasso) take Africa as a muse while modifying "their style of [realistic] representation and experiment[ing] with a nonrepresentational aesthetic" (Lemke 7).[5] These representational tensions and cleavages point toward a myth of Africa as central to what Fredric Jameson describes as a "moment of modernism" in which the sign was disjoined from the referent to create a semiautonomous and "free-floating" realm of representation (96).

In the context of this transdiscursive deployment of Africa as a trope, occasion, and muse for disjunctive representational practices, George Washington Ellis and Henry Francis Downing accepted minor diplomatic assignments in West Africa.[6] After completing their assignments (Downing as consul in Angola from 1887 to 1888 and Ellis as secretary of the US Liberian Legation from 1902 to 1910), they produced writing that shared space with work by Du Bois, Johnson, and Carter G. Woodson in the *Crisis*'s monthly "Selected List of Books."[7] However, by the 1920s, these earlier New Negro writers were, in the estimation of critic Hubert Harrison, unjustly neglected. During the Harlem Renaissance, Harrison suggested that aficionados of black literature who had not read Downing and Ellis were mere dilettantes, enthusiastic about the current Negro vogue but "blissfully ignorant of the stream of literary . . . products which have flowed uninterruptedly from Negro writers from 1850 to the present" (352).[8] Recovering Downing and Ellis from this cultural amnesia, which continues to the present day, requires fleshing out the literary-representational ramifications of their diplomatic work in West Africa, where they themselves emerged less as direct international representatives of the United States and more as semiautonomous diplomatic signs participating in the creation and negotiation of their own unstable attachments to the United States and Africa. As their work in literary and diplomatic representation intersected with African tropes and materialities, Downing and Ellis participated in what Susan Stanford Friedman calls an "expressive dimension of modernity," a modernism sharing "family resemblances" with other aesthetic expressions that also responded to the epoch's tumultuous conditions (432). Their work is a reminder that, during the moment of modernism, innovative representations of Africa and people of African descent were not works of literature and art that experimented with the politically immanent project of dissevering the sign from the referent. Rather, innovation was more likely to arise through sustained contemplation of and engagement with the potentially transfigurative project of suturing African representations to the material world.

Minstrel Mask Diplomacy

Born in Missouri in 1875, George Washington Ellis graduated from high school in Kansas, where he later completed a BA and was admitted to the state bar. In 1897, he moved to New York City and attended the Gunton Institute of Economics and Sociology before passing the US Census Board examination in 1899. He spent the next two years in Washington, DC, working on the 1900 Census while doing postgraduate work in sociology and psychology at Howard University. Ellis's involvement in Republican political campaigns brought attention from Theodore Roosevelt, who in 1902 appointed him to the position of secretary of the United States Legation in Liberia.[9]

Secretary of the United States' Liberian Legation was not a particularly significant diplomatic office. Describing Ellis's position as a type of diplomatic form evacuated of representational content, Downing referred to the office as "a sinecure of the most scandalous kind" (*American* 253). In fact, although Ellis accepted the office because he wanted "to study the Negro African and his social conditions" (Ellis, *Negro* 17), he grew weary of his unchallenging governmental work. During eight years in Liberia, he frequently sought transfers and promotions, occasionally threatening to resign if he were not reassigned. Such threats generated commentary within the State Department that is indicative of the department's regard for its larger corps of black diplomats. Remarking on Ellis's threats, Robert Bacon of the Appointments Office wrote to a colleague that if they wanted to keep Ellis, "there is nothing to do but transfer him." However, alluding to the fact that the department merely tended to rotate the same set of black diplomats in and out of the same posts in small nations and colonies of color, Bacon asked, "Would [Ellis] be better than some new coon?" (qtd. in Fleming 94). Bacon's question lays bare the department's treatment of relations with African-descended nations as a type of minstrel show, with African American representatives becoming the black mask of a white nation less interested in accurate representation in nations of color and more interested in maintaining diplomatic placeholders, with one "coon" just about as good as another in any assignment. In some ways, this was an admission that as long as black diplomatic appointments functioned domestically to remind black voters that their support was not taken for granted, the State Department could make itself amenable to sending what it saw as malapropistic caricatures rather than serious representatives to nations of African descent. Such an approach to international (mis)representation in Africa vividly enacted, on the diplomatic stage, what Houston Baker calls the minstrel mask's "deep-seated denial of the indisputable humanity of inhabitants of and descendants from the continent of Africa" (*Modernism* 17). Like other discourses of the modern moment, US diplomacy took Africa as an occasion to abandon its standard representational practices. Sending forth what it saw as caricatures rather than accurate national representatives, the department engaged in minstrel-mask diplomacy.

Though Ellis was not likely privy to Bacon's comment, he was well acquainted with the semiautonomous status afforded him by the racist diplomatic culture from which the comment emerged. And ironically, it was *because* his assignment was a sinecure—a diplomatic form evacuated of significant representational content—that Ellis found a modest salary, ample spare time, and sufficient pretext to pursue his ethnographical study of the Vai-speaking people of West Africa. By his own account, when the State Department occasionally sent him "into the far interior . . . to report upon the various tribes," he arranged the excursions so that "private studies coincided with official duties" (*Negro* 17). And during the many "times not occupied with his official duties," Ellis "employed Vai scholars to instruct him in the Vai language" and "cultivated the most intimate acquaintances in frequent conferences with Vai savants and elders" (*Negro* 18). Ultimately, it was the State Department's minstrel-mask diplomacy—its denial of Ellis's full immanence to official internationalism—that created for Ellis the autonomy of which he took advantage in performing studies that emphasized Africa's modern mask as a veil of misrepresentation. As Ellis explained it, his "studies in West Africa revealed a Negro substantially different" from what "is described in modern science and literature." He determined that rather than allowing "Caucasian writers" to dominate discourse regarding Africa, "the Negro should explain his own culture and interpret his own thought and soul life, if the complete truth is to be given to the other races of the earth" (*Negro* 19).

By 1910, Ellis had concluded his studies in Africa, and he made good on this threat to resign from the Foreign Service. Settling in Chicago, he opened a law practice but was most truly dedicated to subverting the modern representational practices that had simultaneously framed him as a "coon" and given him the means of conducting African research. He aspired to cast off the mask, to "lift . . . the veil of misrepresentation which . . . has covered the Negro in Africa and elsewhere" (Ellis, "Psychology" 314). With Du Bois and Franz Boas, Ellis was a contributing editor of the *Journal of Race Development*. During this era, he wrote numerous articles as well as a novel and a book-length ethnographical study. His ethnographic work, *Negro Culture in West Africa* (1914), brought together information he collected while studying the Vais as secretary of legation. In some ways, *Negro Culture* was a triumph. Du Bois observed that it proved "the high culture and ability of these black people." Du Bois suggested that the book "ought to be in every colored American's library" ("Pile" 200). Others called it "an important . . . contribution to the knowledge of negro culture in Africa" (Rev. of *Negro Culture*) and maintained it could "be read with profit by all friends of mankind" (Dyson 96).

Mimetic Failure and a Psychological Turn

Yet even as Ellis seemed to succeed in presenting "the Negro African to the world . . . like he really is" (*Negro* 19), other reactions to *Negro Culture* suggested the limits of objective representation. While in Liberia, Ellis carried a camera into the hinterlands with the intention of taking "about 100 pictures of scenes in actual life to illustrate" his manuscript.[10] Ellis's publisher, Walter Neale, reluctantly agreed to include some of these photographs, but Neale also offered the following insult: "Many of the photographs that you have submitted to us tend to disprove your contention that the Vai people are possessed of considerable culture; the bulk of the photographs show a barbarous people, and perhaps a cannibal race."[11] Neale's statement must have seemed revealing, as it underscored the fact that even photography—a supposed mimetic triumph of modernity—could not bridge the disjunction between African representations and African reality for viewers who had imbibed the West's discourse regarding the so-called dark continent. Neale's statement was a reminder that the veil of misrepresentation structured Western reading practices and functioned to disrupt efforts toward objective representations of Africa.

Similar concerns with preconditioned misreading surface in Ellis's novel, published three years later in 1917. *The Leopard's Claw* contemplates the limits of Africa's potential for objective representation in its opening chapters. When Eva, one of the novel's British heroines, arrives in West Africa for the first time, she thinks of the women at a local market "as a replica of an exhibition scene at the Crystal Palace" (16). Here, even as Eva views African reality, she does not *see* African reality but instead imports reading practices that merely permit her to interpret Africa through the distorting lens of England's imperial exhibitions. Eva emerges as analogous to Neale, who saw in Ellis's photographs only the "cannibal race" he had been preconditioned to see. A frustration with the limits of objectivity vis-à-vis Africa may have set the stage for Ellis to respond in substantial ways to a 1915 review of *Negro Culture* by University of Chicago sociologist Robert E. Park. Park drew particular attention to *Negro Culture*'s explanation that the Vai alphabet was developed in response to a dream had by its African inventor. Ellis's study recounts the dream without comment, but Park suggested the dream was "an interesting circumstance . . . from the point of view of recent psychology of the subconscious" (842). Park's suggestion would not have seemed surprising to Ellis given his earlier postgraduate work in psychology, but positive notice from the prominent sociologist must have carried special weight: Park's reference to new psychology suggested that Ellis perform not an objective study of Vai culture in the hinterland but an exploration of the African Negro's psychological hinterland.[12] This would be a move away from attempts at objective representation and toward a realm of psychological symbolism.

Though *The Leopard's Claw* does not eschew commitments to realism,[13] it trucks in psychological symbolism and ultimately becomes a literary exploration that is less wary of the misrepresentative veil and more willing to engage in subjective refractions (rather than objective reflections) of African peoples. If, as one critic has suggested, *The Leopard's Claw* tends to reinscribe "the erroneous impressions of West Africa" that Ellis earlier sought to correct (V. Williams 84), then one of the novel's modes of purveying these erroneous impressions involves the way in which its symbolic approach to representing Africa began to coincide with the State Department's markedly disjunctive approach to representation in Africa. The novel's prefatory materials are illuminating on this point. The title page offers a subtitle billing the novel as "a thrilling story of love and adventure from a European castle through the West African jungle, disclosing a deep insight into the quality and spiritual influence of African social institutions and conditions, and revealing a profound psychic interpretation of African inner life, all clustered about the mysterious function and significance of the Leopard's Claw" (iii).[14] The promise of a "psychic interpretation" associated with "the Leopard's Claw" should direct attention toward the graphic on the novel's front cover (fig. 2).[15] This illustration depicts the front paw of a leopard ripping through the novel's cardboard cover. The paw extends four claws, which are represented as lodged within the cover and placing three-dimensional stretch marks onto the two-dimensional medium. The claws, reaching from the upper left corner to the lower right, suggest the possibility of pulling aside the exterior to reveal an interior that houses the African psyche referenced by the subtitle. In the same motion as the leopard's claws promise insight into African inner life, the claws offer a strong indication of what this inner life will look like. They function metonymically, inviting readers to imagine, behind the front cover, an inner animal existing as a condensation of African psychic life. In other words, as suggested by the commerce between the graphic and the subtitle, readers should allow the metonym of the claw to conduce toward the metaphor of the leopard. The African-psyche-as-leopard is the initiating conceit of the "profound psychic interpretation" promised by the title page. Rather than lifting the "veil of misrepresentation" that Ellis saw as covering "the Negro in Africa," the book's cover becomes the veil, suggesting that the novel will not reveal the African psyche directly but only in snatches of metaphor and metonymy.

The novel's prominent psychological preoccupations (including dream-based memory recovery, sleep-talking, aphasia, and amnesia) suggest that Ellis was indeed interested in turning toward what Park referenced as the recent psychology of the subconscious.[16] Yet these facets of *The Leopard's Claw* pertain to the psychic lives of the novel's European characters, Oliver Montcrief and his family, who spend fourteen years wandering in Sierra Leon and the hinterland in search of riches. Meanwhile, the novel's West African characters are generally "the loyal servants of the English protagonists" (V. Williams 84). This lack of apparent psychological depth on the part of West African characters is curious in light of Ellis's repeated assertion, in his nonfiction, that "the bravery and heroism displayed by many of the African leaders and people in defense of their liberties and their lands . . . contain materials for the most thrilling stories in romance and in fiction."[17] While *The Leopard's Claw*'s title bills it as a "thrilling story," readers might well look at the generally placid West African characters and find themselves at a loss to point toward any African bravery or heroism in the novel. However, recalling the commerce between the novel's title page and its ruptured cover permits a view—in veiled psychic form—of the resistance Ellis held as the ideal in Africa-based imaginative writing.

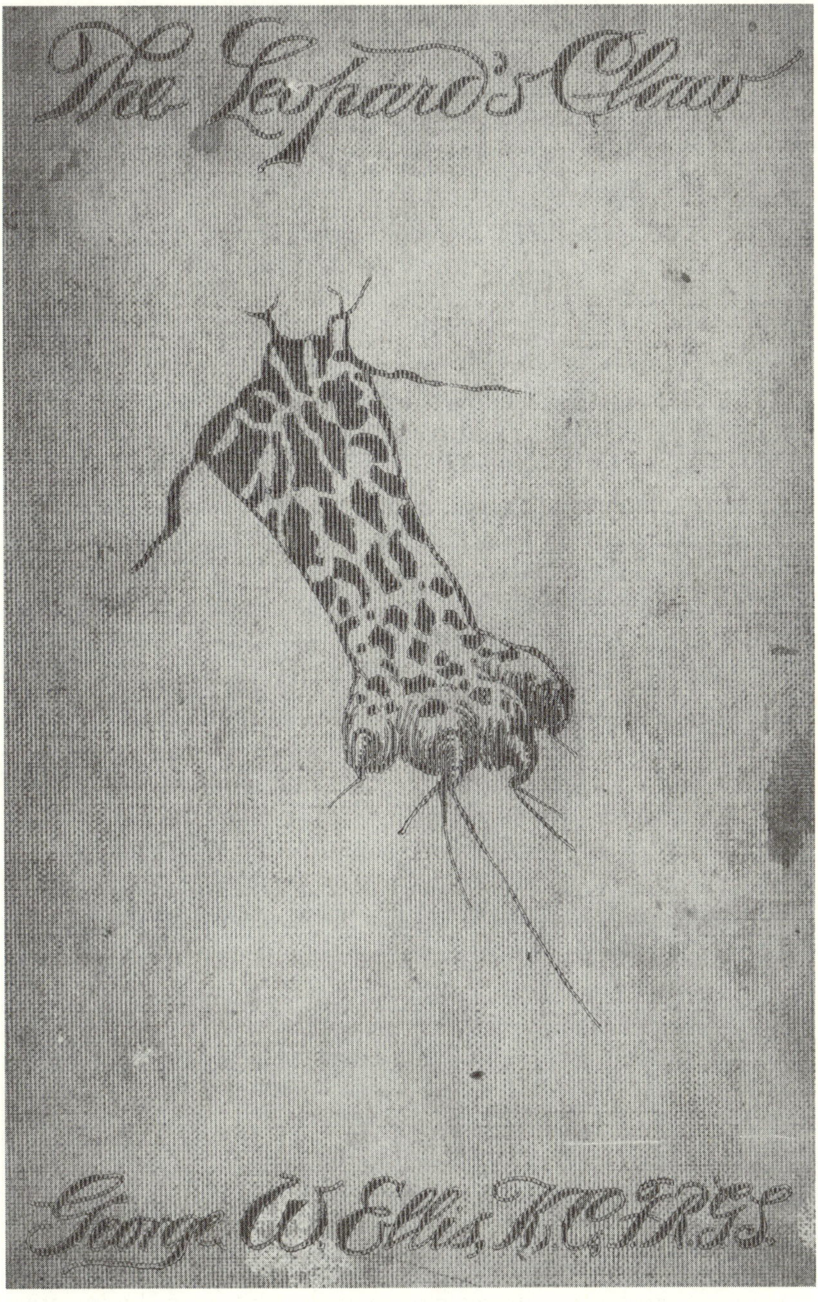

FIGURE 2. Front cover of George Washington Ellis's *The Leopard's Claw.* (Courtesy of the Beinecke Rare Book and Manuscript Library, Yale University)

The first appearance of a leopard within the novel conveys a sense that a leopard is more than a leopard. At one point during the Montcriefs' travels, they spend the night in an African village, and the next morning, Oliver meets one of the few West African characters who seem discontent with the Montcriefs' sense of colonial entitlement. Oliver tries paying for the night's lodging with cloth, rum, and tobacco, but the village chief objects and instead requests a gun and powder. At first, Oliver threatens that Sierra Leon's colonial governor will make the chief "pay for any annoyance," but the chief counters that the land does not "belong to [the] English" and that he and his village are "free people." Oliver subsequently offers the chief a compromise—just the powder and not the gun. Evidently placated, the chief takes the payment and gives Oliver's daughter, Lucretia, "a canine pup" as an apparent goodwill offering (Ellis, *Leopard's* 36). That evening in the jungle, however, as "the owls and other night [animals] protested at what they considered intruders," a leopard jumps out of the darkness, nearly attacking Oliver's wife, Eva, but then carrying the dog into the night (37).

Undoubtedly, readers are meant to draw some parallel between these adjacent scenes, with the jungle scene offering a veiled glimpse at the African psyche that was not fully displayed in the village scene. While the chief merely denies British authority, the night animals register overt protests against the colonial intruders. And while the dog communicates the chief's outward acquiescence to Oliver's compromise, the leopard's attack symbolizes a psychic rescinding of this acquiescence. A glance at West African folklore, furthermore, permits a view of the chief's gift as a type of Trojan horse. As recorded by one of Ellis's folklore-collecting colleagues at the Liberian Legation, the Leopard had long ago sworn to avenge a vendetta against the Dog by "pounc[ing] upon and destroy[ing] him whenever and wherever found" (Camphor 245). In this context, the chief's goodwill offering permits Africans and the Montcriefs to continue their dispute by proxy, through psychologically symbolic animal life. Throughout the novel, the appearances of several other leopards have a similar psychological valence.[18]

This mode of literary representation resonates with some of Marcus Garvey's commentary on black modes of political representation. According to Garvey, the African was wise enough to know he could not succeed in a fight against "the white man" (4: 177). Hence, the African made a tactical choice, refusing to reveal to the white man "his intention and his design" (4: 178) but instead making compromises that should qualify "the Negro" as "the greatest diplomat known to the world" (4:

177). In *The Leopard's Claw*, these compromises call for veiling African "bravery and heroism" in the psychic symbol of the leopard, permitting intention and design to manifest themselves only in brief slips and snatches.

Ellis's novel emerges as problematic not only in its self-evident imitations of white African adventure stories (Gruesser 49) but also in its complicity with many other modernist works that permit blackness to become a psychological trope.[19] As it represents the African psyche via an animal (the leopard) and a fetish (its claw),[20] *The Leopard's Claw* resembles work by modern playwright Eugene O'Neill, whose move away from realism involved writing expressionistic dramas that attempted to symbolize the black psyche by displacing it onto such stereotyped and primitivist manifestations as crocodiles and African masks.[21] Observing this modern family resemblance is far from a celebration of *The Leopard's Claw*'s aesthetic or racial politics.[22] Indeed, as one who was treated as a "coon" in the State Department's minstrelesque program for nations of color, Ellis endured a practical disjunction from his national referent that itself had been a study in the way stereotypes could lead into experimental strategies for representation. However, rather than proceeding with caution in relation to such stereotypes, Ellis's novel borrows significantly from the infamous image of African-descended people as bestial. Taking the leopard as a metaphor for the African psyche, he rehashes in psychological terms a trope that was given biblical force by Jeremiah 13:23, reemphasized by Thomas Dixon's popular Ku Klux Klan novel *The Leopard's Spots* (1902), and hackneyed to the point that during the first decades of the twentieth century, both the Central Park and Bronx Zoos kept a leopard named "Nigger."[23]

Ellis published *The Leopard's Claw* with the hope of supplementing his reputation as a New Negro race representative, a reputation he had begun building through his work as a diplomat. With a novel veiling African resistance in psychological symbolism, he could potentially attract further attention from Park. And Ellis's publisher, while negotiating the contract for *Negro Culture* in 1913, tantalized him with still greater promises of cultural capital: "There seems to be in the air prophecies of notable achievements in literature by members of your race soon to be accomplished. Several noteworthy books by Negroes, if they should be published simultaneously in the near future . . . would bring about a renaissance of Negro literature in America. . . . I think the time near at hand. The rewards of the authors that shall be identified with a movement of the sort, if movement it may be termed, should be very great."[24] It was, then, with the hope of continuing his artistic ambassadorship during an impending renaissance that Ellis responded to modern conditions—ranging from colonialism to the field of psychology to minstrel-mask diplomacy—to arrive at representational refractions bearing familial affinities with the concerns frequently associated with the experimentalist trend in aesthetic modernism. However, Ellis's domestic literary ambitions went largely unrequited. In spite of *The Leopard's Claw*'s psychological bent, the novel apparently elicited no new comment from Park. And although Ellis advertised his novel as "New Race Literature," its depictions of Africa undoubtedly smacked of misrepresentative stereotypes that seemed quite old to the New Negro communities of the 1910s. Before examining the novel, a reporter for the *Chicago Defender* anticipated that *The Leopard's Claw* would follow *Negro Culture* as "another beacon light on [Ellis's] already illuminating pathway of literary progress." The reporter promised that the novel would be "commented upon soon" by the *Defender*'s literary critic ("George"). The literary critic, however, must have found little in *The Leopard's Claw* to suggest innovation and progress, for the review apparently did not appear.[25]

Henry Francis Downing's Problems of Constituency

Reflecting Ellis's intense feelings of ancestral connection to West Africa, he referred to "blacks in the New World" as living in "lands of . . . exile" ("Liberia in the Political" 65). Hence, when he observed that "the Negro should explain his own culture and interpret his own thought and soul life" (*Negro* 19), such a statement was in support of African Americans' work to explain and interpret the lives and interests of Africans. Yet, as evidenced by Ellis's apparent attempt to increase his domestic status by way of a novel veiling Africans behind the hackneyed metaphor of a leopard, a disjunction existed between Ellis's interests (or perhaps judgment) and the interests of the Africans he sought to represent in fiction. In certain ways, this disjunction was as significant as was Ellis's own disjunction, as a diplomatic representative, from the nation he ostensibly represented. Of course, Ellis was not the only New Negro diplomat whose post in Africa seemed to divorce him from (more than bind him to) the United States. Such was also the case with Henry Francis Downing. Yet whereas Ellis used his semiautonomy to pursue independent research interests and eventually to write a novel acquiescing to the modern moment's systematic misrepresentations of Africa, Downing was more obstinate with regard to modernity's tendency to dissever political and aesthetic representations from their material moorings. Downing's resistance did not result in a literary realism that attempted to reattach African representations to their referents; instead, he produced writing that self-consciously theorizes the potential dangers involved when, as in the case with Ellis, African Americans permit non-Afrocentric interests to influence their representations of Africa. Routed through Downing's representationally troubled work in US diplomacy, his literary writings theorize the ways in which New Negro race representatives could become complicit in promoting Africa's veil of misrepresentation.

In a 1917 *Crisis* advertisement, Downing's publisher offered the following description:

> Mr. Downing perhaps has had a more varied career than any other living Negro from the Civil War to the war between the United States and Germany. He was the first colored man to represent the United States at [Luanda, Angola], by appointment of President Cleveland. He introduced Coleridge-Taylor to the London Public. He persuaded Liberia to open its doors to foreign capital. Merely to recount his activities in public life of the past fifty years would take a volume. But his highest renown has been won as a man of letters. ("Books")

This description was more than puffery. In 1917, this endorsement functioned to reintroduce Downing to black Americans who may have forgotten he existed. Although Downing was a New York native, extensive travel had taken him, until his 1917 return to Manhattan, a long way from home. Likely born in 1846, Downing was the son of a restaurateur and the nephew of civil rights leader George T. Downing. By the time Henry Downing was thirty, he had served in the US Navy twice, and his military and personal travels had taken him to the Pacific as well as to West Africa. After his second discharge from the Navy, Downing married and became a prominent black New York Democrat during the 1880s. For his support, President Grover Cleveland appointed him consul to Luanda, Angola, at that time a Portuguese colony.[26]

The *Crisis* advertisement placed this consulship first among the accomplishments leading toward Downing's emergence as "a man of letters." And a glance at Downing's preoccupations while consul suggests a substantial commerce between his early work in international representation and later work in literary representation. Spanning from 1 October 1887 to 3 November 1888, Downing's consulship situated him in a version of West Africa that troubled representational conventions for him as well as for other, more famous modernists. Arriving in Angola just two years after Leopold II of Belgium and Henry Morton Stanley established the adjacent Congo Free State, Downing saw "European countries emptying [the] fertile land of its products, and their citizens growing wealthy."[27] When he learned of Stanley's trespasses against US citizens on the Upper Congo, Downing requested that the State Department commission him to travel up the Congo once a year.[28] His request was not granted. Unlike Joseph Conrad, Downing never traveled up the Congo, but the consul's letters to the State Department occasionally contained passages that would have been more at home in a novel than in a consular dispatch. For instance, whereas Conrad's Marlow wonders if in Africa he has "stepped into the gloomy circle of some inferno" (14), Downing described Africa's "gloom," its "flitting bat, and mournful cry of the owl, with the moon sending her light between the overhanging branches of the trees," as forming "a scene worthy of 'Dante's Inferno.'"[29]

Unlike many other participants in colonial modernity, however, Downing did not take his great lessons in representational distortion from Africa's primeval gloom or its masks and curios; instead, for Downing, these lessons arose from a consulship that asked him to contemplate what could be called (to borrow a phrase from Kenneth Warren) "the problem of constituency," or the fraught question of exactly whom or what he represented in Luanda.[30] As a consul, of course, Downing ostensibly represented US trade interests in Luanda. Yet upon his arrival, he found that the United States had no trade with Angola and seemed uninterested in pursuing it. He observed with some amount of indignation that in spite of the consulate's many years of operation, merchants in Luanda did not even know that US goods existed.[31] It seemed to Downing that the "United States [was] not interested in trade with Angola," and he apparently felt the need to remind the State Department of what ought to have been obvious: "The object of the Government in sustaining a Consulate here is, I judge, to advance the commercial interests of its country."[32] That Downing needed to remind the department of a consul's role, and that he hedged his reminder as he advanced it, points toward an important disconnect between the supposed and actual representational functions of the US consul in Luanda. In the absence of US trade interests, Downing to a large extent became merely representative of the theoretical potential for US representation in Luanda.

Yet Downing felt that this theoretical capacity to represent US trade interests was troubled by the meager salary he received from the State

Department. In Angola, he found his salary "sufficient to pay only 50% of the expense incidental to the place,"[33] and he explained to the department that this level of compensation was "such as will force any one, not enjoying an income independent of his salary, into a position which will launch him into a vortex of embarrassment."[34] The department expected Downing to supplement his consular income by cultivating private trading relationships, but Downing disliked this expectation because it would seem to undercut his immanence to US diplomacy by impinging on his ability to represent US interests. He explained to the department that a "trading Consul not only is at times prejudiced in judgment . . . , but he also often finds occasion to make the performance of public duty give way to private interests."[35] In Downing's mind, cultivating personal trade would have an effect similar to Marx and Engels's *camera obscura* (47), turning the consul's role upside down, converting him from (trade) *representative* to (self-) *represented*. The threat inherent in this conversion lay in its gesture toward the department's complacency with Downing's existence as a diplomatic sign divorced from what ought to have been his national referent. Like Ellis, Downing received his appointment through political patronage. Also like Ellis, he became a diplomatic placeholder in Africa, a "coon" (in the State Department's eyes) with a minimal representative role. Yet compared to Ellis, Downing was more conspicuously discontent with his semiautonomous status. He had not traveled to Africa with the ulterior motive of performing a systematic study of African ethnic groups; his ambitions were more focused on the task and honor of representing the United States, a project aimed at cementing his status as a race representative and promoting African Americans' quest for the full privileges of US citizenship. The State Department's minstrel-mask diplomacy undercut the diplomatic immanence that Downing hoped would further his personal aspirations and racial efforts.

By its conclusion, Downing's work in Africa had indeed launched him into a vortex of difficulties (financial and representational) that later resurfaced in his literary writing. In the meantime, however, he returned to New York, where, recovering from his financial difficulties, he managed a Brooklyn-based weekly newspaper and became a leader in the National Colored People's Protective Association.[36] Then, in 1895, Downing and his second wife relocated to London, where they resided for some twenty-two years. Finding himself at what was becoming a hub of the emerging black internationalist consciousness and community, Downing lodged Dunbar while the poet wrote his first novel, managed Dunbar's first recital with Samuel Coleridge-Taylor, spoke at the Pan-African Conference of 1900, wrote lyrics for black composer Amanda Ira Aldridge, and befriended Nina Du Bois while her daughter, Yolande, attended an English boarding school in 1914 and 1915.[37]

By the early 1910s, Downing had taken a strong literary turn. He wrote serial fiction for Duse Mohamed Ali's London-based (moderately) anti-colonial journal, the *African Times and Orient Review*.[38] Furthermore, in 1913 and 1914, he published at least eight plays and oversaw the Players and Playwrights Association, a society apparently dedicated to helping amateur playwrights place their work with London stage managers.[39] Francis Griffiths, who published six plays by Downing, told the *Citizen* that in Mr. Downing he had found a dramatist "of unusual originality and power" ("Unacted Plays"). Downing's published plays also drew praise from the *African Times* and noteworthy contemporary actors and dramatists including Matheson Lang, John Drinkwater, and Herbert Tree.[40] With these endorsements in hand, Downing "arranged for the production of a number of his plays" at the Royal Court Theatre in 1914. The productions were canceled, however, when the Royal Court shut its doors (due to the First World War) from June 1914 to October 1915. As a result, Downing "lost [the] considerable amount of money which he had already expended" on souvenir medallions for his plays, which led to "arrears with his rent" and subsequent legal trouble.[41]

Aesthetic, Racial, and International Misrepresentation

Although Downing by 1914 had become one of the most prolific African American playwrights to that point, his dramatic work has gone almost completely unexamined. One commentator has suggested that his oeuvre does not deal directly with race questions (Contee 189), a statement which in conjunction with the general unavailability of his work has perhaps stymied interest in further research. Yet even Downing's so-called raceless plays evince preoccupations with race, and a few of his plays include prominent characters of African descent.[42] Among these latter plays, *A New Coon in Town: A Farcical Comedy Made in England* (1914) preoccupies itself with the uses and limits of an African heritage preserved during the Middle Passage. Furthermore, and relevant to the project of coming to a greater understanding of the place and function of international diplomacy within writing of the New Negro era, the play self-consciously treats minstrelesque stereotypes as they relate to interlocking modes of aesthetic, racial, and international (mis)representation. *A New Coon in Town* depicts the London-based misadventures of the African American character Terminus Quoddy, whose dialect and antics clearly allude to a tradition of blackface minstrelsy but who Downing instructs "should act with restraint, and thus avoid debasing the character to the level of the music-hall, minstrel type of Negro" (5). Similar to Cato of William Wells Brown's *The Escape*, Terminus operates within and against minstrel stereotypes—at some moments emerging as tractable but at others as shrewd and intransigent. Susan Stewart has written of "distressed genres" (67) in which the literary stands "in imitation of" older oral and folk forms (68). Such literary reproductions, she explains, create for themselves an "artifactual nature" (67) through "a process of appropriation, manipulation, and ultimately transformation for oral and literary forms alike" (68). Similarly, Terminus emerges as a distressed character, one offering an allusion to minstrelsy's heyday while seeking to transform the "minstrel type of Negro" into a study of the types of Africa-related (mis)representations that operated transdiscursively along diplomatic, racial, and aesthetic lines.

Embodying what Alain Locke later called "the Old Negro," who is "more of a formula than a human being" (3), Terminus arrives in London on a cattle boat that has sailed from Baltimore. Acting on a tradition passed down from his great-grandfather, the traveler is en route to Liberia, where he intends to claim a ruby farm to which he is ostensibly heir. In London, however, Terminus finds himself in trouble with the law and is rescued by—and hence indebted to—a man named Dennis Flynn. Having incurred Terminus's obligation, Dennis enlists the traveler as a reluctant participant in two schemes aimed at deceiving the Hebb family, a household of affluent Londoners involved in the African gem trade. Dennis's two schemes—requiring Terminus to impersonate first an African ambassador and later the statue of an African chief—recall the State Department's treatment of African Americans as diplomatic placeholders, interchangeable "coons" as Bacon crassly stated. As Terminus stands in for a political representative and a work of art, *A New Coon in Town* advances themes harking back to Downing's difficult work in diplomatic representation. Here, Downing no longer covets the diplomatic immanence that the United States' minstrel-mask diplomacy had denied him; rather, his play cautions that African Americans may become immanent to a pervasive system of misrepresentation as they assume the role of transnational race representative, whether aesthetically or politically. Relevant to the type of representational distortions enacted by Ellis's *The Leopard's Claw*, *A New Coon in Town* explores the dangers and pitfalls faced by African Americans as they (especially under white influence) take ancestral ties as credentials to represent Africa.

The play begins on a London street as Dennis greets Serena Hebb, the class-conscious Hebb family matriarch. Serena spurns him, making him feel like a "common plebeian" (8). Angered, Dennis enlists Terminus in a plot aimed at using Serena's aristocratic bent to put her to shame: Terminus is to visit the Hebbs' house while posing as the representative of a facetious African dominion. That afternoon, announced as "Palaver Sauce, Prince of Phoo Phoo" (30), Terminus enters the Hebbs' parlor, where he turns to Serena and says, "Missus, . . . de King o' Phoo Phoo, 'structed me ter come an' smile at yo'." Terminus explains, "I represents de King." To this assertion of representational capacity, Serena's husband, Septimus, replies, "Ah, his Majesty's ambassador?" and Terminus answers "O' co'se!" In hopes of alleviating the strain produced by his "laborious" "duty as Ambassador" (33), Serena offers Terminus food and drink. Terminus replies, "Isn't de mos' 'portant part o' a 'bassador's duty eatin' an' drinkin', and talkin' erbout nuffin?" (34). Before Terminus can begin eating and drinking, however, Dennis blusters into the room disguised as a detective. The detective scandalizes the Hebbs by calling the ambassador a thief and chasing him from the home (35).

Light though this scene may be, it is important because of the way it interrogates the trope of ambassadorship. In portraying Terminus's coerced representation of Africa at the Hebb residence, the play warns that African Americans, when supposedly speaking for Africa, must be wary of serving the interests of a white society in which certain factions have class-based and other interests in seeing African Americans assume the role of ambassador for other populations of African descent. If Terminus is reminiscent (though not wholly reduced to the level) of a "minstrel type of Negro," this is because Dennis's white intentions are operating behind Terminus's black face. In allegorizing certain African American representations of Africa as falling into a mode of minstrel-mask diplomacy, the scene depicts Ambassador Palaver Sauce's highly attenuated relation to an African referent. On this point, Terminus's assertion that an ambassador's primary responsibility is to talk about *nothing* is telling, for it is clear that Terminus the ambassador represents a double portion of nothing: Terminus is no official ambassador but is instead a coerced impersonator of the representative of an ersatz African dominion whose imaginary geography situates it far from any physical continent. Similar to Downing's and Ellis's roles as minor officials in West Africa, Terminus is divorced from his putative object of representation. If Downing's and

Ellis's diplomatic assignments failed to create them as practical representatives of the United States, Terminus's African ancestry conspicuously fails to credential his speech on behalf of Africa.

Terminus's faux-representative role in act 1 is suggestive of representational concerns that resonate with—and trouble—the contemporaneous declarations of experimental modernists such as Ezra Pound. Also writing in London during the year of *A New Coon in Town*'s publication, Pound dismissed the conventions that had traditionally linked art to the objective world. Declaring that "realism in literature [had] had its run," Pound's vision was of a "modern artist" who produced "new wild" art and was the heir "of the witch-doctor and the voodoo" ("New" 68). If Pound's statements were avant-garde in their disdain for the conventions of objective representation in art, his statements (deploying images of the witch-doctor and the voodoo) nonetheless embraced the status quo during an era of colonial modernity that took Africa as a muse for disjunctive representational practices within the arenas of history, politics, economics, and science. As an ersatz African ambassador, Downing's character Terminus functions to interrogate the effects—on Africa itself—of acquiescing to the use of Africa as a rationale for disregarding the conventions that insist on a correspondence between the world of representation and the world of things. In act 1, as a spurious representative, Terminus makes no treaty on behalf of the imagined dominion of Phoo Phoo. Of course, knowing of Terminus's status as an impostor, disinterested onlookers would recognize any such treaty as void—as a misfired attempt to do things with words (Austin 16). But the Hebbs, as self-interested gem dealers, might well insist that a treaty made on behalf of the imaginary dominion of Phoo Phoo ought to be honored by a physically grounded Africa that is susceptible to material exploitation. *A New Coon in Town* saves such an eventuality for acts 2 and 3.

Act 2 finds Dennis in an art studio maintained by his friend Saxon Langston, suitor of Mary Hebb. According to an agreement, Mary and Saxon will marry if Saxon can convince Mary's parents of his talent as a sculptor. In preparation for the Hebbs' visit, Saxon shows Dennis the sculpture with which he hopes to win Mary's hand. Saxon pulls back a curtain to reveal, poised on a platform, a statue of an African chief that according to Dennis appears "so natural-like" (45). Shortly before the Hebbs' visit, however, the statue is shattered, and Saxon panics until Dennis remarks, "The effigy represented a 'nigger' and it could be imitated." Dennis suggests hiring "a live 'nigger'" to stand in imitation of the statue (48). Saxon and Dennis invite Terminus to the studio and (by threat of violence) convince him to "enter into . . . a treaty" to pose as the statue (57). As Terminus changes clothes, the friends notice that their captive is carrying a red stone, which Terminus explains was harvested by his great-grandfather from an African ruby farm to which he himself is heir. Saxon convinces Terminus to sell the stone and ruby farm, and upon making this treaty, Saxon and Dennis agree to form a company called "The Negrobian Grab," with Sir Habisham Jobsdon as manager (63).

Upon the Hebbs' arrival in act 3, Saxon draws the curtain to reveal Terminus posing on the platform. Mary and her father praise Saxon's putative statue, but Serena contends that it is "out of drawing." Ironically, she explains that an African, Palaver Sauce, visited her only yesterday and did not resemble the statue (70). As Saxon apologizes, a wasp stings Terminus, who runs screaming through the studio (72). In the commotion, the ruby falls into Septimus's possession, and Saxon transfers his contract for the ruby and mine to Septimus, who consents to the marriage (80).

Acts 2 and 3 are meant to provoke laughter. Yet we do well to approach Downing's farcical comedy via the remarks of one of his dramatic contemporaries in London, George Bernard Shaw, who explained that through farcical comedy "we are permitted to discuss in jest what we may not discuss in earnest" (34). *A New Coon in Town*'s anticolonial stance is evident. Terminus strongly objects to the name *Sir Habisham Jobsdon*. When told Jobsdon will be managing the Negrobian Grab, Terminus exclaims, "I doesn't know [Jobsdon] . . . but I'se hyeahd a heap o' talk erbout him. He's dat pusson dat said as how de swamps an' jungles, in Africa, was de proper places fur cullud folks ter lib in, while de hills, an' odder healthy spots, should be 'propriated by de white folks." When Dennis tries to placate Terminus by telling him Jobsdon would now "let [Africans] have everything a white man has," Terminus doubts that Jobsdon's prejudice could "melt out o' a pusson sudden-like" (64). Sir Habisham Jobsdon of *A New Coon in Town* bears a striking resemblance to British archcolonialist Sir Harry Johnston, who shared an honorific and initials with Jobsdon as well as a policy that "reserved the [African] Highlands as being suitable for European settlers" (MacPhee 49). Terminus's protests recast Johnston's famous *negotiations for* the Highlands as *appropriations of* the Highlands, thereby undercutting Europe's right to participate in the procurement of African lands.[43] Yet Terminus's negative reaction to the name and history of Sir Habisham Jobsdon is more than a critique of Johnston. Terminus's disdain also functions to criticize those of African descent who had begun warming to the archcolonialist as a friend of the race. While several highly visible New Negro figures had begun performing a politics of immanence by conducting cordial relations with Johnston,[44] Downing's play suggests that even an African American who "doesn't measure knee-high" alongside the "advanced" members of his race (13) should know better than to trust a figure like Jobsdon/Johnston.

In spite of Terminus's objections to Europe's colonization of Africa, he performs his own politics of immanence when he consents to the coercion that asks him, as an African American, to pose as someone capable of treating on behalf of an Africa he has never seen. Here, the play furthers its earlier warning regarding colonial modernity's uses for African Americans as transnational race representatives. Act 1 positions Terminus as the specious political representative of an African king, and now acts 2 and 3 depict him as a specious aesthetic representation of an African chief. As Terminus stands in for an African chief, Downing's play offers implicit commentary on the colonial class's "creation of African chiefs" as a major strategy by which Europeans appropriated African lands (Miles and Brown 125). Indeed, though many African populations did not have "individual chiefs," "it did not prove difficult to find individuals willing to [fulfill] this role when it enabled them to accumulate land and livestock" (Miles and Brown 125). The chiefs, in turn, produced a façade of consolidated power and thereby provided the conditions necessary for colonialists to negotiate for African land ownership (Miles and Brown 125–26).[45] When Terminus stands in for an African chief that has been created by Saxon (whose name is allegorically suggestive), we see a reflection of the strategy discussed earlier—especially inasmuch as Saxon negotiates with this imitation chief for the possession of a ruby mine. Yet the scene emphasizes that Saxon's coercion does not operate in the absence of Terminus's consent. Indeed, when presented with the opportunity to acquire fifty pounds sterling, Terminus is pleased for Saxon to interpret his African descent as constituting the authority to speak on behalf of Africa (Downing, *New Coon* 63). This facet of the scene communicates the play's caution that New Negro representatives, like native African "chiefs," may play into Europe's colonial designs, facilitating Africa's material exploitation in exchange for the acquisition of personal wealth, power, or prestige. The validity of this power and prestige is undercut by the play's representation of Terminus, who imitates a voiceless object and whose visibility is mediated by a misrepresentative veil (the curtain surrounding the platform) controlled by Saxon.

I do not want to suggest that Downing looked askance at all representations of Africa by African Americans, but the play, through Terminus's borderline minstrelesque performance, conveys reservations regarding the "reconstructed" status of New Negro figures whose representations of Africa acquiesced to the modern notion of Africa as an occasion to disregard the conventions attaching representation to the material world.[46] *A New Coon in Town*, like Antonio Gramsci's later hypothesis, warns of "American negroes" as "agents in the conquest of the African market" (Gramsci 21). Unlike Gramsci, however, who hypothesized that African Americans would be specifically useful to "the extension of American civilisation" in Africa (21), Downing's play emphasizes that African Americans must be wary of serving as ersatz African representatives to any political or economic entity in need of a transnational chief willing to speak illegitimately on behalf of African interests.

Significantly, *A New Coon in Town* turns to the conventions of aesthetic representation to comment on the dangers of Africa's political and economic misrepresentation. Serena's words upon seeing the putative statue permit the play to cast Africa's misrepresentation in terms of mimetic failure. When the curtain is drawn, Serena protests that the statue is "out of drawing," that it incorrectly represents "the human form," and that it is covered with "eccentric curves" and "botches" (70). Serena's phrases invite us to consider Terminus's political and economic misrepresentation of Africa in terms of aesthetic modernism's radical representational experimentation. In describing Terminus as "out of drawing," Serena's language is homologous with descriptions of Picasso's early work and other "modern picture[s]," which were also described as "out of drawing."[47] Meanwhile, Serena's dissatisfaction with Saxon's "eccentric" rendering of "the human form" resonates with the stance of Cambridge University art professor Sir Charles Waldstein, who in 1914 cautioned young artists against the emergent trend of portraying "eccentric forms" that were in "opposition to the broad laws of nature" (47). Clearly, Serena does not worry that the putative statue constitutes an avant-garde aesthetic statement. She merely sees it as bad. But, as Ernest Hemingway intimated to Gertrude Stein, there is a distinction between bad (as in poorly rendered) and bad (as in rendered according to a modernist aesthetic).[48] The former indicates a lack of artistic proficiency, while the latter performs its mimetic infidelity with self-conscious knowingness. Regardless of whether Downing meant for Serena's words to equate the living statue's misrepresentations of Africa with aesthetic modernism's self-conscious representational disruptions, his play *A New*

Coon in Town undoubtedly evinces a self-conscious knowingness in its treatment of the aesthetic and political disruptions surrounding African representations. In 1917, Downing carried this knowingness with him when, driven out of London by German bombing raids, he returned to Manhattan, where he eventually settled in Harlem and wrote during the Renaissance of the 1920s.[49]

A Lost Generation of New Negro Internationalists

A New Coon in Town's knowingness, as well as the self-conscious if uneven representational efforts of *Negro Culture* and *The Leopard's Claw*, should position Downing and Ellis as important figures in a truly lost generation of internationally oriented black modernists. Their work in Africa during the late nineteenth and early twentieth centuries created them as sites on which modernity's assault on traditional notions of representation was vividly enacted, and their subsequent writings grapple with the legacies of this assault as it relates to the myth of Africa as an occasion to suspend conventional representational practices. Though the other writer-diplomats treated in this study did not spend their diplomatic careers in the African heart of colonial modernity's assault on representation, they also were treated as the United States' internal colonials and generally sent by default to colonies and nations held under direct or indirect imperial sway. Like Ellis and Downing, they encountered in the United States' relations with the darker world the "veil of misrepresentation" that Ellis observed "covered the Negro" not only in Africa but "elsewhere" ("Psychology" 314). These diplomats produced writings that worked within and against the modern moment's representational disruptions surrounding people of color. On one hand, in light of Pound's and Picasso's deployments of blackness for representationally disjunctive aesthetic purposes, the black writer-diplomats' self-conscious and uneven efforts toward an ideal of objective and salutary African representation might be considered a type of antimodernism. However, more in keeping with Friedman's notion of modernist family resemblances would be to draw on Paul Gilroy's framing of Black Atlantic denizens as not antimoderns but as countercultural participants in a capacious modernity (*Black* 1–5). Along these lines, the expressive culture growing out of New Negro diplomacy emerges as part of a capacious modernism defined less by a particular aesthetic program and more by a set of protean aesthetic engagements regarding Africa, African descent, and experiments in representation.

4 / Metonymies of Absence and Presence: Angelina Weld Grimké's *Rachel*

In the 1910s, as George Washington Ellis and Henry Francis Downing brought their foreign service to bear on their literary efforts, poet and playwright Angelina Weld Grimké was gaining recognition for her drama *Rachel.* Set entirely within the living room of a middle-class African American home, the play seems to exist in a domestic sphere quite separate from the internationally oriented space inhabited by the New Negro era's world-traveling writer-diplomats. Further seeming to steer the drama away from international preoccupations, *Rachel* focuses on the difficulties of African American motherhood while critiquing the national problem of lynching. Regarding Grimké's literary use of motherhood to create a transracial alliance among women within the nation, she explained, "If anything can make all women sisters underneath their skins it is motherhood. If, then, the white women of this country could see, feel, understand, just what effect their prejudice and the prejudice of their fathers, brothers, husbands, sons were having on the souls of the colored mothers . . . and upon the mothers that are to be, a great power to affect public opinion would be set free and the battle would be half won" ("Rachel" 414). Grimké's statement, of course, suggests that *Rachel*'s antiracist project seeks to meld national citizenship into familial ties, as black and white women in the United States become "sisters underneath their skins." This reliance on the trope of family ties has been observed in discussions of the play's domesticity.[1]

In correctly commenting on questions of *Rachel*'s domesticity, however, critics have been less attentive to recent discussions of "the domestic" as a term describing and forging conceptual ties between the spaces of home and nation. Importantly, Amy Kaplan has observed that "*domestic* has a double meaning that links the space of the familial household to that of the nation," with familial and national spheres imagined "in opposition to everything outside the geographic and conceptual borders of the home" (*Anarchy* 25). Similarly commenting on the construction of domestic spaces, Rosemary Marangoly George remarks that "homes" are created by "closed doors" and "closed borders" (18), an observation suggesting that spaces existing beyond restrictive doors and borders share a common *foreign* quality. In light of such observations, Grimké's drama emerges as doubly domestic in its overlapping concerns with familial and national homes. And if we take seriously the proposition that domestic spaces exist *as domestic* only in relation to that which is foreign, then we may productively ask about the foreign spaces in relation to which Grimké's drama defines itself. Clearly, the domestic space of the living room has been disrupted by a lynching, an event whose foreignness to the home is foregrounded when the mob is described as breaking "down the front door" and "dragging . . . out" its victims (Grimké, *Rachel* 25). Yet we should also ask about the drama's reliance on a less evident foreign—a foreign that exists in tension not necessarily with the familial home but with the domestic space of the nation that is Grimké's focus. The question of the foreign in *Rachel* finds important elucidation as we consider the fact that Grimké's father, Archibald Grimké, left home in mid-October 1894 to travel to a consular post in Santo Domingo, where he worked until 1898. Comprising four years during Angelina's adolescence, Archibald's consulship loomed large enough throughout the Grimkés' lives that, thirty years afterward, Angelina remarked, "it was thought best not to take me down [to Santo Domingo] but so often and so vivid [*sic*] have I had the scene and life described that I seem to have been there too."[2]

Archibald's four-year consulship in Santo Domingo usually receives a cursory nod in narratives of Angelina's life, with his diplomatic work framed as merely incidental to his daughter's literary production. In some ways, this is fitting, since Archibald lived in Santo Domingo before Angelina came into her own as a poet and playwright. In other ways, however, the critical elision of Archibald's four-year consulship seems incongruous. After all, Angelina's loss of her mother at age seven has been a factor in assessments of the playwright's literary life, with Grimké's biographer, Gloria Hull, focusing on this loss and suggesting, "It is psychologically interesting that in her literary works, motherhood is a major theme" (109).[3] Yet after being sent away from her mother to live with her father, Angelina came to look to her father as "a gentle mother" (Grimké, "To My Father" 38), and she wrote that "without him" she had "no desire absolutely for life" (qtd. in Hull 114). In light of this intense relationship with her father, it would seem that, similar to Angelina's childhood loss of her mother, Archibald's four-year diplomatic absence should not be overlooked. Archibald's four-year consulship constitutes a repressed yet pivotal and defining foreign presence within *Rachel*'s domestic project. This foreign presence not only lends structure to the play's narrative and geopolitical orientation but also insinuates itself into the very heart of *Rachel*'s domestic concerns. Tracing metonymies of this foreign absence and presence illuminates the voids created by diplomacy's occlusion of racial activism among the black men and women who participated in the matrices of official internationalism.

Silence, Violence, and the End of Pleasant Days

Rachel is set in a Northern city during the first decade of the twentieth century, with its action revolving around the date of October 16.[4] Act 1 takes place on this date, which is the day that teenagers Rachel and Tom learn from their mother, Mary Loving, that exactly ten years earlier their father and brother were lynched. Rachel, who feels called to be a mother (Grimké, *Rachel* 12), is horrified by Mary's account, realizing that her own children might also be lynched (27). Act 2 takes place four years later, also on October 16. During the four-year hiatus, Rachel has begun entertaining a suitor, John Strong, and has adopted a child named Jimmy. On this day, she learns that some white children have called Jimmy a "nigger" (61), an incident she connects to the lynchings fourteen years earlier. Act 3 takes place a week later. Rachel is psychologically distressed and terrified by the hate that her biological children might face, and she rejects Strong's marriage proposal. As the play concludes, Rachel plaintively addresses her unborn children: "Your little, brown, beautiful bodies—I shall never see. . . . You may be happy now—you are safe" (96).

On the face of it, *Rachel* seems thoroughly domestic, but a closer examination suggests that this domesticity is achieved in relation to an intense dependence on a repressed foreign presence within the drama. To begin to appreciate this presence, we may direct attention to a handful of *Rachel*'s narrative devices and preoccupations: the play's representation of a shattered middle-class African American household, its portrayal of a mid-October loss of the father, its focus on a distraught daughter mourning his loss, and its inclusion of an abrupt four-year hiatus. These are not merely key elements of Grimké's *Rachel* but are also defining facets of Angelina's life from age fourteen to eighteen, the era of Archibald's consulship, when Angelina's own middle-class African American home was shattered by the loss of her father, who departed in mid-October 1894 to begin a four-year Dominican hiatus.[5] It is telling, in light of these temporal and thematic resonances, that just as *Rachel* features a cyclical "time [that] loops around to the anniversary of the lynching" (C. Allen 69), Archibald's absence relentlessly looped through Angelina's memories of childhood and adolescence. In an unpublished biographical sketch of her father written after his death in 1930, Angelina offered a series of narrative loops, giving a recursive presence to Archibald's consulship. She wrote,

> Eventually he became the secretary of the Board [of trustees of Westboro Insane Hospital] and is still remembered for important services rendered the Hospital. He was on the Board until he went to Santo Domingo in 1894.
>
> When I was seven years old [in 1887] my mother sent me back to my Father. At that time he was living in Hyde Park, then a suburb but now a part of Greater Boston.
>
> He had a hard time. When he was appointed by [Grover] Cleveland as consul to Santo Domingo he was almost down to his last dollar.
>
> I forgot to say that Carlos Martyn editor of the True Reformer Series . . . engaged my Father to write the two volumes, "Life of William Lloyd Garrison," and "The Life of Charles Sumner." This was a couple of years before he became the American Consul.
>
> My Father was four years in Santo Domingo, and served so well that his work was commended highly by the State Department.
>
> In 1898 he returned to the U.S. and for a number of years lived half of the year in Boston and half in Washington.[6]

Only one of these paragraphs dedicates itself to narrating Archibald's consulship, but on every occasion Archibald's absence disrupts the linear flow typical of other sections of Angelina's biographical sketch. Similar to the saturating power of Mr. Loving's lynching in *Rachel*, Archibald's consulship recursively insinuates itself into Angelina's recollections of his work at the hospital, his financial troubles, his writing pursuits, and his reunion with his daughter.

While Angelina's staccato paragraphs and temporal loops point toward an *unspoken* psychological stress regarding Archibald's absence, she provides more overt commentary in her essay "A Biographical Sketch of Archibald H. Grimke [*sic*]," published in *Opportunity* in 1925. In this sketch, she recalls her childhood from age seven to fourteen and remarks that "some of [her] pleasantest recollections" are of life with Archibald in the "living room." However, she complains, "In 1894 all these pleasant days came to an end, for it was at this time President Cleveland appointed [my father] as Consul to Santo Domingo" (47). For Angelina, the mid-October end of "all these pleasant days" not only reverberated through her personal life (as her unpublished narrative attests) but also found refraction in *Rachel*, a play in which the mid-October loss of a father has a recursive presence, resulting in what David Krasner calls the lynching's "repetitious cascade of sounds spoken in a murky void" (103).

Rachel was not the first twentieth-century African American text to offer an implicit analogy between lynching and diplomacy. Jacqueline Goldsby has described the lynching in James Weldon Johnson's *The Autobiography of an Ex-Colored Man* as borrowing emotional energy from Johnson's outrage at the State Department's refusal to transfer him from Nicaragua to the consulate in Saint-Étienne, France. "The State Department's affront," Goldsby observes, "haunted the writing of the novel" (*Spectacular* 182). But whereas Goldsby situates Johnson's novel as locating violence in the State Department's refusal to acknowledge the full equality of its black representatives, Angelina's *Rachel* implicitly locates violence in the diplomatic institution's racial inclusiveness, which functioned to send New Negro race men to foreign locales far from their familial and national homes. Of course, the traditions of lynching and New Negro diplomatic service are so disparate that their equation borders on metaphysical conceit, especially when we consider the sharp contrast between lynching's torture and murder of African Americans and diplomacy's provision of material benefits and prestige to a select few black US citizens. Yet recent studies have outlined lynching's contested tropological life within US culture,[7] and *Rachel* itself, as Angeletta Gourdine convincingly observes, turns Mr. Loving's lynching into a metaphor for violence that is "psychically and metaphorically" oriented (535). Hence, without eliding the incongruities between lynching and diplomacy, we may approach *Rachel* with questions regarding the structural convergences that inspired the commonalities between the parallel losses of Mr. Loving and Archibald. Beyond mid-October dates and four-year temporal lapses, Mr. Loving's lynching and Archibald's consulship share the common function of silencing African American writers who were outspoken in their insistence on racial equality within the United States. Focusing on this functional parallel permits an illumination of the theme of silence in Angelina's dramatic work while also shedding light on certain upshots of New Negro immanence to US diplomacy.

In *Rachel*, the lynching is aimed at silencing an African American activist. Mrs. Loving explains to Rachel and Tom that their father was the editor of an African American newspaper in which "he said a great many daring things" in defense of his race. After a local lynching, Mr. Loving "published a most terrific denunciation of [the lynch] mob." He received a letter requesting that he retract his words, but Mr. Loving's next issue "contained an arraignment [just] as frightful." That night, Mrs. Loving tells Rachel, a mob appeared and "your father was finally over-powered" (24–25). The physical and social violence of lynching relied on myriad pretexts to meld promiscuously with a motivating white-supremacist ideology, but Mrs. Loving's account frames Mr. Loving's lynching as operating according to a poetics of black silence. This is a departure from the era's dominant discourse on lynching, as showcased in Theodore Dreiser's 1901 story "Nigger Jeff," which projected lynching as a white response to black predations on white womanhood (157). For the mob in *Rachel*, lynching is a threat aimed at silencing black protest. And when Mr. Loving refuses to retract his protest, lynching moves beyond the realm of threat and becomes a physical method of silencing him, with his death functioning to remove him from a position in which he can speak in defense of the race.[8]

In a statement reminiscent of the silencing function of Mr. Loving's lynching, historian Allison Blakely observes that periods of diplomatic service tended to lead "highly successful" African American men to "mute . . . their public protest . . . in opposition to the [white-supremacist] establishment" ("Black" 5). Indeed, Archibald's letters from Santo Domingo provide a view of his consulship as resulting in a silencing that was analogous (on a discursive level) to Mr. Loving's murder. Before Archibald's consulship, he had, like Mr. Loving, been a black newspaper editor and writer, but, as his biographer Dickson Bruce observes, Archibald's entrance into international diplomacy had the effect of removing him from "the political, social, and economic concerns that had [previously] occupied so much of his time and effort" (*Archibald* 69). The adolescent Angelina had a clear view of this effect. If her father had only recently written biographies of Garrison and Sumner for Funk and Wagnalls' American Reformer Series, Archibald now wrote home that as a consul he could not act as "a reformer" but only as "the representative of [the US] government." Archibald explained that he "must be content to hold himself strickly to the performance of this single role."[9] In another missive, he worried that his stray words could become "chickens . . . coming home to roost . . . & cause [his] recal [*sic*]."[10] Diplomacy's rhetorically and politically hobbling effect on Archibald clearly surfaces in a *Washington Evening Star* article, published during his last days with Angelina, after his consular training but before his departure for Santo Domingo. Here, Archibald answers a question regarding African Americans' troubled relationship to the Democratic Party, which was at the time infamous for discriminating in the assignment of public offices and failing to combat epidemic lynching in the largely Democratic South.[11] Archibald responds, "I have nothing to say politically. As a United States consul, and a representative of the government, I don't think it becoming in me to speak of the present political situation. I have never been active in politics, but I am a great admirer of the President. . . . I hear that there are some disaffections among the colored democrats, . . . [but] I have not given much attention to political affairs" ("Consul"). It is unsurprising that Archibald opted to remain silent. After all, the State Department regulations and rules of thumb discussed in chapter 2 applied to Archibald as well as to James Weldon Johnson. What is perhaps more remarkable about Archibald's response is his claim that he had "never been active in politics." This claim reveals an Archibald whose politics of immanence not only silenced him in the present but also created him as always already silenced, with a present diplomatic expediency effacing his past antiracist and squarely political efforts.

The commonalities of political silencing, a four-year hiatus, and a mid-October paternal loss suggest a correspondence between Mr. Loving's lynching and Archibald's consulship. Yet Angelina's representation of the lynching does not constitute a mere transposition of her father's departure for Santo Domingo. Instead, Angelina's early personal loss operated in the spirit of Freud's explanation of repressed material entering into, and priming itself by way of, "the modifying influence of . . . [later] experience" (*Moses* 122). In other words, memory of this early personal loss apparently entered into a mutually reinflecting relationship with Angelina's mature disdain for a nation sanctioning the racial prejudices and practices that culminated in lynching. In this relationship, the public tragedy of lynching is infused with an intimacy inspired by Angelina's personal loss of her father, and this personal loss of a father (to a nation permitting lynching to go unchecked) emerges in literary form as a racial complaint directed toward a nation that sought to silence its black citizens. To borrow from Anne Anlin Cheng, *Rachel* is a site at which Angelina converts herself from "being subjected to grief to being a subject speaking grievance" (7). Drawing attention to *Rachel*'s overlay of early and later psychological stressors permits Mr. Loving's lynching to shed important perspective not only on the place of Archibald's consulship within Angelina's psychic life but also on the epistemic violence occasioned by New Negro involvement in international diplomacy more generally. In Gayatri Spivak's narrative of "epistemic violence," the dominating culture silences the native voice while reconstructing certain comparatively elite members of the dominated culture as "native informants."[12] Analogously, the United States deployed an elite group of black citizens to nations and colonies of color, where they were tasked to perform as (in Archibald's words) silenced representatives rather than speaking reformers.

Hence, while John Mercer Langston and James Weldon Johnson framed international diplomacy as a path toward racial liberation, *Rachel*'s domestically oriented refractions of Archibald's consulship bring important focus to the interrelated categories of silence and absence—not necessarily Archibald's particular silence or his absence from Angelina but rather the more difficultly assessed *absence of black speech and activism* occasioned by New Negro diplomatic service more generally. This is an absence partially constituted by the stances Archibald *might have expressed* had he not worried about his "chickens . . . coming home to roost." It is an absence driven by the same forces that played a role in convincing James Weldon Johnson to publish his novel anonymously for fear that "a diplomat should not affix his name to so controversial a book" (Tarry 215). It is the negative rhetorical space left unfilled by the newspaper articles George Washington Ellis *did not publish* after receiving a warning advising him that the State Department "discouraged press contributions by its diplomatic staff" (Fleming 90). It is a locutionary void of whose existence we are alerted by Frederick Douglass's suggestion that he at one time declined to defend himself against racist allegations for fear that self-defense of his diplomatic work could function to the "detriment [of] the public interest" by exposing "the secrets of the negotiations in question" (*Life and Times* 1026). This is a silence left unfilled by the strong antilynching stance that John Stephens Durham *might have adopted* had he not spent his later life in hope of receiving another diplomatic appointment. Of course, the silences we may retrospectively attach to these relatively prominent figures merely constitute the negative traces of a more profound silence surrounding the scores of late nineteenth- and early twentieth-century New Negro diplomats (many of whom are now nearly anonymous) whose racial activisms were obviated by and within the international world's diplomatic matrices.

Much of the archive surrounding such figures remains to be recovered and assessed, but in self-reflexively approaching this archive, it is also important to remember that the archival limits do not merely reside within the white-supremacist biases of their compilers. Certain limits are prearchival and epistemic, involving activisms that were anticipated and diffused by the ambassadorial scripts that gave rise to New Negro diplomats' political performances. Of course, speculation about *what New Negro diplomats might have said or done had they not been diplomats* is at best a counterfactual exercise. And beyond the relatively safe claim that this group of African American men would have spoken and acted in more racially insurgent ways, I am not presently interested in making further (and exponentially more speculative) projections. Yet, in light of counterfactual historians' particular interest in questions of international relations and also in light of their tendency to draw on imaginative literature for methodological models,[13] we may be justified in turning toward *Rachel* for a metaphor for the absence left by the voices and activisms occluded by New Negro participation in official US diplomacy. Rachel's unborn, counterfactual children do not speak in any physical way but instead speak to Rachel, who in turn mediates their voices to the play's audience (Grimké, *Rachel* 94). Just as the audience has access to these metonymies of absent speech only through Rachel, our access to black diplomats' silences also must be indirect, mediated by traces of absence inferred from the reserved statements of the diplomats themselves as well as from texts (such as *Rachel*) that bear the impress of—and theorize—that absence in perhaps unconscious ways.

Travel So Beautiful It Hurts

Beyond functioning to obviate racially insurgent speech, diplomacy has played a significant if traditionally overlooked role in what Robin D. G. Kelley has described as black people's overarching historical trope of "movement—real and imagined" (16). On the question of travel, the commentary of John Stephens Durham (Archibald's predecessor in Santo Domingo and Douglass's successor in Haiti) showcases certain tensions that emerge from the contrast between African Americans' subjugated domestic status and the New Negro diplomats' international representation of the nation that offered that subjugation. Durham sympathized with those who "hated the conditions" in the United States ("Confessions" 170), and he viewed work in the "foreign service" as a mode of egress from "the inconveniences and real discouragements" faced by "a colored man" living within the nation's borders (*BTWP* 6: 327). Diplomatic service offered a mode of travel whose flight from domestic insults resonated with the liberative energy of antebellum escape narratives, but, ironically, this travel created the fugitive as an international extension of the very nation that nourished the racial conditions he was escaping. Like Durham, Angelina knew the discouragements of being black in the United States, but to her these conditions underlined the expediency of fighting a racial "battle" within the nation (Grimké, "Rachel" 414) rather than escaping to—and being co-opted on—foreign and ostensibly friendlier shores. A reading of Angelina's published biographical sketch of her father, in conjunction with Archibald's letters from Santo Domingo, helps highlight the motives and methods behind what emerges as *Rachel*'s infantilizing and pathologizing treatment of travel.

In "A Biographical Sketch of Archibald H. Grimke," Angelina outlines her father's life as one of tireless dedication to the advancement of African American domestic interests and implicitly situates his consulship as a hiatus in that fight. According to Angelina, Archibald was (like Mr. Loving) among the class of "fighters" who used "pens and tongues . . . as efficient weapons" (45). His early credentials on "the race question" (46) were impressive. Angelina observes that he was editor of "a colored newspaper," he was "president of Boston's famous colored literary society," he played a role in the "long unpleasant fight" to erect the Crispus Attucks Monument on Boston Common, and he delivered the eulogy upon the death of famed abolitionist Wendell Phillips (47). Then, when young Angelina arrived on the scene at age seven, Archibald performed a perfect melding of his domestic racial concerns and his domestic familial concerns. Angelina remembers that he stayed at home with her while writing newspaper articles and books at the table in the "living room." Archibald's doubly domestic work (writing for a national audience from the living room) later constituted some of Angelina's "pleasantest recollections." Hence, when Archibald's consular appointment brought "all these pleasant days . . . to an end" (47), international diplomacy was doubly foreign: it disrupted the domestic space of Angelina's childhood home, and it offered Archibald an escape from the national racial battle.

In the essay, we see an implicit contrast between Angelina's celebration of Archibald's sustained battle of "tongues and pens" and her comments on his consulship. Of Archibald's consulship, Angelina offers the seemingly innocuous explanation that her father "enjoyed the tropics and . . . his days were busy, eventful and happy ones. His one big accomplishment was the settling [of] a law suit over a bridge in favor of an American citizen named McKay, a suit that had been pending for years and a source of great annoyance to this government" (47). After this four-year absence from the racial fight, Angelina observes, "he returned to this country and . . . has given his time and his energies to the writing of addresses and pamphlets on the race question, to the making of speeches and to the fighting of race prejudice wherever found" (47). The essay presents this fight as culminating in 1919 when Archibald received the NAACP's Spingarn Medal, "for a long lifetime of service to his race" (47).

While maintaining appropriate public respect for Angelina's father and the office of consul, "A Biographical Sketch of Archibald H. Grimke" champions Archibald's domestic fight while detracting from his foreign service. We must wonder about the illocutionary aims of Angelina's reference to Archibald's "one big achievement" as "a law suit over a bridge." To be sure, the question of the bridge had been an "annoyance" to the United States, but Angelina's sketch implicitly invites readers to contrast the value of Archibald's status as a resolver of the United States' international annoyances with the value of Archibald's domestic "fighting of race prejudice wherever found." Interestingly, before Angelina wrote the published essay, she seemed nonplussed by Archibald's accomplishments as a consul. Although she had heard many vivid accounts of the Dominican scene and life, her prewriting outline mentions only the "Bridge [in] Santo Domingo" and asks if her father had done "anything else in [Santo Domingo]?"[14] The published narrative publicly answers this private question: No, "his one big accomplishment was the settling of a law suit over a bridge." The narrative intimates that Archibald may have "enjoyed the tropics" and that his days may have been "eventful and happy," but these days were a distraction and an escapist interruption in a life otherwise dedicated to the national racial battle.

Angelina would have had ample reason to conceive of Archibald's consulship as inconsistent with the generally resistant tenor of his life, given that her father's Dominican reminiscences were vivid and frequent but were nonetheless apparently lacking in descriptions of many significant achievements. Archibald's nostalgic recollections no doubt retraced the diplomatic life to which Angelina earlier had been exposed by the four years of letters he sent home from Santo Domingo. These missives reveal an Archibald who (like Durham) found a haven in diplomatic service inasmuch as international travel permitted him to escape US-based race prejudice. Before Archibald left home, his family joked that going to Santo Domingo might have a degenerative effect, turning him into "a big, greasy black man" and leading him to strut "around barefoot & eating acorns."[15] But as his letters reveal, once in Santo Domingo, Archibald found himself in a position of privilege that he, as an African American, could not have occupied if he lived in the capital of the nation that sent him. Shortly after his arrival, he wrote to Angelina, "I am living in one of the finest houses in the city, in the best part of the city."[16] His letters have him frequenting luxuriant banquets and dances at the residences of Dominican and diplomatic elites.[17] In one missive, he recounts the "cosmopolitan . . . character" of a grand ball held by the Dominican president for a "very select" group of people "who move in the highest society." He was pleased to see "every color of the genus *homo* . . . represented," from "royal black . . . through all gradations to pure white." He saw no "hint . . . of the existence of such a thing as prejudice against color, not even among the Americans," who "after they live here a while . . . seem to lose their diabolic ability in detecting the presence of a drop of black blood in one of us. The gift seems to be reversed for they seem to have a marvelous faculty for finding . . . a drop of white blood." He enthusiastically reported, "people whom [white Americans] would call 'colored'" in the United States are treated "as white down here!"[18] In light of his contentment with life beyond the ken of US-based race prejudice, it is unsurprising that, entering the fourth year of his consulship, he wrote to Angelina that living in Santo Domingo "certainly agrees" with him, and he could "ask nothing better than to retain [his] position several years to come."[19] He projected that if he could get a raise in salary "from $1500 to $2500," then he and Angelina "shall be happy ever after!"[20] But if Archibald enjoyed life as a diplomat, this enjoyment required that he repress his discomfort with what he discussed as the white "merchants & planters" "getting the lions share of the business & wealth" in the Dominican Republic. In early letters home, Archibald described these conditions as pitiful and a regret, but evidently as he saw the benefits of representing white interests, such laments dropped out of his letters.[21]

African American internationalism and cosmopolitanism often have been framed as productively reminding black US travelers that the United States' oppressive racial conventions are culturally specific rather than universal, and Dickson Bruce has suggested that Archibald's "Santo

Domingo experiences showed him that an alternative to the segregated society of the United States was possible" (*Archibald* 73). Undoubtedly this sense of racism's cultural and geographical contingency was reemphasized to Archibald by his consulship, but Angelina, viewing her father's fight as a "lifetime of service," may not have seen her father as *needing* this reminder. After all, according to Angelina's narrative, Archibald fought to banish the effects of race prejudice both before and after his consulship. What, then, was the upshot of international travel? As Archibald's letters suggest, going to Santo Domingo meant supplanting participation in a domestic racial battle by adopting a life of banquets, palaces, high-society balls, and living "happy ever after." Indeed, though several of his missives deal with the serious side of international diplomacy, many letters suggest that his life had some of the escapist qualities of the novels that Archibald, while in Santo Domingo, warned Angelina against reading.[22]

A view of internationalism as a distraction from the domestic fight certainly resonates with Angelina's adulthood frustration regarding US newspapers that focused on international "barbarities" while offering just "a careless word or two dismissing" the United States' racial tragedies (qtd. in Hull 130). We might conceive, then, of this adulthood interest in the domestic fight as founded in opposition to Angelina's most profound experience with internationalism, which involved descriptions of a racially egalitarian Santo Domingo that were so vivid and frequent that she felt she had seen them herself. Understanding this juxtaposition does much to contextualize *Rachel*'s geopolitically aware construction of travel and domesticity.

Within *Rachel*, the audience's introduction to the question of travel is coeval with Rachel's first appearance. In the first scene, she arrives home late, leading Mrs. Loving to ask if her daughter will ever "grow up." Rachel replies that she wants to remain "irresponsible" for the next few years at least and explains that presently her irresponsibility has taken the form of imaginary travel with Jimmy, a toddler whom she has just met outside. Enthusiastically, Rachel explains that she and Jimmy have "been everywhere: New York, Chicago, Boston, London, Paris and Oshkosh" (4). However, back in the apartment, a sense of maturity settles on Rachel. She concedes with a sigh, "I've got to grow up it seems" (7), and shortly thereafter the family's conversation turns toward the difficulties of a college-educated family friend (John Strong) who has searched for work but failed because of the "handicap of being colored" (8). Now, rather than enthusing about irresponsible fantasy travel with a toddler, Rachel evinces a mature interest in protesting conditions within the United States. She condemns John's treatment: "Just because he is *colored*! . . . We sing a song at school . . . about 'The land of the free and the home of the brave.'" Rather than continuing this conversation, Mrs. Loving directs Rachel to practice the piano, and Rachel begins singing Jessie Gaynor's lullaby "Slumber Boat":

> Sail, baby, sail,
> Out upon that sea,
> Only don't forget to sail
> Back again to me. (9)

Concluding, she says, "Ma dear, it's so beautiful—it—it hurts" (10).

If Rachel feels hurt by "Slumber Boat," then the lullaby's themes of fantasy travel and childhood invite readers to contextualize this pain with Rachel's own recently completed fantasy travel. Just a few minutes earlier, Rachel has traveled "everywhere" with Jimmy. But now, after being reminded of race prejudice in the United States, she tells "baby" to sail "out upon that sea." Meanwhile, as is suggested by her request that "baby" sail "back again" to her, she herself remains on the shore of a nation that uses a test of skin color to selectively apply its egalitarian ideals. The hurt wrapped up in "Slumber Boat," then, pertains to Rachel's newfound maturity: first, it represents a heightened realization of the difficulties of being black in the United States; second, it represents a maturity that *confronts* these domestic difficulties rather than lending itself to the type of fantasy travel that the drama conflates with childhood. In other words, baby may enjoy the fantasy of sailing out to sea, but committed adults will remain on the home shore to face—and to protest—racial prejudice in the land of the free.

Whereas act 1 codes travel as childish escapism, the third act resumes and revises *Rachel*'s treatment of travel in powerful ways. Rachel has now adopted Jimmy, and she presently tells him a bedtime story about two boys who lived with a man and woman who forced them to work and "beat them when they did not move fast enough" (69). The children escape and set out in search of the Land of Laughter. Finally, they reach this happy land, where "they grew old, laughing" (73). After the story, Jimmy requests that Rachel sing "Slumber Boat." Rachel obliges, repeating "almost against her will" the closing refrain:

> Sail, baby, sail
> Out upon that sea,

Only don't forget to sail
Back again to me.[23]

Afterward, Jimmy says he plans on traveling to the Land of Laughter in "the 'Slumber Boat'" (75).

Act 3 reiterates act 1's conflation of travel and childhood, but if act 1 depicts Rachel's resolution to abandon the irresponsible fantasy of travel, then act 3 depicts Rachel's eventual failure in this mature resolve. Interestingly, the bedtime story portrays protagonists living in harsh conditions suggestive of slavery and racism in the United States. In contemplating a response to these conditions, the story is double voiced, speaking at once to its two audiences, both to Jimmy and to the drama's audience. For Jimmy, the presence of child protagonists frames travel as an acceptable fantasy for children like himself. But to an audience who has earlier observed Rachel's decision to grow up, the bedtime story's juvenile protagonists reaffirm the drama's conflation of travel with childhood. Yet despite Rachel's earlier recognition that she must grow up, her resolve is now faltering, as she sings the refrain "almost against her will."

It seems unsurprising, then, that when Jimmy asserts he will travel to the Land of Laughter on the Slumber Boat, Rachel collapses in her mature resolve and seeks to travel once more with Jimmy: "Jimmy! honey! . . . Don't go without Ma Rachel. Wait for me, honey. I do so wish to go, too, to the Land of Laughter. Think of it, Jimmy; nothing but birds always singing, and flowers always blooming, and skies always blue" (76). Tellingly, this vision of travel as an escape to a perpetual springscape resonates with Archibald's letter home upon first viewing the island of Hispaniola: "We steamed on our way under the most beautiful of skies . . . with breezes blowing as . . . delicious as if they were blowing straight out of the gates of Paradise. . . . Think of me . . . under the vast vault of the heavens stained with the softest blues . . . flashing with thousands of stars." He continued: "I woke next morning in sight of the island. . . . I had no conception of its beauty & grandeur. . . . It is a wonderfully grand sight . . . at sunrise."[24] Jimmy's proposed voyage on the Slumber Boat absorbs and infantilizes Archibald's Caribbean voyage, which years earlier had carried him away from the racial fight and through the gates of Paradise as he slept.

In this light, Rachel's renewed enthusiasm for travel is not meant to embody an adequate response to the United States' racist culture. Rachel is, in Angelina's words, a "highly-strung" figure who is "ill . . . in mind and soul" ("Rachel" 413, 416). Using travel as a psychic crutch may be expedient for those who are "highly-strung," but adequate participation in the domestic racial battle does not involve the fantasy of travel, whether to the Land of Laughter or to happy days in Santo Domingo. Instead, a psychically healthy participation involves working domestically, fighting (as stated on *Rachel*'s performance program) to "enlighten the American people relative to the lamentable condition of ten million of colored citizens in this free Republic." This is a domestic fight, and its method is written not into Rachel's character but into the subtitle with which *Rachel* was advertised, which billed the drama as "A Play of Protest."[25]

Rachel's representations of travel spoke to conversations of its time. Distinct from Downing's *A New Coon in Town*, Grimké's drama suggested that New Negro travel was less dangerous to black diasporan populations abroad and more dangerous because it detracted from the efforts of the portion of the diaspora that was fighting a racial battle in the United States. *Rachel* also spoke to the question taken up in Eugene O'Neill's *All God's Chillun Got Wings*, which during the subsequent decade problematized African American impulses to go "abroad where a man is a man" (108) by couching such travel as "run[ning] away and giv[ing] up [the] fight" (113). Within Angelina's drama, New Negro travel became not a nostrum for the effects of US-based racism but a symptom exhibited by the "highly-strung" who are made "ill . . . in mind and soul" by this racism.[26] Interestingly, as *Rachel* found its greatest audiences among a post–First World War readership, the literary legacy of Archibald's consular travel would have taken on special relevance in relation to the many African American men who had chosen exile by refusing to return from Europe after service in the war.[27]

Travel and Childlessness

In positioning travel as an infantile and regressive fantasy, *Rachel*'s geopolitically aware domesticity brings a sharp focus to the interface between racial discourses and domestic questions pertaining to the family and nation. Again, as Angelina explained, the play's object was to fuse familial and national homes via the trope of motherhood. While several scholars have commented on the question of motherhood within the play,[28] William Storm has offered particularly useful commentary. Storm notes that Rachel finds "models of motherhood" in two figures, namely, Mrs. Loving and the "Blessed Virgin, pictured on the wall of the living room in a reproduction of Raphael's *Sistine Madonna*" (464).

Of course, Mrs. Loving's name, Mary, suggests that both of these models allude to the Blessed Virgin. Hence, when Rachel at first responds positively to the call to be a mother, her view of herself in analogy to "Mary . . . at the 'Annunciation'" (Grimké, *Rachel* 12) is overdetermined by the two models to which she has access.

In many ways, Angelina's decision to write the Virgin Mary into *Rachel* was also overdetermined—in part by an African American spiritual tradition valorizing Mary, in part by a predominantly Christian United States that had taken Mary as a type of universal mother, and, I would suggest, in part by the transcultural jolt Archibald received during his consulship as he left the northeastern United States for the Caribbean.[29] In light of Mary's sustained cultural life in African American and US culture, it would be unwise to look to Archibald's consulship for the origin of Mary's presence within *Rachel*. But remembering Gloria Hull's observation that Archibald loomed large as a motivation and audience for Angelina's writing (114–15), it seems appropriate that in approaching Mary's apparitions within *Rachel*, we take into consideration Archibald's Dominican insights into Christian iconography and everyday life. Archibald's letters home offer a window into the Marian themes that undoubtedly surfaced in his postconsular lifetime of Dominican reminiscences.

Archibald's ideas on the intersection of motherhood, aesthetics, and everyday life were altered by life in Santo Domingo. Before arriving at his Caribbean post, he was displeased with the disjunction between everyday realities and conventional representations of the Madonna and Child. As he explained in a letter from Santo Domingo, he vividly remembered visiting Boston's Williams and Everett Art Gallery, where he had seen a contemporary German representation of the Madonna and Child. Of this representation, he explained, "The mother is . . . fully & warmly clad while she holds in her well covered arms a perfectly nude child. This contrast at the moment struck me as an inartistic incongruity. . . . But after I reached this island the scales fell from my eyes, & the mystery was solved." Archibald went on to describe the mystery's solution:

> For just what we see in the old masters I see here, women completely & comfortably clothed carrying naked babies in their arms. I perceived at once that Raphael & that mighty throng of Italian artists painted from life what they saw in Sunny Italy. Every where in the street, & house, & field they saw the fully robed mother & the naked child. They had but to idealize this common & lovely picture

> of life about them, to lift the simple & common into the universal & devine [*sic*] Motherhood & Child-Lord of the race.

Envisioning sunny Italy and sunny Santo Domingo as part of an expansive and transnational South, Angelina's father saw that Southern painters had long painted from life, while Northern painters merely imitated those in the South. He asked, "But while the Italian painters painted from life, do German & English & American artists paint from life when they paint a Northern Mother & Child as the great masters painted a Southern Mother & Child? Ought not Northern Art to conform in certain respects to the life about it, as Southern Art conformed so gloriously to its environments?"[30]

Archibald's displeasure with Northern artists for failing to "paint from life" suggests his reverence for realism's conventions of verisimilitude. Yet his missives did not simply prescribe a one-to-one correspondence between the world of things and the world of representation. Life in Santo Domingo also prompted Archibald to meld his inclinations toward verisimilitude with a practice of reading everyday life as if it were a shadow cast on the screen of material existence by a transcendent essence. He complemented his praise for "every day life" with a concurrent valorization of artists' efforts at mining the "simple & common" and seeing within it "the universal." Archibald's subsequent explanations within the letter reveal that he himself applied the reading practice of the "old masters" as he took everyday scenes from Dominican life and sought to access the actuality beyond the actuality. He wrote to his family, "I was passing a dirty hut one afternoon, in the door was a woman in an incredibly dirty frock, but she had . . . that indescribable pose & grace of Santa Barbara in Raphael's greatest Madonna & Child." He explained that recognizing a "hint of the goddess in . . . common workaday folk" could be achieved by forgetting the "bare feet & homely face." While this type of reading could be accomplished "as in a glass darkly to the Modern eye," the "old masters used to see [the divine] so vividly in the every day life about them."[31] With everyday life in Santo Domingo offering these insights into the aesthetic practices of the Old Masters, Archibald himself approached women as everyday texts awaiting a revelation of their transcendent essence through the readings he offered in his letters.[32]

Archibald's Dominican-inspired practices of reading and rewriting the everyday world constitute just the type of theoretical and practical currents that *Rachel* clearly engages in its treatment of motherhood. As the *Sistine Madonna* hangs over *Rachel*'s dramatic action, Angelina's depiction of Mary Loving within *Rachel* takes seriously Archibald's suggestion that Northern artists, like Southern artists, should draw on everyday life in constructing their images of the Madonna and Child. Mary Loving's concerns are markedly everyday as she sews (2), plans the family menu (14–15), looks after supper (17), and works to help support her children (78–80). Yet at the same time, *Rachel* offers details that point toward a reading of Mary as divinely universal. Complementing the allusion constituted by her name, Mary attempts to buoy up her children's faith in God (28, 42) and orients herself (in analogy to the Madonna on the wall) toward universalism when she claims at one point that her own "experience is every mother's" (13). But Mary Loving's is more than a universal motherhood. Her performance of motherhood is a study in what happens when black female particularity responds to the putatively universal call of motherhood. Unlike the *Sistine Madonna*, Mary Loving is not removed from time, frozen in a perpetual Mother-Child idyll on the wall. Instead, the conditions of everyday life in the United States dictate that a black woman must exist in time, watching her child suffer and even die like the biblical Mary.

By the moment of *Rachel*'s opening scene, the script of crucifixion already has been enacted. As Mary relates the terrible scene to Rachel and Tom, she tells not only of her husband's lynching but also of the death of her son George. She explains that when the mob took Mr. Loving, George tried to rescue him, but the mob took her son as well. Mary remembers the moments before George was taken and hung on a tree: "He never made an outcry. His last words to me were: 'Ma, I am glad to go with Father'" (25). George's death is reminiscent of the biblical account, in which Jesus "opened . . . not his mouth" (Acts 8:32) and was "hanged on a tree" (5:30). As a drama that reads everyday particularity in terms of a divine universal, *Rachel* not only deploys Archibald's Dominican reading practices to render Mary as a black Madonna but also renders George as a black Christ. In this way, *Rachel* presages Langston Hughes's "Christ in Alabama" or W. E. B. Du Bois's "Jesus Christ in Texas."[33] Like these later texts, *Rachel* depicts white Christians ironically crucifying a figure possessing the sacrificial mantle of Christ. Yet *Rachel* redoubles the scandal by making its audience privy to the killing's traumatic effect on Mary (Loving), which emphasizes that—in contradistinction to Archibald's idealizing hermeneutics of the universal—reading black women as Madonna figures conduces away from the ideal and toward an intense reminder of rampant black tragedy.

As Mary's daughter, the character Rachel seems poised to offer a second view of the way in which African American women may suffer as they become texts for the type of reading practices Archibald deployed in his Marian rewritings of everyday life. Forces ranging from other characters to inanimate objects seek to interpellate Rachel, with the intention of exposing the spark of her divine motherhood. At first, Rachel acquiesces to this maternal hailing, as during the opening scene, "her expression becomes rapt" after she raises "her eyes to Raphael's 'Madonna' over the piano" (11). She tells her mother of a dream in which a voice announced she was "to be a mother to little children"; she says she knows "how Mary felt at the 'Annunciation'" (12). Later, John Strong reinforces the maternal call. He admires the Lovings' reproduction of the *Sistine Madonna* (7) and then hangs "pictures of Madonnas" in what is to be his and Rachel's conjugal apartment (92). Social and ideological forces within the play are unrelenting in their insistence that Rachel has always already been the divine Mother in whose image she is to be created.

But Rachel's identification with the Madonna is complicated by her lament that her own children—in the path of George rather than of the forever-static Child in the *Sistine Madonna*—must "grow up" (10). Growing up means living a life "blasted by the white man's prejudice" (93), becoming subject to epithets, employment discrimination, and lynching. Finally, Rachel rejects the gaze attempting to arrogate to her (rather than to locate within her) the role of divine Mother. Referencing her personal Annunciation scene (62), she speaks back to the force she perceives as issuing the call: "You God! . . . I swear—and may my soul be damned to all eternity, if I do break this oath—I swear—that no child of mine shall ever lie upon my breast." She then approaches the roses that John Strong has sent her, taking each flower in her hand and ripping off its head (63). Given the play's conflation of children with roses (11, 60, 61), the stems symbolize the children she has resolved never to bear. Yet in light of the rose's status within Marian symbology,[34] this deflowering is also a rejection of the call to become—or to be read as—an African American Madonna. This is a denial of the divine that Archibald, in Santo Domingo, claimed existed behind the dark glass of the "workaday." It is a denial of what he termed the hidden "hint of the goddess."

Rachel's decision to remain childless functions, like foreign travel, as a means of escaping the horrors of US racism. In the case of childlessness, the escape occurs via the ghostly proxies of one's counterfactual children. This mode of childlessness is also analogous to travel in its effective capitulation to the traditional and great white hope that whiteness might somehow be left alone to become the United States' sole heir. But within *Rachel*'s economy, Rachel's final denial of fertility is no more valorized as a mode of escape than is travel. The scandal of Rachel's denial supersedes even the play's scandalous image of a Christian nation crucifying Christ in the person of George. Rachel's rejection of the call issued at her personal Annunciation frames white racism as writing God out of existence, causing a Madonna figure to reject the Annunciation scene and thereby stymieing the birth of a Child-Lord. This is a scandal aimed at what Angelina called "one of the most conservative elements of society," the "white women of this country," whom she hoped to mobilize as a means of counting a coup in the domestic battle against race prejudice ("Rachel" 414). Ironically, this central domestic trope had routes in—and responded to—reading practices that Archibald honed during his international work as a diplomat in what he saw as a transnational South that spanned from sunny Italy to sunny Santo Domingo.

Toward an Unmaking of Properly Conditioned Americans

This chapter has highlighted metonymies of absence—traces of Archibald's diplomatic absence within *Rachel*, voids unfilled by diplomacy's occluded black activisms, the absence of maternal essence intimated by Rachel's rejection of her Annunciation scene. But metonymy is a representational cul-de-sac in which a presence represents that which is absent, and absences (in the archive, in the historical record, in physical space) are illuminated by partial presences. One such partial presence is at the heart of Angelina's claim regarding Archibald's life in Santo Domingo—that she "seem[ed] to have been there too." In Angelina's assertion of virtual presence, we see a gesture toward what might be called, borrowing from Homi Bhabha, a "'partial' presence" or "metonymy of presence" (*Location* 86, 89). Bhabha has discussed partial presence in relation to his famous treatment of colonial mimicry, but the notion of metonymic presence may be instructively redeployed in approaching black women's situation within the complex of African American racial, literary, and official international representation. While black women were not permitted to assume representational roles in the State Department until the mid to late 1950s, black men began making inroads into the diplomatic corps after gaining the franchise in the 1860s, and white women assumed representational roles in diplomacy soon after the passage of the Nineteenth Amendment in 1920. If, as Claudia Tate has observed, black men's nineteenth-century enfranchisement secured for black women "political representation through male mediation" (*Domestic* 91), then in the post-1910s United States, black women were afforded access to official internationalism via the parallax mediations of the black men and white women who performed on the international stage. Black women of the day could draw on the familial and generic ontologies of race and gender to claim international representation, but the incompleteness of this representation was inevitably reemphasized because when black women looked at their representatives, they could merely say (to signify on an old folk expression), *My color but not my kind* or *My kind but not my color.* Like Angelina listening to Archibald's stories, black women "seem[ed] to have been there too"—with a semblance of their presence emerging on the official international stage via the indices of race and gender affixed to the international actors that the United States permitted to assume the role of diplomat.

Yet locating black women's presence on the diplomatic stage by positing a race- and gender-based mediation affords short shrift to black women's material presence, a presence to which relevant archives give us only metonymic traces. While this chapter has argued that *Rachel* gestures implicitly toward diplomacy's rhetorically hobbling effect on New Negro men, it is important to emphasize that diplomatic service also functioned systematically to preserve large (and largely untapped) quantities of official writing by these men. Hence, we have ample access to the official actions taken by black men in the service of the United States. However, diplomatic archives and public representations of black women's roles on the stage of official diplomacy have been occluded systematically (because black women did not officially represent the United States until the 1950s) as well as on personal, contingent, and informal bases. For instance, Archibald considered his personal letters from Santo Domingo to be highly important; thinking he might "need them hereafter," he instructed that Angelina and his other family members "be very careful to preserve *all* that [he] may write."[35] Yet Archibald apparently did not preserve Angelina's letters, which likely contained (especially as she entered her late teens) passages in which she commented on Archibald's status as a consul or perhaps offered opinions on the Spanish-American War, of which Archibald wrote to her during his final months in the Caribbean.[36] Because the letters were not preserved, however, we have no way of knowing. Black diplomats' disinclination to account for their female family members' engagements with official diplomacy was not confined to the case of the Grimkés. In a similar case, James Weldon Johnson's autobiography, *Along This Way*, offers extensive details on his own consular work but accounts for his wife Grace Nail's twenty-month presence in Nicaragua with a mere handful of references, including notes on the clean house she kept with the help of two Nicaraguan maids (268), a dispute between Grace and a laundryman (274), and Johnson's assertion that "no woman from a northern climate ought to stay longer than two years at a time in the tropics" (273). However, what Johnson failed to make known in the public record of his diplomatic life, he conceded in earlier personal letters from Nicaragua, in which (after Grace's return to New York City) he repeatedly confessed to missing his wife's "help" with his "official duties."[37] Grace's unpaid and publicly unacknowledged surrogation of diplomatic performances at the consulate not only aided Johnson in fulfilling his official duties but also freed up time for him to pursue his literary interests, which included revising his novel and drafting portions of his first book of poetry.[38] Hence, we may consider *The Autobiography of an Ex-Colored Man* and *Fifty Years & Other Poems* to be metonymies of Grace Nail's publicly unacknowledged and unofficial performance of Johnson's official role on the international stage.

In part, black diplomats' biases against preserving or reporting their female family members' engagements with official international diplomacy may be explained via the well-documented tendency to read the international world as a masculine space. Certainly, Johnson communicated his sense of the masculinity of his own consular life when he commented that women from the North ought to limit their time in the tropics. Meanwhile, Archibald led Angelina to believe that he did not take her with him to Santo Domingo because she "was too young" (Grimké, "Biographical" 47). This age-based rationale seems adequate at first glance, but a more likely explanation for Archibald's decision not to take the fourteen-year-old Angelina can be found in his insistence, repeated with great frequency in his letters from the Caribbean, that she "be always under all circumstances a young lady of refinement & high breeding" and that she "develop into a sweet & noble woman."[39] Prep schools in the United States were the place for this feminine development, not Santo Domingo. In approaching New Negro diplomats' tendency to keep female family members removed from the physical sites and narrative accounts of their international diplomatic posts, some of John Stephens Durham's commentary becomes illuminating. Durham candidly asserted that "no properly conditioned American would be satisfied to rear his family in a Latin community. If without children, he could not be satisfied to see his wife vegetate in it" ("Confessions" 171). As this gendered geography intersected with the State Department's de facto policy of sending black men almost exclusively to tropical and Latin posts, the project of keeping black women away from diplomatic posts became a method not only of performing masculinity but also of asserting one's status as a "properly conditioned American."

This effort, accomplished within physical and narrative realms, involved an imperfectly executed erasure that has left us with metonymies of black women's official internationalist presence that await further exploration. Angelina Grimké's *Rachel*, in its contemplations and revelations regarding Archibald's work in diplomacy, is one such partial presence. Others include the currently unknown international engagements of the wife of George Washington Ellis, Clavender Sherman Ellis, who is described in the dedication of *The Leopard's Claw* as a "promising writer of short stories" with "special knowledge of African life and conditions." Clavender exhibited "unfaltering fealty and fidelity to the cause of presenting the African before the world as he really is" (v). Unfortunately, today we have neither her stories nor a record of the convergences of her "special knowledge of African . . . conditions" with Ellis's diplomatic work. Another figure who to this point is only partially present on the stage of official internationalism is consular clerk Lillie Mae Hubbard, whose photograph was published in the *Crisis* in 1929 with the caption, "Miss Lillie Mae Hubbard, of the United States Consular Service in Liberia and Portugal, and her collection of African art now on exhibition in Chicago" ("Miss").[40] Bringing sustained focus to one such metonymy of presence, the following chapter draws attention to the case of Ida Gibbs Hunt, whose official internationalist and Pan-Africanist engagements vividly reveal that black women before the 1950s accomplished much more than merely *seeming* to have been there too.

PART III

Hip-to-macy

New Negro Internationalism and American Studies

Continuing to travel and write long after the New Negro era, Langston Hughes emerged during the 1960s as one of the commentators who has most provocatively theorized the integration of diplomatic and African American cultures. In his 1965 collection *Simple's Uncle Sam*, Hughes presents readers with a scene in which Harlem folk character Jesse B. Semple discusses how best to "take up the international situation." "I would call a Summit Meeting," Simple explains, "and get together with all the big heads of state of the world." Simple's interlocutor replies, "I gather you would . . . become a diplomat." But Simple retorts, "A hip-to-mat, . . . minding everybody's business but my own, . . . looking like an Englishman. But what would be different about me is I would be black. . . . [I would say,] 'Gentlemens of the Summit, I want you-all to think of how you can provide everybody in the world with bread and meat. Civil rights comes next. Let everybody have civil rights, white, black, yellow, brown, gray, grizzle, or green. . . . So many leaders is in the game for payola. . . . But me, self-appointed, I am beholden to nobody" (162–63). Continuing his hypothetical Summit address, the hip-to-mat asks, "Do I hear some of you-all say, 'It do not matter what Harlem thinks'?" He gives his reply: "I regret to inform you, gentlemens of the Summit, that IT DO!" (164).

Clearly, Simple's vision for international engagement involves none of the knee-pants, poodlism, or curtsying that Wright deplored in the role of New Negro artistic ambassador. Instead of worrying about protocol or state-generated performance imperatives, Simple is brassily self-appointed and apparently beholden to no one. To describe his status, he coins the term *hip-to-mat*, a neologism splicing the phrase *hip to that* into the term *diplomat* and thereby integrating the hip knowingness of black vernacular culture into official diplomacy's traditionally staid approach to internationalism. "Looking [not quite] like" white diplomats, Simple's model hip-to-mats would be diplomats but ersatz—with their ersatz status introducing a subversive parody to the international stage as the practitioners of hip-to-macy go over world leaders' heads and under their noses.

Hughes, as a black intellectual whose travels often brought him into close quarters with official internationalism,[1] was in an excellent position to imagine a conceptual category through which to theorize the long-established African American practice of signifying on international diplomacy by making use of its tropes and methods in unofficial ways. In fact, to the degree that New Negro consuls and diplomats permitted official diplomacy to inform their unofficial work in racial and literary representation, each of them may be thought of as a hip-to-mat *avant la lettre*. This study's final part, however, is less concerned with black US citizens whose work in diplomacy became an enduring component of their public identities. Rather, part 3 draws attention to figures including W. E. B. Du Bois, Ida Gibbs Hunt, and Richard Wright, whose modes of hip-to-matic internationalism developed in dialogue with a sustained and often strained contact with official internationalism. Du Bois, Hunt, and Wright function as bridges between the New Negro era's corps of official diplomats and the larger group of writers and intellectuals who have contributed to the African American (and indeed black diasporan) internationalist tradition. This larger tradition of black internationalism is constituted by the many self-appointed commentators whose work has critiqued, intersected with, and taken inspiration from a twentieth-century internationalism invested in traditional diplomatic encounters as well as new formations and institutions such as the League of Nations, a burgeoning proletarian internationalism, the United Nations, and the Non-Aligned Movement. Riffing on these modes of internationalism, uncounted African American writers and commentators have, like Simple, taken up the international situation.

In complement to its interpretive consequences for New Negro diplomacy and the larger black internationalist tradition, Hughes's theorization of hip-to-macy has significant heuristic value in relation to the field of American studies. Since the fall of the Soviet Union, the discipline of American studies increasingly has assumed an attitude of critique in reference to the American exceptionalism that frequently characterized Americanist scholarship during the Cold War.[2] Many new Americanist scholars, attempting to distance themselves methodologically from the state-supportive and state-complicit exceptionalism of the past, have routed their literary and cultural analyses through transnational geographies that seek to subvert, on epistemological levels, the circumscribing geography of the nation-state.[3] As a result, several new cultural geographies have animated the postnationalist American studies: cultures of US imperialism, the global South, the borderland, Americanity, the Atlantic world, the Pacific Rim, the hemisphere, and the planet, among others.[4]

Yet even as these proliferating transnational geographies have sought to defetishize the nation-state, prominent voices have expressed a suspicion that the transnationalized American studies still may advance a cultural politics supportive of the US state's political culture. Looking back on the "cold war years [of] American studies" as "practically defined by the field's investment in American exceptionalism" (107), Michael Bérubé has wondered if the postnationalist American studies' current relation to the US state might not "be uncomfortably similar" to that cultivated during the Cold War: might the transnational turn in American studies ultimately be found to be "encouraged by enlightened multinationals, and their supporters in government, who [are] interested in the propaganda value of a critical, anti-imperialist, internationalist American studies?" (110). This is a self-reflexive suspicion that reframes some of the field's most resistant and postnationalist scholarly endeavors as functionally—if not intentionally—supportive of a globalized neoliberal regime whose center of gravity is the United States. Bérubé suggests that many such complicities will remain imperceptible to academics who are inattentive to university funding models (104–05), but American studies scholar Richard P. Horwitz has offered candid and sound commentary on the more overt levels at which transnationalized American studies and the state emerge as mutually reinforcing. Recalling his own experiences as an Americanist Fulbright Scholar whom the state sent abroad neither as "a policy analyst" nor as "an ambassador," Horwitz remarks that "simple decorum and intellectual integrity can turn a [seemingly autonomous] Fulbrighter into a spin-controller for the powers that be" (466).

In light of Horwitz's and Bérubé's commentary, the putatively autonomous figure of the hip-to-mat emerges as a potentially crucial exemplum for a field whose disciplinary history suggests the urgency of contemplating the gradations of complicity that can arise in scholarly and teaching activities that at first glance seem unbeholden to the state. If, as Shelley Fisher Fishkin has pointed out, "the experiences of black U.S. . . . diplomats . . . provide a promising avenue of research" for the transnational American studies (49), then I would argue that the histories of New Negro diplomacy and black hip-to-macy come together to create a story that at some moments might be taken as a prehistory—and at some moments should be taken as a parable—of American studies' variegated state complicities as the field has transitioned from the Cold War era into an era of globalized neoliberalism. Gilles Deleuze and Félix Guattari have described a world in which transnational commerce and international class stratification precipitate the state's escalating detachment from physical territory. In this environment, write Deleuze and Guattari, "The State . . . must invent specific codes for flows that are increasingly deterritorialized" (218). If two of the planet's major deterritorialized flows have been a black diaspora (preconditioned largely by Atlantic world slavery) and a planetary community of scholars (created through borderless intellectual exchange), then two of the US state's corresponding transnational inventions have been New Negro work in US diplomacy and an American studies that emerged during the Cold War as an ideological apparatus. As a conceptual mediator between these two political-cultural inventions, Hughes's figure of the hip-to-mat does not offer easy answers to the problematics of complicity and autonomy that become major factors in African Americanist scholarship and American studies. However, advancing hip-to-macy as a conceptual category promises to help map the terrain that links both the New Negro era and the field of American studies to the official diplomatic performances of some of the most prominent international representatives of the early twenty-first century.

5 / Diplomats but Ersatz: The Hip-to-matic Pan-Africanism of W. E. B. Du Bois and Ida Gibbs Hunt

Because Langston Hughes's archetypal hip-to-mat is the organizer of a "Summit Meeting," hip-to-macy emerges as an apt trope through which to interrogate the international and representational questions surrounding a series of landmark summits—the meetings held by the Pan-African Congress (PAC) in 1919 and the 1920s. Within the context of these watershed moments of black internationalism, the lens of hip-to-macy becomes especially crucial to assessing the activities and writings of two of the PAC's founding African American organizers, W. E. B. Du Bois and Ida Gibbs Hunt. Cofounder of the NAACP and longtime editor of the *Crisis*, Du Bois was the most famous Pan-Africanist of the twentieth century. He spoke at the Pan-African Conference of 1900, and in 1919, he was the founder and secretary of the First Pan-African Congress, which took place in Paris on 19, 20, and 21 February.[1] Indicating his sense of centrality to the movement and revealing the degree to which official internationalism undergirded that sense of centrality, Du Bois at one point described himself as "a sort of ambassador of Pan-Africa," self-consciously redeploying the official representative character he attained through his one-month stint as Calvin Coolidge's minister plenipotentiary to Liberia.[2] If Du Bois, as the PAC's founding secretary, has found pride of place within discussions of the organization's activities, quite the opposite can be said of the Congress's founding assistant secretary, Ida Gibbs Hunt. Nearly anonymous alongside her famous PAC collaborator, Gibbs Hunt hailed from a family that was long intertwined with the State Department. Her father, Mifflin Wistar Gibbs, had been consul in Madagascar from 1898 to 1901, and he was succeeded by another African American consul, William Henry Hunt, who gained a position at the consulate largely through the efforts of his romantic interest (and Consul Gibbs's daughter), Ida Gibbs.[3] William Hunt's ensuing diplomatic career was long and varied, and after Ida married him in 1904, she accompanied him to his posts in Madagascar (through 1907), France (1907–27), Guadeloupe (1927–29), the Azores (1929–31), and Liberia (1931–32).[4]

Though the State Department's sexist employment practices would have prevented Gibbs Hunt from representing the United States abroad, her position on the margins of official diplomacy did not preclude her from—and actually aided her in—her work with Du Bois as "a sort of ambassador of Pan-Africa." Du Bois and Gibbs Hunt enjoyed a close and abiding friendship. They likely met while Ida (before her marriage to William) taught at Washington, DC's M Street High School, and they afterward exchanged a cycle of letters lasting decades. Acknowledging the significance of this relationship, David Levering Lewis has speculated that Gibbs Hunt "may have served as a model for Carolyn Wynn" in Du Bois's novel *The Quest of the Silver Fleece* (*W. E. B. Du Bois: Biography* 568). In any case, when the *Crisis* editor arrived in Paris to organize the Pan-African Congress of 1919, Gibbs Hunt left her husband at his consulate in Saint-Étienne and "dashed off to work for several months in Paris with Du Bois" (Alexander 175). Claude McKay once represented Consul Hunt's work in official diplomacy as stymying inclinations toward racial solidarity (253), but Gibbs Hunt was unfettered by consular regulations and State Department protocol. And ironically, even as the State Department denied passports to African Americans seeking to attend the 1919 Congress, it was "the tireless Ida Hunt," wife of a US consul, who collaborated with Du Bois to arrange the "ingenious publicity campaign" that led to the conference's fruition.[5] Serving as assistant secretary of the Congress of 1919, Gibbs Hunt also had a strong presence at the Congress of 1921 and was a chief speaker and one of three signatory committee members at the Congress of 1923.[6]

Historicizing the representational questions brought to a head during this landmark moment of black internationalism, and recovering Gibbs Hunt's quasi-diplomatic work as an instance of what chapter 4 calls a metonymy of presence, this chapter draws attention to the ways in which Du Bois's novel *Dark Princess* and Gibbs Hunt's poetry exist as literary theorizations of the PAC's efforts on the international stage. Bringing Hughes's notion of hip-to-macy to bear on the PAC organizers' literary endeavors directs important focus toward black internationalism's parallels with official diplomacy, its rationalizations of self-appointment, and its investments in the trope of messianism as a means of fulfilling its aspirations.

Rationalizing Pan-African Self-Appointment

When Langston Hughes's Simple highlights his status as "self-appointed . . . [and] beholden to nobody," his description is meant to convey the hip-to-mat's ability to speak in ways unfettered by governmental purse strings and state-generated performance imperatives. As Simple imagines it, self-appointment leads to an honest directness that distinguishes the hip-to-mat from the traditional diplomat, whom Sir Henry Wotton memorably described as a "man sent to lie abroad for the commonwealth" ("Casual Comment" 9). In contrast to the traditionally disingenuous diplomat, the self-appointed hip-to-mat seems appealingly authentic. In theory, self-appointment offers an ethical alternative to the strategic indirection employed by characters such as Shiny, Booker T. Washington, the Ex-Colored Man, and James Weldon Johnson himself in *The Autobiography of an Ex-Colored Man*. In practice, however, self-appointment poses its own set of ethical difficulties. A view of these difficulties—and their stopgap solutions—emerges quite clearly from an examination of Du Bois's *Dark Princess*, Gibbs Hunt's poem "To France," and both writers' commentary on their roles in the Pan-African Congress.

When Du Bois sailed for Europe to organize the 1919 Congress with Gibbs Hunt, he took passage on the *Orizaba*, a ship sharing a name with the vessel aboard which Matthew Towns, protagonist of *Dark Princess*, flees the United States.[7] The opening page of *Dark Princess* finds Matthew standing on "the deck of the *Orizaba*" in a fury over the color discrimination that has driven him out of medical school in New York City (3). He knows the *Orizaba* will deliver him to Belgium, from whence he anticipates traveling extensively throughout Europe and perhaps Asia (5). However, after landing, he is sidetracked in a Berlin café, where he meets "Princess Kautilya of Bwodpur, India" (17). The princess invites him to a dinner with some associates and repeatedly interrupts herself while issuing the invitation: "We represent—indeed I may say frankly, we are—a part of a great committee of the darker peoples; of those who suffer under the arrogance and tyranny of the white world." She continues: "We have among us spokesmen of nearly all these groups—of them or for them—except American Negroes" (16). During dinner the following evening (in the presence of a committee composed of persons from Japan, China, India, Egypt, and the Middle East), Kautilya turns to Matthew and offers an explanation similar to the one she gave earlier. This time, however, she delivers the explanation without interrupting herself: "You will note, Mr. Towns, that we represent here much of the Darker World. Indeed, when all our circle is present, we represent all of it, save your world of Black Folk" (19). Matthew has been invited to help the committee decide whether people of African descent are worthy of representation within this august assembly.

The question of whether to include black folk is the committee's overtly expressed concern, but the significant differences between Kautilya's two descriptions of the committee's mission suggest that the princess is preoccupied with more fundamental questions regarding international representation and self-appointment. Kautilya's second description flows as if it followed an implicit script approved by the committee, but her first description (offered in private) is riddled with self-interruptions indicative of a discomfort with the committee's official representational claims. During the committee meeting, the princess unequivocally states that except for "Black Folk," the members of the committee "represent all" of the Darker World. However, during her initial explanation, Kautilya's assiduous efforts at specification betray an intense confusion. She begins, "We represent—indeed I may say frankly, we are—." As Kautilya replaces representation ("We represent") with ontological status ("we are"), she calls into question the adequacy of the mediated presence offered by representation, and she grasps for the seeming authenticity of original presence. Thus, Du Bois situates the erudite princess within a tradition harking back to Socrates, who worried that an object can be straight when seen directly but nonetheless "look crooked" when viewed through the insidiously refracting "water" of representation (Plato 323).[8] Wary of such refractions, the princess drives toward authentic presence with the phrase "we are."

But if the committee offers direct presence rather than representation, what is that presence? Kautilya was about to assert that the committee members *represent* the Darker World, but she knows she cannot credibly claim that the committee members *are* the Darker World. Instead, as she treads carefully forward, she can only assert that she and her coterie *are* a "committee of the darker world," a description that necessarily reinserts representation into her explanation by implying that the committee is entitled to speak *for* the darker races because its members are *of* the darker races. This is an attempt to insert roots-based ontological status into the committee's representational work. In the princess's next breath, however, she reveals the unevenness of roots-based representation within the committee. She claims the committee has "spokesmen of nearly all these groups—," but she then interrupts herself by specifying, "—of them or for them." Her deliberative choice of prepositions concedes that some of the spokespersons do not hail from the groups for which they speak. At best, then, the committee members validate their self-proclaimed representative status by recourse to racial roots, but they often speak for groups of which they admittedly *are not* (certainly a thorn in the side of someone anxious to replace "we represent" with "we are").

The differences between Kautilya's committee and Du Bois and Gibbs Hunt's Pan-African Congress are readily apparent. Yet *Dark Princess* emerged from the heyday of Du Bois's work with the Pan-African Congress, and Kautilya's concerns over the validity of self-appointed representative status were shared by Du Bois and Gibbs Hunt as they contemplated their own roles as ambassadors of Pan-Africa. Indeed, with the apparent confidence of Kautilya before the committee, Du Bois at the Second Congress read a resolution listing demands made by "the Negro race through its thinking intelligentsia" ("To the World" 8). However, he admitted one month later in the pages of the *New Republic* that while attending the Congress, he had been nonplussed by the Congress's representational claims. Calling the question of representation the Congress's "subtler and more fundamental problem," he recalled that "Europe asked, What do these hundred, more or less, persons of . . . Negroid ancestry really represent? Is this a real Pan-Negro movement or the work of individuals . . . enthusiastic with an idea but representing little?" Du Bois remembered the delegates' insecurity: "And we ourselves could not answer. Of the hundred and fifty millions of African Negroes, few were conscious of our meeting." Then, undercutting the language he had earlier used to assert the Congress's capacity to represent, he described the Pan-African delegates as "an intelligentzia [*sic*]" but wondered, "how far did we really represent and voice" the concerns of the black world "and how far were we merely floating in the air of our dreams and ambitions?" ("Second Journey" 42).

On occasion, Du Bois himself was willing to let "dreams" stand in for "really represent[ing]." This was the case when he reported on the Third Pan-African Congress and evidently dreamed into existence a group of Pan-African delegates. Before the Congress convened in London, Isaac Béton of the Congress's French Committee wrote to Du Bois and told him that his committee refused to send any delegates to the session. Du Bois, however, reported in the *Crisis* that the French Committee "sent . . . delegates" to the London session. He even implied that "propositions were offered" by some of these imaginary French delegates ("Third Pan-African Congress" 122). When Ida Gibbs Hunt read Du Bois's summary in the *Crisis*, she was perturbed by the liberties Du Bois had taken in asserting the presence of French delegates at the meeting. Gibbs Hunt and Rayford Logan had traveled from Paris to the London session and had served with Du Bois on the Third Congress's three-person executive committee, and Gibbs Hunt now intimated that she recognized some of her own words (as well as those of Logan) in Du Bois's description of the "delegates to London from France." With evident pique, she wrote to Du Bois, "Certainly Mr. Logan and I went independently and paid our own expenses. We represented no one but ourselves."[9] It may be that Gibbs Hunt and Logan, as longtime African American residents of France, took it upon themselves to informally represent the French Committee's position to Du Bois. Or it may be that Du Bois, wishing the Pan-African Congress to make good on its stated purpose of "unit[ing] . . . representatives of the main groups of peoples of African descent,"[10] simply used his summary to ascribe to them this representative capacity. In either case, Gibbs Hunt was not pleased with Du Bois's public implication that she represented French people of African descent, and in reaction she disavowed representing anyone besides herself at the recent meeting. In privately claiming to represent only herself, Gibbs Hunt was arriving at what Du Bois later wrote into *Dark Princess* as Kautilya's ideal, which was to replace representation with ontological status, or to have what one represents become coextensive with what one is, at which point representation seemingly collapses into original and authentic presence. In claiming to represent only herself, Gibbs Hunt implicitly acknowledged the representational tautology of the PAC's project, calling into question the significance of her signature (with those of Du Bois and Logan) "for the Third Pan-African Congress" on the meeting's resolutions (Du Bois, "Third Pan-African Congress" 122). This signature, appended to a public document, had implied a confidence that she represented a Pan-African constituency, but her letter to Du Bois voiced a private discomfort with the self-appointment that ostensibly forged a representational link between herself and the African-descended world.

Du Bois and Gibbs Hunt had real doubts about the validity of their status as self-appointed representatives, but the fact that they continued in this capacity suggests they found some provisional answers. A literary representation of one such answer surfaces in *Dark Princess* at the committee meeting. As Matthew listens, he finds among the delegates a bias toward "royal blood" (23) and a prejudice against the world's "rabble" (24). Believing people of sub-Saharan African descent to be part of this rabble, the committee members question the "real possibilities of the black race" (21). At first, Matthew sits silently, but eventually he indignantly begins to tell his audience of the "high-born blood" among African Americans. He wants to explain, "We've had our kings, presidents, and judges—," but then he stops. Distancing himself from the committee's fetishization of high-born blood, he speaks the words of "some great voice, crying and reverberating within his soul." This voice, as the narrator tells it, "spoke for him and yet was him." With this new voice, Matthew calmly acknowledges, "we American blacks are very common people" (23). Matthew's unabashed emphasis on "common people" produces silence, but eventually the committee members again begin casting aspersions on people of African descent as "canaille" (25). At this return to insult, Matthew at first turns inward but then suddenly finds himself powerfully singing (in the same unbeckoned voice that spoke for him and yet was him) the Negro spiritual "Go Down Moses" (25–26). A "chorus of approval" erupts from the committee, and Matthew says triumphantly, "That . . . came out of the black rabble of America." He continues: "America is teaching the world . . . that ability and capacity for culture is not the hereditary monopoly of a few, but the widespread possibility for the majority of mankind if they only have a decent chance in life" (26). Eventually, Kautilya and the committee draw on Matthew's commentary to arrive at a vision of "democracy" (225): "Only Talent served from the great Reservoir of All Men of All Races, of All Classes, of All Ages, of Both Sexes—this is . . . real Democracy" (285). As the international committee arrives at what is widely familiar as the notion of the talented tenth, *Dark Princess* internationalizes Du Bois's long-term project of arguing "that the Talented Tenth . . . [are] worthy of leadership" ("Talented" 34), or worthy of self-appointedly representing others.

Because the rubric of the talented tenth depends on the cultural framing of the exceptional as the representative, *Dark Princess* must work to naturalize talent as the most important credentialing attribute of a representative. This naturalization takes place during the committee meeting. The committee's prejudice against black folk prompts Matthew to speak on behalf of the folk constituencies associated with his genealogy—his slave grandfather, his washerwoman mother, and his father who died in jail (23). But the narrator mystifies the scene by framing Matthew's voice as one that "spoke for him and yet was him." This phrase denies that Matthew is self-appointedly speaking for the folk and instead implies that the unbidden voice is a folk voice that speaks for Matthew. Even when the narrator claims that the voice "was" Matthew, this is not an acknowledgment that Matthew has appointed himself to speak for the folk but instead an assertion that the folk voice has a right to represent Matthew because Matthew has folk heritage. In muddying the water regarding Matthew's speech on behalf of the folk, *Dark Princess* enacts what Kautilya and Socrates fear—that representation distorts rather than reveals, that the refracting waters of representation can make a straight stick look crooked. But in deploying a vernacular voice, Du Bois's novel—which is invested in blurring the line between what "is really Truth—Fact or Fancy" (312)—seeks to take this crooked stick (of self-appointed international representation by the talented) and hit a straight lick with it. Matthew's mystical speech on behalf of the folk becomes a prophecy resulting in an egalitarian selection of representatives from all races, all classes, all ages, and both sexes. Similar to the term *hip-to-mat*'s evocation of the international representative as invested in a hip black vernacular tradition, *Dark Princess* seeks to validate the talented tenth's self-appointment by finessing a mystical yet allegedly authentic black folk voice into a putatively natural logic for self-appointed race representation in the international arena.

Dark Princess reveals a Du Bois who was concerned with validating the self-appointment of leaders purporting to represent a preexisting entity (the black world) on the international stage, but Ida Gibbs Hunt's literary work showcases a PAC organizer who sought to bring a new entity and constituency into existence via the interactions of self-appointment and the conventions of diplomatic representation. Keenly interested in literary writing, Gibbs Hunt received a BA and MA in English from Oberlin College. Afterward, she taught English at the M Street High School in Washington, DC, where she was also a member of the original and influential Booklovers Club.[11] By the turn of the century, she was instructing talented New Negro associates and students to "read broadly for culture and [then] enter upon the field already settled by Dunbar, Grimke, [and] Chestnut [*sic*]" (Gibbs Hunt, "Reading" 25). She herself was well read, and during her life in the United States and abroad, she likely submitted and published poetry under a pseudonym.[12] Currently, however, our access to her poetry is quite limited, with her two positively identified poems titled "To France" and "To Belgium." These two poems—preserved as signed, unpublished manuscripts among the Kendrick-Brooks Family Papers—likely found their way into the Brooks family collection via Antoinette Brooks Mitchell, who lived with her husband (jazz musician Louis A. Mitchell) in Paris during the era of the Pan-African Congresses. Gibbs Hunt's biographer, Adele Logan Alexander, suggests that the PAC organizer wrote her poetry during the months that she and Du Bois collaborated to organize the Congress's first meeting, and if such is the case, then Gibbs Hunt in all probability shared her poems with Du Bois and perhaps passed them around among friends and associates attending the Congress.[13] In any case, the poems are consistent with the PAC's tendency to address and evaluate nation-states, and like *Dark Princess*, they offer important insight into the ways in which one of the Congress's principal organizers conceived of the relation between self-appointment and black international representation. Particularly relevant to this question, "To France" is worth quoting in full.

TO FRANCE

O land of right and justice!
O land of people true!
Here is a hearty handshake,
And homage due to you.
You that some thought feeble,
You that some thought vain,
Have crowned the world with glory,
And caused the truth to reign.

Type of sublimest courage,
Through woe and sacrifice,
Fainting yet undaunted,
You rushed to pay the price;
Your life for home and country,
Your life for Freedom's cause,
Against a foe relentless,
Bent to make you pause.

Beacon of Liberty,
You alone was brave,
Brave in that highest courage,
All men's rights to save.
All men were your brothers,
Black and white and brown,

You scorned to bow to others
Who'd crush a fellow down.

In form and tone, "To France" is conservative compared to the poetry produced by more famous US expatriate writers of the day. But dwelling on Gibbs Hunt's poetic relation to the Anglo-American modernist zeitgeist is less interesting than interrogating her poetry's relevance to plotting a poetics of the PAC's efforts at validating speech on behalf of millions of African-descended people throughout the world. In light of her familial ties to official diplomacy and her status as an organizer of a Congress seeking to insert itself into negotiations at the Paris Peace Conference and the League of Nations,[14] we do well to consider the poem's overarching trope—that of apostrophe—as operating according to a logic of international diplomatic address. Certainly, the poem's assertion that France "alone was brave" in saving "all men's rights" is a prewriting of the PAC's official declaration that "France alone . . . has sought to place her . . . black citizens on a plane of . . . equality with her white" citizens (Du Bois, "To the World" 8). I would further suggest that a close analysis of this poetic representation of an international diplomatic address can reveal a great deal regarding certain facets of the PAC's rationalization of self-appointment.

Beginning with an apostrophic "O," the poem's first stanza addresses France as if the nation were a person, calling France "you" and granting the nation a human corporality by offering it "a hearty handshake." The presence of a handshake asks readers to conceive of the speaker as engaged in a peer relationship with a nation. Hence, with a handshake that simultaneously personifies a nation and nationalizes a persona, "To France" causes the interpersonal and international to intersect in a way that finds its best analogy in the event called a diplomatic encounter, or a meeting during which nations personified by diplomats (or persons nationalized by the states for which they are envoy) come together to speak for symbolic or practical reasons. This handshake is especially important to the project of the poem (and indeed the PAC) because, as an international gesture implying amity between two nations, it seeks to remove the black speaker from a realm of nationless international vagabondage by evoking a sense that the speaker is an envoy from what is indeed an emergent national entity.[15]

"To France" does not name the new nation on behalf of which the persona speaks; instead, the second and third stanzas triangulate the new nation's identity by naming its interests in relation to other nations—creating a sense of national content, as it were, for the national form evoked by the handshake. The speaker frames the nation for which she speaks as France's ally when she cites common enemies. In the second stanza, when the poet-diplomat praises France's work "in Freedom's cause, / Against a foe relentless," readers assume with relative certainty that the "foe relentless" is Germany, France's primary rival during the First World War. But the ambiguity of the phrase "foe relentless" permits the third stanza to broaden the poem's conceptualization of the enemy of Freedom's cause. Here again, the poem praises France for its commitment to Freedom: "Beacon of Liberty, / You alone was brave, / Brave in that highest courage, / All men's rights to save." Now, the foe emerges as a nation rejecting the conviction that "All men [are] . . . brothers, / Black and white and brown." Hence, rather than focusing on Germany as the enemy, the third stanza creates the "foe relentless" in the image of the United States, which, even as it sent African American soldiers to fight for the Allies, "sought desperately to reproduce in . . . France the racial restrictions of America, on the theory that any new freedom would 'spoil' the blacks" (Du Bois, "Essay" 79).

The animosity that the speaker's nation feels toward the United States is further reflected in the grammatical aberration that surfaces when she tells France, "You alone was brave." The presence of the third-person "was" rather than the second-person "were" suggests that in earlier drafts of "To France," Gibbs Hunt likely included the line as "France alone was brave" but that she finally decided to be true to the poem's overarching form of apostrophe by changing the subject to "You." In replacing "France" with "You," I would suggest, she may have forgotten to replace the third-person "was" with the second-person "were." Hence we are left with the grammatically hybrid phrase "You alone was brave." The subjective tension between the line's second-person subject and third-person verb conjugation is a symptom of two competing impulses within "To France": the impulse to be true to the apostrophic form by speaking *to* France and the impulse to cast aspersions on the United States by speaking glowingly *of* France to an international community that includes the United States. This impulse to address a larger audience while claiming through the title to be making an address specifically "To France" resonates with Henry Louis Gates, Jr.'s discussion of loud-talking: "One successfully loud-talks by speaking to a second person remarks in fact directed to a third person. . . . A sign of the success of this practice is an indignant 'What?' from the third person, to which the speaker responds, 'I wasn't talking to you.' Of course, the speaker was, yet simultaneously was not" (*Signifying* 82). The erratum constituted by the presence of "was" reflects the poem's internationally loud-talking impulse. It is a trace mistakenly carried over from an earlier draft, analogous to an inadvertent glance shot at the loud-talker's implicit third-person audience—in this case Pan-Africa's most powerful foe, the United States. By positioning the United States and Germany as the common enemies of France and Pan-Africa, "To France" suggests that US race prejudice and German military aggression are cut from the same cloth—a banner flown in opposition to "Freedom's cause."

Classically, R. W. B. Lewis has described Walt Whitman as poetically speaking a nation into being via the process of naming or cataloging its component parts (51–52). Gibbs Hunt's poem also aspires to national creation but relies instead on international diplomatic conventions. As "To France" speaks to and about other nations in the voice of a peer entity, the speaker's performance on behalf of African-descended peoples drives toward national sovereignty, which is commonly held to be constituted in part by an entity's "capacity to enter into relations with other States."[16] This notion of national realization through international representation has significant implications for the questions that vexed Du Bois and Gibbs Hunt regarding self-appointment. If the national status of an entity does not antedate its international representation (and indeed if international representation can be seen as an act of constituting a nation), then the protonational entity's initial international representatives cannot be appointed by a national constituency and instead, like Simple's hip-to-mat, must be in some way self-appointed. Rather than making a romantically racialist argument that relies on supposedly natural representative capacity (as showcased in *Dark Princess*'s justification of the talented tenth), Gibbs Hunt's poem approaches the representative character of the PAC's delegates as constructed and contingent, with a representation-effect emerging from recognition by other national entities. We might take Gibbs Hunt's "To France" (and by extension the quasi-official proclamations produced by the PAC and published in the *Crisis*)[17] as forerunners of Hughes's hip-to-mat, who appoints himself to represent Harlem and then certifies his representative status not by an appeal to his constituency but by implying that the "big heads of state" at the Summit Meeting recognize that he does indeed speak for Harlem (Hughes, *Simple's* 163–64).

Testing Diplomacy's Messianic Potential

Hughes's hip-to-mat is not merely self-appointed; he is also a type of internationally oriented black messiah. This hip-to-matic messianism comes to the fore as Simple imagines himself standing at the Summit, seeking to save the world from race prejudice by declaring (in resonance with the famous declaration "Let there be light"), "Let everybody have civil rights." Presently, Simple admits that he himself "cannot do much" but predicts that "some sweet day" he may have to "wham the world so far up into orbit until [all the white folks] will be shaken off the surface of the earth" (*Simple's* 163). Racially oriented messianic imagery is far from unique to Hughes's figure of the hip-to-mat. The image of a racially liberating black messiah has deep roots and frequent flowerings in African American cultural and literary traditions. Du Bois has been discussed as both a participant in and shaper of this messianism through works such as "Jesus Christ in Texas" and "Of the Coming of John," yet none of his works relies more extensively on messianic tropes than *Dark Princess*, a novel whose prominent "messianic vision" has been recognized as mixing with thematic elements including "proletarianism, Eastern mysticism, [and] aristocratic notions" (Moses, *Black* 154).[18] Indeed, the topic of *Dark Princess*'s messianism is well-trod critical terrain, but reading this messianism through the internationally oriented trope of hip-to-macy, and in conjunction with Gibbs Hunt's poem "To Belgium," brings new focus to significant though generally overlooked moments during which the novel fuses the messianic with questions of darker peoples' official international representation.

Dark Princess culminates in a final messianic spectacle. The finale finds Kautilya and Matthew in the Virginia countryside with their newborn son, Madhu, who is called the "Messenger and Messiah to all the Darker Worlds" (311). The infant's birth has galvanized a meeting of the "Great Central Committee of Yellow, Brown, and Black" (296). And in what Claudia Tate describes as a scene "reminiscent of the Magi's adoration of the Christ child" (*Psychoanalysis* 63), Madhu is greeted into the world by "a pageant" of twenty men who walk slowly out of the nearby woods. From among this group emerge "three old men: one black . . . and magnificent in raiment; one yellow and turbaned . . . ; and the last naked save for a scarf about his loins" (Du Bois, *Dark* 310). Such preternatural pageantry may seem incongruous within a novel that frequently aspires to literary realism, but Madhu's moment of messianic arrival has been anticipated throughout *Dark Princess*, first presaged during Kautilya's initial encounter with Matthew. During this encounter, the princess feels that her meeting with Matthew holds providential significance for the prospect of black representation within the Committee of Darker Races. She explains to Matthew that today she has been at the Palace of Art, where she gazed at an exhibition of paintings while "thinking absently of Black America." Then, suddenly, "one picture there intensified and stirred [her] thoughts—a weird massing of black shepherds and a star" (17). Primed by this "allusion to biblical events before Christ's birth" (Blum 169), Kautilya now tells Matthew that she feels their present meeting demonstrates "that the Powers of Heaven [have] bent to give [her] the knowledge which [she] was groping for" in her earlier thoughts on Black America's potential for representation within the committee (Du Bois, *Dark* 17). *Dark Princess*, then, not only concludes by mixing messianism and black international representation; it begins with this mixture.

Several critics have sought to flesh out the geopolitical implications of the novel's messianic finale,[19] but less attention has been directed toward Kautilya's early report that her thoughts on black international representation have been stirred by a painting alluding to Christ's birth. In referencing this painting of the "black shepherds and a star," Du Bois may have meant to allude to a specific work on display at Berlin's Palace of Art.[20] But as he created a scene in which Matthew, after disembarking from the *Orizaba*, meets a woman linking a piece of messianic artwork to black international representation, it is also likely that Du Bois drew on his own experience in 1918, when he himself disembarked from the *Orizaba* and met with a woman who, as she coordinated the Pan-African Congress, took political inspiration from a piece of art alluding to the birth of the Christ child. Notably, Ida Gibbs Hunt's poem "To Belgium" prefaces itself with an acknowledgment that it is modeled "after the picture of Lucien Jonas, The Three Wise Men of Our Day." Jonas was at the time a popular French painter who had illustrated many scenes inspired by the First World War. His illustration "Les Nouveaux Rois Mages" (fig. 3) foregrounded people of color within a messianic scene, and this representation stirred Gibbs Hunt's thoughts to the point that she responded in an instance of poetic ekphrasis. Jonas's "Les Nouveaux Rois Mages" takes as its subject matter Germany's August 1914 invasion of Belgium and the Allies' successful efforts to bring the German occupation to an end. The illustration allegorizes this situation by depicting Belgium as the Christ child surrounded by the Allies' colonial soldiers ("le Sénégalais, l'Indien, l'Arabe," as noted by the caption), whose gift-bearing presence creates the colonial soldiers as "Les Nouveaux Rois Mages" or (in

FIGURE 3. Lucien Jonas's "Les Nouveaux Rois Mages." (*L'Illustration* 26 Dec. 1914)

Gibbs Hunt's translation) "The Three Wise Men of Our Day." In light of Gibbs Hunt and Du Bois's shared interests and common project during their months in Paris, it would be surprising if the Congress secretary and assistant secretary failed to discuss "To Belgium" and the political inspiration Gibbs Hunt took from Jonas's illustration. If such was the case, then Gibbs Hunt's fascination with "Les Nouveaux Rois Mages" would seem a likely inspiration for Kautilya's interest in the painting of the "shepherds and the star." Yet even if Gibbs Hunt refrained from telling her friend of the inspiration she took from Jonas's illustration, her poem "To Belgium" buoys up an examination of *Dark Princess*'s messianism because it reveals the ways in which one of Du Bois's major Pan-Africanist collaborators conceived of the messianic in relation to the project of securing international representation for the darker races.

TO BELGIUM (AFTER THE PICTURE OF LUCIEN JONAS, THE THREE WISE MEN OF OUR DAY.—"L'ILLUSTRATION," 1914).

O little babe of Flander's [*sic*] farm,
Hid in a stable poor,

The Wise Men come from every clime
To keep this Christmas Day
And bring to thee their gifts sublime
From near and far away.

Above thee, robbed of hearth and home,
The star of Freedom hangs,
And guides men to the battle's edge.
Allied in common fealty,
Allied in hope and faith, they pledge
Their strength of arms to thee.

The dusky sons of Afric's soil
And India's mosque-clad hills,
And Asia's incense laden crests,
From mountain, plain and sea,
In mingled ranks with Europe's best,
Offer their all to thee.

In commenting on Germany's invasion of Belgium, "To Belgium" meticulously masks Gibbs Hunt's personal feelings, expressed during the war, that "poor Belgium is reaping what [King] Leopold sowed. . . . How many Congo natives had their hands cut off . . . ?" (qtd. in Alexander 164). Rather than framing Belgium's invasion as retribution for its depraved actions in the Congo, "To Belgium" utilizes a diplomatic voice that imitates the decorum and indirection typical of international negotiations. Fittingly, given what Gibbs Hunt recalled as the hand's role in Belgium's colonial activities, Belgium (unlike France) receives no offer of a handclasp. But the poem decorously follows the generous precedent set by Jonas's illustration by inserting Belgium into the messianic position conventionally occupied by the Christ child. And having acquiesced to Belgium's messianic *position*, the poem takes, in return, the opportunity to subtly undercut Belgium's messianic *function*. Traditionally, the Magi are drawn toward the star because it signifies the Christ child's presence. Yet within "To Belgium," as "the Star of Freedom," the star becomes a sign unto itself by bringing with it its own signified in the notion of Freedom. In other words, it is the ideal of Freedom, not a messianic Belgium, that motivates and "guides men to the battle's edge." In fact, if any figures in the poem can be said to have a messianic *function* (rather than merely a hollowed-out messianic *position*), they are the colonial soldiers, the "dusky sons," who arrive with the "sublime" gift of salvation for an otherwise helpless Belgium. The dusky sons, furthermore, have an ambassadorial function in that they have traveled from African and Asian climes to stand iconically within the poem for all peoples of African and Asian descent. In their commitment of "strength of arms" (if not of hands) to Belgium's cause, these ambassadorial figures create for Belgium and the Allies an obligation toward the dusky sons' African and Asian constituencies.

We see a proposal for the fulfillment of this war-generated obligation in the Pan-African Congress's various demands of Belgium and other European nations. The PAC asked that Belgium give African-descended people "a voice in [the Belgian Congo's] government."[21] The PAC also requested that African natives "shall have equitable representation in all the international institutions of the League of Nations" and that the League "appoint direct diplomatic representatives in the Mandated territories [seized by the Allies from Germany's colonial possessions]," with "representatives of the NEGRO race on the [League's] Mandates Commission."[22] In these requests, the legacy of Gibbs Hunt's "dusky sons" persists past the "battle's edge," promoting a vision of African-descended peoples mingling with "Europe's best" in the arena of postwar diplomacy. We have a gesture toward this vision in Gibbs Hunt's translation of Jonas's title, which rewrites "Les Nouveaux Rois Mages" as "The Three Wise Men of Our Day." Standing in for a more literal translation of *nouveaux* as *new*, the phrase *of our day* communicates *nouveaux*'s sense of currency while making use of a possessive pronoun that lays claim to a voice for the darker races in the new day of official internationalism arising out of the war's ashes. This translation seeks to move people of color from the realm of geopolitical outsiders by resituating them as diplomatic insiders. The poem's tack is unsurprising in light of a letter that Gibbs Hunt wrote to Du Bois less than five months before he sailed on the *Orizaba*. She explained, "Observation and experience have taught me that one can fight more effectively from within than from without."[23]

If "To Belgium" seems subtle in its aesthetic reworkings of geopolitical power relations, this is all the more reason to consider the poem in relation to the PAC, especially during the Belgium session of its second meeting. Jessie Fauset's description of this session cannot help but resonate with the poem's diplomatic willingness to forgo voicing Gibbs Hunt's grievances against Belgium. As Fauset reported, "Belgian officialdom was well represented" at the session, and under "the careful Belgian eye," the PAC speakers presented "three days [of] . . . pleasant generalities." They neither referenced "the atrocities of the Leopold regime" nor offered "a word of criticism of Colonial Governments." Fauset, feeling that she herself was also subject to Belgium's "shadow of Colonial dominion" ("Impressions" 14), joined other PAC attendees in silently reflecting on the "smothering power which made it impossible for men even in a scientific Congress to be frank and to express their inmost desires" (15). Like Fauset, Gibbs Hunt also came to see the dangers of working from within the international world's diplomatic matrices. After her husband's 1932 retirement from the Foreign Service, she spoke publicly of diplomacy itself as productive of a racist geopolitical culture. She described the League of Nations (which had been unresponsive to the PAC's overtures) as "a mighty union . . . to uphold Nordic supremacy" and condemned "diplomats [for] . . . barter[ing] away the rights of the weaker nations." She ranked "diplomacy" with "imperialism and exploitation" as a few of the international world's "old worn-out methods" ("Price" 80). Evidently, she came to see diplomacy as a means of maintaining the European-descended world's international status quo: rather than permitting nations of color to speak as peer entities (as Gibbs Hunt attempted in "To France" and the PAC attempted in its efforts to engage the proceedings of the Paris Peace Conference and the League of Nations), diplomacy produced an international hierarchy that systematically precluded peer relationships between European nations and peoples of color. Rereading "To Belgium" through Gibbs Hunt's later perspective requires a recognition of the dusky sons as envoys to a world of European internationalism that systematically precludes them from emerging as saviors of the African-, Asian-, and Arab-descended peoples they ostensibly represent.

Like Gibbs Hunt and Fauset, Du Bois approached black participation in twentieth-century internationalism with questions regarding the relative empowerments afforded by positions both *inside* and *outside* of international diplomacy. And, similar to Gibbs Hunt's move from diplomacy as messianism to diplomacy as white supremacy, *Dark Princess* abandons diplomatic messianism for a new skepticism regarding diplomacy's potential to save the darker races. In doing so, the novel theorizes the improbability that a person will emerge as a messiah when he or she operates in a mode that is inside rather than outside—immanent rather than exterior to—the world of official internationalism.

This question finds its major episodes of literary contemplation in Du Bois's representation of the events immediately following Matthew's attendance at the committee meeting. After the meeting, Kautilya has a private interview with Matthew during which she explains her interest in gaining further knowledge regarding African Americans' readiness for representation within the committee. She tells Matthew of a black nationalist organization in the United States and asks him to find its leader. Matthew is to "report to her [his] impressions and recommendations" (*Dark* 29). He returns to New York City and finds the leader, a West Indian named Perigua, living in Harlem. Matthew enters a room rife with "bad air, voices, and gesticulations" (43) and gains an audience with the leader. When Matthew tells Perigua that he has brought a "message . . . from—abroad," the leader leaps to his feet with a sense of urgency regarding his "State business" (44). Perigua turns to his acolytes and says, "*Le jour de gloire est arrivé!* . . . Men, I have news—great news—the greatest! Salute this Ambassador from the World—who brings salvation." Perigua explains, "Now all is well. We are recognized—recognized by the great leaders of Asia and Africa. Pan-Africa stands at last beside Pan-Asia, and Europe trembles" (45). The leader's baroque nationalist pretensions amid the "stale smells of food and tobacco" create the scene as decidedly bathetic. Matthew can see that Perigua is "no leader, he [is] too theatrical" (45).

Perigua's pronouncement regarding Matthew—that he is an "Ambassador" bringing "salvation"—represents an overt conflation of the messianic and diplomatic themes earlier condensed into Kautilya's reading of the painting. And significantly, Du Bois places this articulation into the mouth of a figure he represents as a charlatan. If, as has often been argued, Perigua is a thinly veiled reference to Marcus Garvey,[24] then Du Bois's representation of Perigua's enthusiasm for the "Ambassador" might well be taken as a critique of Garvey's assessment of the role of official international diplomacy in black racial liberation. Garvey's Universal Negro Improvement Association sent "ambassadors" to the League of Nations, Cuba, Abyssinia, France, and other nations.[25] And Garvey was a great believer in diplomacy, explaining that the "Negro must learn . . . diplomacy": "We must learn to give and take. If we want Africa, as we surely do, we must . . . yield some things and make concessions in America and other white countries by sane and proper arrangements" (6: 220). He told his followers that "the white man" was presently "on top," and he asked, if the white man "has to use keen diplomacy to keep him on top, how much more has the fellow down below to lift himself to the position of the white man by kee[n]er diplomacy [?]" (5: 527). Du Bois and Garvey had long been engaged in a bitter feud by the year of *Dark Princess*'s publication, and the novel's bathetic portrayal of Perigua undoubtedly parodies Garvey's tendency to look to diplomacy (in both its geopolitical and methodological senses) for salvation. Yet *Dark Princess*'s portrayal of Perigua's equation of ambassadorship with salvation also may have permitted Du Bois to transfer ownership of the PAC's own naive position regarding international diplomacy's saving potential. Interestingly, to Perigua's way of thinking, an "Ambassador" brings "salvation" because the ambassador's arrival implies that Perigua's "State" is now recognized internationally: "Now all is well. We are recognized." Certainly, the PAC's addresses to the League of Nations and individual European nations also relied on a logic seeking black national legitimization by way of international recognition. Both Perigua and the PAC attempt to answer European diplomacy with a "keener diplomacy," a position that counterproductively creates them as immanent to the international logic that prewrites the oppression of nations of color into its script.

Matthew's initial interactions with Perigua set in motion events that permit the novel to further consider the messianic avenues opened and closed by assuming positions that are immanent and exterior to international diplomacy. Matthew sends reports to Kautilya but does not receive any response from the princess. Despondent, he becomes part of Perigua's plot to avenge a recent lynching by dynamiting the Klan Special, a train carrying passengers to Chicago for a large meeting of the Ku Klux Klan. This is a suicide mission: Perigua plans on blowing up a railroad trestle and dying in the explosion, and Matthew volunteers to be a porter on the Special as it speeds toward the demolished section of track. The plan is foiled, however, when Matthew discovers that Kautilya is a passenger on the Special. She is traveling at the invitation of the Klan, which has asked her to deliver an address at the convention. Unable to bear the thought of killing Kautilya, Matthew pulls the brake. He saves the day, and the passengers come "forward with a big purse to reward him for his services" (98). However, Matthew refuses the Klan's gesture and is put on trial for conspiring to kill hundreds of people. Kautilya, meanwhile, is loath to see Matthew go to jail. She attempts to transfer the appearance of complicity from Matthew to herself, telling the court that Matthew had no knowledge of the plot until she made him aware of it just minutes before he stopped the train. Significantly, it is Kautilya's "diplomatic immunity" that provides her with a "refuge," as it would permit her to implicate herself in the conspiracy (and thereby to spare Matthew) without fear of legal consequences. One character explains Kautilya's diplomatic immunity this way: "The English Embassy, which represents her country abroad, backs her reputation, vouches for her integrity, and promises her immediate withdrawal from the country" (97). Matthew, however, refuses what Kautilya calls the "little sacrifice that [would have] cost [her] nothing and meant everything to [him]." He replies that Kautilya's little sacrifice might cost "the whole future of the darker world" (103). Going to prison, he tells her, is "the only effective . . . atonement that I can [make] to the Great Cause which is ours" (104).

This sequence of events—culminating in a discussion of who will play the role of savior—places Kautilya on the inside and Matthew on the outside of diplomacy, which here is represented as both a realm of geopolitics and strategic compromise. Kautilya has decided to engage in a dialogue with the Klan;[26] Matthew, in contrast, is attempting to destroy the Klan Special and refuses the Klan members' money even when it might be used for his defense during the trial. Matthew and Kautilya also differ in their relation to the international community. Whereas Kautilya feels it would "cost . . . nothing" to take advantage of the diplomatic conventions that free one nation's leaders and diplomats from the laws of other nations, Matthew sees a nearly incalculable cost. He sees that relying on the princess's diplomatic immunity (routed through the British embassy, which "represents her country abroad") would reaffirm the international status quo, which attempts to naturalize white nations' domination and representation of darker peoples throughout the world. Matthew sees, in other words, that Kautilya's attempt to save him is grounded in an acquiescence to the West's determination that darker peoples "cannot represent themselves; they must be represented."[27] On this point, the aim of *Dark Princess*'s analogical work is clear: by portraying Kautilya and Matthew as differing in their willingness to make tactical compromises with both the Klan and postwar internationalism, the novel suggests that these two institutions—one domestic and the other international—share the common mission of (in Gibbs Hunt's words) "uphold[ing] Nordic supremacy." (This is hardly a revelation regarding the Klan but is nonetheless an important critique of an early twentieth-century official internationalism that almost uniformly refused international representation of darker peoples except via white proxy.) In Matthew's divorcing himself from tactical and geopolitical diplomacy while claiming to make an "effective . . . atonement . . . to the Great Cause which is ours," his actions reach toward a contradiction of Perigua, Kautilya, and the PAC's conflation of Ambassador and Savior. Yet Matthew's atonement, even as it strives to remain exterior to the international world's diplomatic matrices, is still unwittingly imbricated in those matrices. His atonement sends him to prison, leaving Kautilya, who has demonstrated a willingness to make tactical compromises with the Klan and the international world, to carry on without him in the great cause. If Matthew is a test case in acting as an international outsider, then his case would suggest that there is no point outside of diplomacy's circle that is not structured by and complicit in what is inside the circle.

The events growing out of Matthew's interactions with Perigua permit *Dark Princess* to explore the differences and functional overlaps between positions that are immanent and exterior to the West's postwar internationalism, but the novel's messianic finale reminds us that exteriority is only one of immanence's binaries. Another is transcendence. As *Dark Princess* concludes, the African, Asian, and Indian wise men of "To Belgium" reappear, emerging now from the Virginia woods. But the dusky sons no longer seek to play the role of savior to Belgium. They now have seen that the West has created an internationalism that systematically precludes evenhandedness in white nations' interactions with darker peoples. Hence, rather than attempting to create an obligation that Europe is diplomatically prescripted to dishonor, they approach the infant Madhu. Du Bois's literary creation of Madhu releases the trope of black messianism from its perpetual tension, which Wilson Jeremiah Moses notes involves a simultaneous "rejection of white" culture and "a participation in one of its most sacred traditions" (*Black* 14). Within the novel, Madhu's presence brings an end to the conflict over messianism's immanence or exteriority to white-supremacist culture; the child reminds readers that the trope of messianism transcends cultural specificity. Madhu is a Christ figure at the same time as he is "King of the Snows of Gaurisankar," "Protector of Ganga the Holy," "Incarnate Son of the Buddha," and "Grand Mughal of Utter India." He is, finally, the "Messenger and Messiah" (Du Bois, *Dark* 311). His messianism is transcendent, situated above and comprehending regional and sectarian messianic traditions. And his status as "Messenger" transcends the traditional compromising role of diplomatic envoy. Madhu's birth is a sign assuring that the "Dark World" will be liberated and that this liberation—whether via "Peace and Reason" or "Blood and Storm"—will be incontingent on negotiations with "the Pale Masters of today" (297). At the novel's conclusion, this liberation has not taken place (it is, in fact, still twenty-five years distant), but the incontingency of liberation is affirmed as Kautilya discusses it not in future tense but in present tense: "In 1952, the Dark World goes free" (297). This new logic of international relations is neither inside nor outside of diplomacy's circle: it is a dimensional shift, transcendent and transfigurative of the current geopolitical plane.

Interestingly, *Dark Princess*'s narrator concludes with an "Envoy," a device that acknowledges the novel's preoccupations with—and efforts at intervention in—the arena of international representation. In this literary sending forth, the narrator summons "all the sprites who . . . have clustered around [his] hands and helped [him] weave this story" and sends them as his envoys to "the Queen of Faërie," who has aided him in writing his story by lending him the "gossamer of dream." The narrator instructs the sprites to return this dreamy gossamer and to relay to the Queen of Faërie his "fond obeisance" (312). That the author uses the Envoy to send forth envoys to the Faërie Queen ought to direct our attention to the novel's enigmatic dedication, "To Her High Loveliness TITANIA XXVII . . . QUEEN OF FAERIE." Just as *Dark Princess*'s "Envoy" self-consciously deploys bivalently literary and diplomatic language, we might also read the phrase "To Her High Loveliness . . . QUEEN OF FAERIE" as not merely a dedication but also a salutation marking the novel as a long address that itself is envoy to an otherworldly queen. This reading of *Dark Princess* is evocative of the literary and diplomatic fusions of Gibbs Hunt's "To France" and "To Belgium," but *Dark Princess*'s fusion attempts to imagine not just a keener diplomacy but a new diplomacy, a diplomacy that has undergone a sea change as it has been touched by forces transcendently messianic. Within certain messianic traditions, such radical changes in content have been reflected in subtle yet diacritical alterations in nomenclature: Abram's transformation to Abr*ah*am, Sarai's emergence as Sara*h*, or Saul's conversion to *P*aul. In *Dark Princess*'s vision, we see a messianic rewriting of diplomacy as *hip-to*-macy.

Hip-to-macy and the New Negro Era's End

In July 1928, Ida Gibbs Hunt sent Du Bois a letter from her husband's new consular post in Guadeloupe. "I'm writing," she told her erstwhile co-conspirator, "to order your book, 'Dark Princess' for Mr. Hunt's birthday. We are both anxious to read it." In response, Du Bois had his new novel "sent right off."[28] It would be interesting to know if Gibbs Hunt thought of "To Belgium" and Jonas's "Les Nouveaux Rois Mages" when she read Kautilya's account of seeing the messianic painting, or if she remembered Du Bois's fanciful creation of her as a French delegate when she read the Envoy's question "Which is really Truth—Fact or Fancy?" But her subsequent preserved correspondence with Du Bois does not return to the topic of *Dark Princess*. One also wonders what

Consul Hunt—who was quite proud of his "more than thirty years in the harness" of the State Department (1)—might have thought upon reading *Dark Princess*'s vision for a new hip-to-matic internationalism. Apparently, it did not make an impression he wanted to share. In spite of his wife's Pan-Africanist collaborations with Du Bois and Du Bois's publicized visit to the Hunts' home in Saint-Étienne,[29] William Hunt's detailed autobiography mentions Du Bois only once in passing (56) and completely ignores the Pan-African Congress and the deficiencies the PAC revealed in the racial logic of the twentieth century's official internationalism. Of course, it is easy to see how *Dark Princess*'s preternatural vision for transforming the international world could leave a realist and career diplomatist feeling uninspired or even defensive. Hip-to-macy's drive toward integrating racial grievance into international diplomacy could prove an embarrassment to certain black US diplomats, who often strove internationally to draw attention away from the discrimination they received at the hands of their fellow citizens in the United States. Such was the case of William Henry Hunt's colleague black US consul William James Yerby, who in 1929 became angry upon learning that a copy of *Dark Princess* was being passed among staff at his consulate in Oporto, Portugal.[30]

Hunt and Yerby were two of the last remaining officials of black US diplomacy's first generation. African American monadnocks within the diplomatic landscape, they weathered the Wilson administration's racialized purging of the State Department and maintained their consular positions as the following decades further eroded the small remaining group of New Negro diplomats. By the time they retired in the 1930s, the first generation had effectively come to an end. And by the end of this first generation, the hip-to-matic legacy of the New Negro writer-diplomats had long since outgrown a State Department that functioned both to promote and to stymie New Negro cultural figures' engagement with the international world. When the New Negro writer-diplomats had practiced hip-to-macy, it took place anonymously (as in the case of James Weldon Johnson) or after official diplomatic service had concluded (as with John Stephens Durham, George Washington Ellis, and Henry Francis Downing). But through Ida Gibbs Hunt's collaborative work with Du Bois during the late 1910s and early 1920s, hip-to-macy departed radically from the State Department's strictures. The first Pan-African Congresses, pivotally co-organized by the wife of a black US consul in France, stood as prominent models for the twentieth century's subsequent African American hip-to-mats and paved the way for the international conceptualizations of figures such as George Schuyler, Nella Larsen, Langston Hughes, and Zora Neale Hurston. Hip-to-macy, in conjunction with a wider swath of antiracist and anti-imperialist movements, was destined to play a role in restructuring white privilege within the world of official internationalism.

6 / The Practice of Hip-to-macy in the Age of Public Diplomacy: Richard Wright's Indonesian Travels

During James Weldon Johnson's early twentieth-century work in Venezuela, he added a new dimension to his role as a consul. His primary duties involved aiding US sailors and facilitating trade between Venezuela and US wholesale houses, but on his own initiative, he helped organize two Venezuelan baseball clubs. In some ways, organizing baseball teams was a creative answer to Johnson's commercial duties: it spurred "an order for complete outfits from a New York sporting goods house." But to Johnson's mind, the emergence of baseball teams in Venezuela had ideological implications extending beyond standard diplomatic protocol. "When I left Puerto Cabello," he recalled in his autobiography, "there were indications that our national game was gaining a foothold in that section of Venezuela" (*Along* 249). Through the ambiguous phrase *national game*, Johnson intimated his sense that deploying US culture could generate goodwill and hence promote US regional influence.

Johnson's foray into baseball diplomacy fell outside the era's diplomatic norms. During the early twentieth century, diplomacy was conceived of as an activity carried out on a government-to-government basis, and attempts at influencing foreign publics on a cultural level were seen as undiplomatic.[1] Much has changed since then. With the Second World War, the United States recognized the importance of strategically deploying its culture as a means of predisposing foreign publics toward US foreign policy. During the past half century, such cultural deployments have been known as *public diplomacy*, and in recent years, Joseph Nye has discussed US cultural influence across the globe as a major component of the nation's *soft power*, or its ability to use the attraction of its "culture and ideology" to achieve its geopolitical ambitions (10).[2] Some of the United States' conspicuous and enduring public diplomacy initiatives have been the Fulbright exchange program, the Voice of America radio broadcasts, and the maintenance of free lending libraries serving populations outside the United States.

Whether public diplomacy initiatives have been conspicuous and enduring or discreet and ephemeral, black US culture and citizens have played major roles in US efforts to generate soft power. By the late 1940s and early 1950s, certain US officials began recognizing that the country's dismal record in domestic race relations was becoming an Achilles heel as the nation wrestled with the Soviet Union in an international system increasingly accountable to decolonization and anticolonial sentiment.[3] In response, the United States' overwhelmingly white diplomatic apparatus developed what I term *hipster diplomacy*. To borrow language from Norman Mailer's often troubling account of hipsterism in the 1950s, this was a "postwar generation" of US diplomacy dominated by white officials but drawing on "the source of Hip"—"the Negro for he has been living on the margin between totalitarianism and democracy for two centuries" (340). Consistent with Mailer's description of hipsterism, hipster diplomacy absorbed African American performances and performance practices (341). It operated under an assumption that "the Negro's experience," which derives authority from years of "tortured senses," might be "the most universal communication" that the West could offer the planet's reeling postwar populations (364). Hipster diplomacy had various instantiations. The Cold War State Department orchestrated the Asian, African, Middle Eastern, and European travels of "Jazz Ambassadors" such as Dizzy Gillespie, Louis Armstrong, and Duke Ellington. In the late 1950s, African American contralto Marian Anderson traveled and sang throughout Asia as a US "Goodwill Ambassador." During this era, the United States Information Agency (USIA) distributed thousands of radios to Asian, African, and Middle Eastern populations and then made jazz a prominent feature on its Voice of America radio broadcasts. And in 1962, Langston Hughes read his famous poem "The Negro Speaks of Rivers" at the opening of the USIA's free lending library in Accra, Ghana. During his presentation, Hughes observed that "America has often fallen far short of . . . her basic dreams," but he maintained that these American dreams were nonetheless "always *seeking*" and "sometimes finding . . . expression" ("American" 1).[4] In arranging for Hughes and Satchmo to perform as unofficial cultural representatives abroad, the United States was working to democratize its international face by reconscripting the antihierarchical practices that earlier black internationalists innovated as they drew on and departed from official internationalism. By engaging in hipster diplomacy, the United States was initiating a long-term reliance on the modes of hip-to-macy developed during the New Negro era.

As someone who incisively remarked on the ambassadorial stances that gained purchase among the previous generation of African American writers, Richard Wright emerges as a fitting site for a treatment of official US diplomacy's later efforts at co-opting its hip-to-matic geopolitical cousin. Wright himself became a cultural ambassador of sorts when in 1946 he grabbed the US State Department's attention by traveling to France, where the department recognized that his commentary could offer foreign publics a more immediate familiarity with US culture's virulent racism.[5] Wright in France was emerging—in resonance with his description of Langston Hughes seven years earlier—as a literary figure poised to "represent . . . the Negroes' case . . . at the court of world opinion" ("Forerunner" 600). At this time, the "Negroes' case" was most certainly against the United States. Yet Wright felt torn. On one hand, he wanted to speak internationally on behalf of African Americans (Wright, "I Choose" 8), and he resented the State Department's efforts to coerce "any American going abroad" into "behav[ing] like an ambassador" for the United States (Henriques). Yet he also wished that somehow he could help the United States in its tactless and ill-informed interactions with the international world ("I Choose" 17).

These competing racial, governmental, and ethical exigencies came to a head in early 1955, when Wright read about and decided to attend the landmark anticolonial Asian-African Conference. The conference, he learned, would be held in Bandung, Indonesia, and would be a gathering of over two dozen independent Asian and African nations. It would be "a meeting of almost all of the human race living in the main geopolitical center of gravity of the earth" (Wright, *Color* 12). Wright's decision to attend the Bandung Conference was a personal one inspired by the event's evident world-historical significance, but his travel to Indonesia as a freelance writer was arranged and financed by the Congress for Cultural Freedom (CCF).[6] In the 1950s, the CCF presented itself as an independent congress dedicated to peace and intellectual freedom in the face of Soviet-style totalitarianism (CCF, "Manifesto"), but Wright believed it was a semiofficial organization with indirect support from the State Department. By agreement with the CCF, he was "*officially* . . . not covering" the conference for the CCF but would in an ostensibly unaffiliated way write several articles on the conference to be published in the CCF's internationally distributed magazines—*Encounter* in English, *Preuves* in French, *Der Monat* in German, and *Cuadernos* in Spanish. The terms of the agreement also permitted Wright to publish these articles in book form.[7] Since the late 1960s, it has been clear that Wright was indeed making this agreement with a semiofficial organization—backed not by the State Department but by the CIA.[8]

Critical approaches to Wright's Indonesian travels typically have exhibited two major trends. First, they frequently have approached Wright in Indonesia as a largely independent writer. Second, they have tended to bring focus to *The Color Curtain*, Wright's book-length report on the Bandung Conference.[9] While such approaches have proven enlightening, a recent forum on the cultural study of public diplomacy suggests the imperative of complicating these trends. Observing that analyses of public diplomacy have suffered from privileging the United States' overt initiatives over its "covert practices," Liam Kennedy and Scott Lucas draw attention to the United States' "state-private network," which they describe as the "collaboration between 'official' U.S. agencies and 'private' groups and individuals in the development and implementation of . . . programs in support of U.S. foreign policy" (312). In the same forum, Ron Robin draws attention to the urgency of examining public diplomacy's "effects and reception" within global culture and affairs (351). Kennedy and Lucas's observations would suggest that reading Wright as an independent writer in Indonesia distracts from his evident participation in the United States' state-private network, ultimately contributing to a critical effacement of the black presence within a major arena of US diplomatic activity during a key moment in anticolonial history. At the same time, Robin's emphasis on public diplomacy's reception would suggest that Wright's *The Color Curtain* should not be taken as the representative text of his Indonesian cultural diplomacy. While *The Color Curtain* offers Wright's perceptions of the conference's place within world history, it conveys only a limited sense of Indonesians' reception of one of the United States' most famous hip-to-mats.

Such acknowledgments precondition a scholarly stance toward Wright that is committed to exploring his presence in Indonesia not simply as a conference attendant and observer but as a world-famous author capable of building or reinforcing significant cultural bridges between the United States and Indonesia. This approach helps shift focus toward a constellation of shorter English-, Dutch-, and Indonesian-language texts, documents that bring to light three major facets of Wright's participation in the United States' state-private network: his Indonesian lectures, the interview he granted for the prominent Indonesian literary column *Gelanggang*, and the Indonesian intelligentsia's reception of his travel writings. Wright's foray into public diplomacy reveals the way in which the hip-to-macy of an earlier New Negro era resurfaced during the second half of the twentieth century to become a constitutive logic of US diplomacy's neoliberalizing willingness to replace old strictures with new hipsters.[10]

Questions of Intercultural Bridges

After three and a half centuries of occupation by Dutch colonizers, three and a half years of occupation by the Japanese during the Second World War, and a postwar period during which the Netherlands fought to regain its lost colonial possession, Indonesia emerged as a sovereign and unified nation under President Sukarno on 17 August 1950 (Vickers 115). Within a year of this date, the newly sovereign nation afforded Richard Wright a place within an official and internationally circulated narrative of its literary culture. In 1951, the Indonesian embassy in Washington, DC, published *The Cultural Life of Indonesia*, a booklet whose foreword, written by Indonesia's ambassador to the United States, announced that "Indonesia is no longer isolated or remote" (Sastroamidjojo vii). Tracing Indonesian literature's transition from the "traditional to the modern" (Embassy of Indonesia 49), the booklet pointed toward Wright's influence on Indonesia's literary innovations. With John Steinbeck and Antoine de Saint-Exupéry, Richard Wright had exerted special "influence" on the work of Pramoedya Ananta Toer, a prize-winning Indonesian "prose writer who has attracted attention in recent years" (54–55).[11] Destined to emerge as the most prominent of Indonesian writers, Toer made the nature of Wright's influence explicit in a 1953 essay that praises Wright's *Black Boy* for refusing to strive for beauty. Instead, *Black Boy* offers its readers "bitter realism," insisting that "reality be swallowed raw." Toer maintained that Wright's readers "will tremble as they realize the danger of genocide." Toer believed that Wright's bitter realism—together with naturalism, psychologism, and surrealism—offered guidance for a modern vision of literary writing ("Definisi" 176).[12]

In light of the way Wright was incorporated into the narrative of Indonesian literary development during the early 1950s, when Wright sought CCF funding in 1955, the CCF undoubtedly saw an opportunity to create and reinforce strategic dialogues between US and Indonesian literary scenes. Making arrangements for Wright's trip, CCF director and CIA agent Michael Josselson told Wright that Mochtar Lubis, member of PEN Club Indonesia and chief editor of the independent socialist newspaper *Indonesia Raya*, would meet him at the airport in Jakarta. Josselson wanted to do more than finance Wright's travels to the Bandung Conference. He wanted to orchestrate Wright's interactions with arbiters of Indonesian culture. The director wrote, "I am sure that Mr. Lubis will be delighted to be of assistance to you and on the other hand you will find him charming, interesting, and well informed. I have suggested to Mr. Lubis that while you are in Djakarta you may want to give a talk at the Pen Club there."[13] How did Josselson know Lubis to be charming and well informed? Lubis had been associating freely with American diplomatic staff in Indonesia (Hill 52), and the CCF had recently brought the prominent newspaper editor into its orbit when he attended and made formal comments at the CCF-sponsored Conference on Cultural Freedom in Asia, held in Burma in February 1955.[14]

Because Wright was a highly successful representative of African American culture, CCF organizers also undoubtedly felt that his interactions with Indonesian cultural arbiters could function as an answer to the efforts of the Indonesian Communist Party (PKI). Consistent with other Communist publications of the era, the PKI's newspaper, *Harian Rakjat* (*The People's Daily*), was publishing articles that attacked the ideal of US democracy by underscoring the United States' segregated and racially unequal society.[15] Of course, Wright's autobiography and novels were anything but complimentary of racial conditions in the United States, but experience with the horrors of US racism had not lastingly convinced Wright that communism was the natural alternative to US democracy. As if to emphasize Wright's stance in preparation for his visit, the CIA-sponsored Indonesian Anti-Communist Front published a translation of the anticommunist collection *The God That Failed*, which contained Wright's scathing renunciation of the Communist Party, "I Tried to Be a Communist."[16] The translation appeared in February 1955, and by the time Wright arrived in Jakarta two months later, Indonesian artists and intellectuals were well aware of his status as a contributor to the anticommunist anthology.[17]

Evidence suggests Wright understood that in striking a deal with the CCF, he was becoming part of covert efforts in US cultural diplomacy.[18] In a February 1955 letter, he told his literary agent, Paul Reynolds, that in obtaining a travel visa from the Indonesian consulate in Paris, he had purposefully concealed his CCF affiliation and simply presented the consular officials with the line that he and the CCF had agreed on—that he was a freelance writer. Wright closed the letter with a postscript emphatically demanding that Reynolds tell no one of his involvement with the CCF.[19] It is easy to see why remaining silent about the CCF would have served Wright's purposes. As a famous African American writer and expatriate, Wright was seen as someone self-appointed, beholden to no one, and free to speak the truth. He was interested in maintaining his hip-to-matic ethos. Here, Wright's interests overlapped with those of the CCF. As part of a state-private network dedicated to covertly shaping international culture and politics, the CCF also benefited when people in its pay appeared as if they were self-appointed, beholden to no one, and hence free to advance noncommunist messages without seeming to toe the United States' line.[20] While Wright apparently did not accept CCF sponsorship out of a specific desire to participate in US international diplomacy, his need for travel funding dovetailed with a mode of US diplomacy that was abandoning the traditional diplomatic model in which delegates are given "*authoritative* instructions [which they are] bound blindly to obey" (Burke 110). Now, Wright and others traveled as concomitant hip-to-mats and public diplomats tasked to speak more or less according to their own judgments and consciences. For US diplomacy, this was a hip move from a mandate-based representation to a weak ambassadorial mode of standing symbolically for others on one's own terms.[21]

Arriving on 12 April and departing on 5 May, Wright spent over three weeks in Indonesia. During his visit, he devoted a week to attending the Asian-African Conference (18–24 April) but spent most of his time meeting and speaking with Indonesian intellectuals. Jotting notes on the trip, Wright explained that certain organizations placed pressure on him to deliver speeches and that he spoke on the topics of black literature and industrialization ("Retreat"). Mochtar Lubis's *Indonesia Raya* represented these speeches as two of the trip's highlights. On Sunday morning, 1 May, Wright spoke on African American literature to a group of Indonesian writers gathered at the mountain bungalow of Takdir Alisjahbana, one of Indonesia's pioneering novelists. On 2 May, Wright spoke to PEN Club Indonesia and the Indonesian Council for Deliberations on National Culture at Jakarta's cultural center, Balai Budaya ("Siapa"). Just the type of events that CCF director Michael Josselson had hoped to orchestrate, these speeches became occasions for Wright and his Indonesian hosts to contemplate the possibilities and difficulties of constructing bridges between their countries' respective cultural scenes.

Wright's speech at Alisjahbana's bungalow was given during a gathering of the Studieclub Konfrontasi, a culturally oriented Indonesian study club that published the little magazine *Konfrontasi*.[22] The magazine printed the full text of Wright's lecture, "American Negro Writing," in its subsequent issue. An earlier version of this lecture had been published in French in a 1948 issue of Jean-Paul Sartre and Simone de Beauvoir's *Les Temps Modernes* as "Littérature Noire Américaine." A later version in English was published in Wright's 1957 collection *White Man, Listen!* But the Indonesian magazine *Konfrontasi* offered the piece its first English-language publication. The speech's three published iterations line up closely and usually verbatim. They begin with the same joke, and they subsequently proceed to "use Negro poets and their poems as . . . examples; for poets and poems have a way of telling a lot in a compressed manner" ("American" 2; "Literature" 106; "Littérature" 193). Through the poetry of Phillis Wheatley, Frances E. W. Harper, Paul Laurence Dunbar, James Weldon Johnson, and Margaret Walker, Wright traced African America's relationship to the cultures of the United States and the wider world.

Yet the lecture's three versions are not identical, and the differences reveal Wright in Southeast Asia as someone under the influence of a concern that Indonesia might abandon its nonaligned status by embracing communism. Interestingly, in the lecture's 1948 version, Wright had credited "Soviet Russia" for rising and sending out "its calls to the oppressed" ("Littérature" 218) and thereby providing "the first real break" in African Americans' "continuity of hopelessness" (217).[23] But while speaking to the Studieclub Konfrontasi, Wright supplanted "Soviet Russia" with "Trade Union Leaders" and now credited *these* leaders for issuing calls that resulted in a departure from black American hopelessness ("American" 22). And whereas the 1948 version had celebrated Langston Hughes's visit to "the headquarters of Lenin, the father of the Soviet Republic" ("Littérature" 218), Wright's Konfrontasi lecture elided Hughes's visit to the Soviet Union ("American" 22). Tellingly, Wright restored these positive Soviet references in the 1957 version of his lecture. The decision to refrain from praising the USSR while in Indonesia may reflect Wright's own sense of the varying contexts in which he felt it was politically appropriate to praise things Soviet. Or perhaps Wright's decision was precipitated by a factor observed by one of the Studieclub's officers—that the speech was attended not only by the Studieclub but also by "a number of Americans" who had invited themselves to the event (Vuyk, "Weekend" 808). Wright's discipline in representing the Soviet

Union may have arisen from a sense that these self-invited Americans might be affiliated with the organization presently financing his Indonesian travels. Alternatively, the organization itself—or perhaps the CCF working collaboratively with the Studieclub Konfrontasi—may have seen to it that the published lecture elided in print the positive references to the Soviet Union that Wright possibly voiced while giving his talk.

But the changes made to Wright's Konfrontasi lecture are perhaps less interesting than the changes the lecture underwent as a result of its altered geopolitical contexts. The 1948 and 1957 lectures were offered to the white Western world on behalf of people of color, but the Konfrontasi lecture was presented mainly to the Indonesian intelligentsia.[24] At Alisjahbana's mountain bungalow, as Wright spoke of poetry because it could "tell . . . a lot in a compressed manner," the visiting writer framed himself in tandem with poetry as a second site of representational compression. He implied that he spoke on behalf of multiple and traditionally disparate constituencies: African Americans and the US population more generally, the wretched of the earth and Indonesians specifically. Certifying his speech not only on behalf of African Americans but on behalf of the United States, Wright told the Studieclub, "We black folk, our history and our present being, are a mirror of all the manifold experiences of America. What we want, what we represent[,] what we endure is what America is." He told his audience, "If we black folk perish, America will perish" ("American" 24). Situating the United States' status as contingent on African Americans' status, these words unintentionally recall the diplomatic work of Frederick Douglass, John Mercer Langston, and John Stephens Durham, who decades earlier deployed the ambassadorial trope of representative character to assert that their status as US representatives could reconstitute the nation they represented. Speaking before the Studieclub Konfrontasi, Wright framed African Americans as representative Americans.

This framing would have gained increased significance for the Studieclub audience in light of another of the lecture's assertions regarding African American representation. African Americans were not merely Americans' truest representatives—they were the truest representatives of the wretched of the earth. Wright claimed, the "voice of the American Negro is rapidly becoming the most representative voice of oppressed people anywhere in the world" ("American" 24). As Wright himself embodied the voice of the American Negro before his Indonesian audience, he presented himself in analogy to the poems he recited. Just as the poems represented "a lot in a compressed manner," Wright represented himself as a bi-tenored metonymic vehicle of sufficient capacity to provide a meeting space for US citizens and the world's oppressed.

Emphasizing to the Indonesian audience members' minds that they were to be included in the meeting that their guest proposed to facilitate, Wright finished the scripted part of his lecture and then, as reported by *Konfrontasi*'s editors, made the following plea: "Lihatlah kepada kami, kenallah kami dan saudara² akan kenal diri sendiri, karena kami adalah saudara², kami jang memandang kepada saudara dari katja gelap kehidupan kami!"[25] ("Synopsis" 28). This remark was not part of his script and not recorded in English, but the editors' Indonesian-language rendition of the statement clearly suggests that Wright was drawing on a sentence in his book *12 Million Black Voices*: "Look at us and know us and you will know yourselves, for *we* are *you*, looking back at you from the dark mirror of our lives!" (146).[26] Fourteen years earlier, when Wright had included this plea in *12 Million Black Voices*, he was speaking on behalf of a black constituency to a white readership. But as he redeployed the request before the Studieclub, he seemed to be hailing his Indonesian audience, calling on them to recognize their reflections in a dark speaker who also claimed to be the mirror reflection of the United States. Wright in Indonesia apparently felt he was speaking without taking his script from the semiofficial organization that was sponsoring his travel, but the CCF would have been hard-pressed to write a better script than Wright's own: his lecture presented African Americans as a bridge between—and accurate reflection of both—the United States and Indonesia.

It may have been in preparation for this weekend event at Alisjahbana's bungalow that someone (most likely Lubis) handed Wright a cheat sheet listing several Indonesian artists and authors. The list offered typed descriptions and contact information for these figures, but a handwritten addendum drew Wright's attention to Pramoedya Ananta Toer: "novelist (in my personal opinion in some way influenced by R. Wright)."[27] The presence of this note suggests that the construction of intercultural bridges between Indonesia and the West was already in process and that, through the worldwide circulation of Wright's literary works, he had already taken part in building bridges. But as is indicated by Wright's very presence in Indonesia, the CCF was not depending solely on the vicissitudes of unguided cultural and literary exchange for the construction of these bridges. Just a few months before Wright's visit, the CCF had recruited not only Lubis but also Alisjahbana, the Studieclub's leader, to attend and deliver an address at its Conference on Cultural Freedom in Asia.[28] Hence, regardless of whether any of the several self-invited Americans at the

Konfrontasi gathering were US agents, Wright's CCF-sponsored Indonesian travels were inserting him bodily into a transnational community of cultural contacts covertly engineered by the CIA. During his Konfrontasi lecture, Wright's self-presentation positioned him as a meeting ground for this transnational community.

If Wright presented himself to the Studieclub as a bridge between US and Indonesian constituencies, certain aspects of his lecture the following day at the Balai Budaya seem to have troubled this image. With an audience that included Indonesian PEN Club members ("Siapa"), this was the lecture that Josselson had suggested to Lubis. During the lecture, Wright spoke of the artist's place in the planet's fragmented modern society. He remarked that there comes a time when "tradition, custom, old values" can no longer offer a guide for human life. During this time, new leaders arise who bring "new ideologies, and through force/violence form a new society." Wright told his audience that an author becomes very important during these moments: an author whose writings are in tune with the leaders can become "a priest to replace Holy Scriptures such as the Bible, . . . the Koran." Wright cited the way Russian authors had become the richest class in Russia, and he mentioned that one of his own friends, who had written for a political party that did not win, had been found dead a few years previously (Wright, "Seniman"). Later, Wright referred to this lecture as one given on the topic of industrialization ("Retreat").

Apparently, Wright's thoughts on industrialization were not well received by some people in his audience. According to Wright's lecture, effective industrialization involved new leaders seeking to build new societies by violence if necessary. But many of Wright's Indonesian hosts disliked their own leader, President Sukarno (Roberts and Foulcher 800), and they viewed Sukarno's Bandung Conference as a "circus" geared toward distracting from the administration's "weakness and blunders" (Vuyk, "Weekend" 803, 807). Yet Wright had told them that Sukarno was "a great man" and also had insisted that Gold Coast prime minister Kwame Nkrumah was "a great man," in spite of what some of his hosts perceived as Nkrumah's fascist governing strategies (806–07). Indeed, these hosts were repulsed by Wright's commentary on industrialization (Wright, "Jakarta" 190), which in Indonesia seems to have taken the tenor of other commentary Wright offered on industrialization during the mid-1950s. At the 1956 International Congress of Black Writers and Artists, Wright gave a speech titled "Tradition and Industrialization," during which he pointed to Nkrumah and Sukarno and averred that they "must be given *carte blanche* to modernize their lands . . . , and we must understand the methods that they will feel compelled to use" (100). In calling Sukarno and Nkrumah great men, was Wright endorsing fascism or the possible use of force or violence to forge a new, modernized society? Could the *carte blanche* held by such leaders empower them to force writers and artists to become priests of the dictatorial state, with the invention of this artist-priesthood justified by the resultant modernization? Less than a month after Wright left Indonesia, one of his hosts observed that Wright did not give enough attention to the perils of Nkrumah's "dangerous and alarming path" (Vuyk, "Black").

Wright's travel journal does not refer directly to this lecture's reception, but at one point, it has him spending an evening eating and talking about industrialization with a group of Indonesian artists, writers, and intellectuals. This event, perhaps occurring after the lecture, seemingly offered Wright the chance to perform and reconsider certain moments from his 1953 novel *The Outsider*, which has protagonist Cross Damon arguing the futility of fleeing "from [the] industrial machine and find[ing] haven in some tropical island." Cross explains: "Those little islands, too, are being caught up in the global tide of industrialization and soon there will be no hideaways" (477). Now among the islands of Indonesia, Wright had offered a specific and (to his Indonesian hosts) disturbing vision of industrialization, and he wrote in his journal of listening to his hosts resist the idea of industrialization because they worried about preserving their traditions. Wright replies that if they do not industrialize, their islands will be recolonized by other nations ("Jakarta" 190).[29] Wright was speaking from what he thought of as a "third point of view";[30] he was speaking from a position that *The Outsider* had theorized as the gifted "double vision" of one who is "both *inside* and *outside*" of Western culture (163). Yet his journal entry describes his feelings during the evening when members of the Indonesian intelligentsia resisted his thoughts on industrialization: "I felt alone, lost"—he was Western and yet had dark skin; his hosts accepted him to a degree but also reminded him that he was not one of them. From amid these feelings of geoethnic solitude, Wright called into question an assumption undergirding his Konfrontasi lecture. In his journal, he asked, "What bridges could be built between these two worlds? And who would build them? And what kind of bridges could be built?" ("Jakarta" 190). Earlier in the journal, he had dismissed the efficacy of overt public diplomacy, claiming that non-Western nations see cultural ambassadors and food aid as instances of Western subterfuge (66). Now he questioned even the capacity of the hip-to-matic voice—apparently beholden to no one as it spoke from a third point of view—to become a bridge of sufficient capacity to accommodate the meeting of East and West.

Hermeneutic Tensions and Wright's Indonesian Reception

Wright's questions on bridges were apropos when he wrote them in 1955, and, in rearticulated form, they are also helpful in considering current critical approaches to black internationalism. What bridges might be built between the two worlds of black internationalism and the United States' official internationalism? Who might build them? And what kind of bridges might be built? These questions are less historical and more critical. They speak less immediately to the New Negro era and its hip-to-matic legacy and more to the ways black internationalism and official internationalism have figured into late twentieth- and early twenty-first-century critical treatments of US and African American expressive cultures. Recent decades have seen the emergence of an American cultural and literary studies that approaches the United States' official internationalism with a hermeneutics of suspicion. This body of scholarship has fleshed out the image of a United States whose imperialism has been not an aberration but a persistent attribute. Concomitantly, studies of African American internationalism frequently have been animated by a hermeneutics of recovery, as they have worked to elucidate long-obfuscated interconnections among African Americans, denizens of a wider black diaspora, and populations of color more generally.[31] Suspicion and recovery come to a crossroads in the study of African American participation in the United States' international diplomacy. After all, official internationalism has played a role in forging race- and color-based connections to the degree that the United States sent New Negro and later black diplomats to nations of color. In turn, the transnational connections forged by such assignments have functioned bivalently to transnationalize antiracism even as they at times have facilitated US economic and cultural imperialism.

Some of Penny Von Eschen's work on US jazz diplomacy is illustrative of the hermeneutic tension produced at this crossroads of official and black internationalisms. Pointing to the ways in which jazz propaganda became a two-edged sword for the Cold War United States, Von Eschen draws attention to moments during which famed jazz musicians used their State Department–sponsored travel to disrupt "claims to an exclusively American identity by promoting solidarities among black peoples" ("Who's" 126). "Ironically," Von Eschen observes, "many of

[Dizzy] Gillespie's ties to Brazilian and South American artists were built partly through his State Department tours" (127). Von Eschen is correct in observing irony in this situation, but a sense of the situation's irony should arise less from an image of Gillespie's transnational rapport as constituting a self-undercutting facet of US public diplomacy. Rather, Gillespie's race-based ties to South American musicians would have contributed to what one US official described as public diplomacy's effort to "provide the United States with . . . stable cultural bridges to Latin America."[32] I would suggest, then, that the irony Von Eschen notes in Gillespie's situation is more a function of the present-day critical default position that sees color-based transnationalism as official internationalism's subversive counterdiscourse. Ironically, we might say, US efforts in international coercion actually sought to promote the precise mode of color-based connections that present-day cultural criticism would normally celebrate as subversive to the nation-state. To be sure, black internationalism and official internationalism have frequently run counter to each other, but in approaching US public diplomacy in general, and in assessing Wright's Indonesian travels in particular, it is important to recognize the United States' international deployment of culture as a complex site of détente between two often divergent internationalisms. Acknowledging this détente promotes an increased recognition of the hermeneutic crosshatching that black and official internationalisms' intersecting archives repay. An interpretive back-and-forth between recovery and suspicion reminds us that the stymying of transnational connections between a black envoy and people of color may function to disrupt US efforts at generating soft power.

Clearly, Wright felt a racial connection to the nations of color whose delegates were descending on Bandung for the Asian-African Conference. Before leaving for Asia, he told his wife, "I'm an American Negro; as such, I've had a burden of race consciousness. So have these people" (*Color* 15). He was so confident that common racial concerns would ingratiate him to the people at the conference that, before traveling to Indonesia, he prescripted this bonding by writing in his journal what he imagined he would publish upon his return. Describing future events as if they had already occurred, he wrote that the Asians and Africans were more open with him than they would have been with a white American or European because Wright had "talked to them as a brother who shared all of their virtues . . . [and] failings" ("Jakarta" 74). During his stay in Indonesia, this sense of brotherhood was showcased in the Konfrontasi lecture's concluding unscripted plea.

But as is suggested by Wright's private acknowledgment that the Indonesians accepted him while also reminding him that he was Western, his Indonesian contacts were reluctant to see their reflections in the dark mirror that Wright alleged his presence offered them. Commenting in *Konfrontasi*, the Studieclub's editorial board was measured in its response to the outlines of African American literary development that Wright presented in his lecture. The editors prefaced their Indonesian-language summary of the lecture by noting that Wright had described African American literature from a "political-sociological angle" and that "this limited view presents questions and doubts to the reader—What truly is the value of Negro literature?" ("Synopsis" 25). After the summary, the editors offered a translation of Wright's closing color-based plea without comment. But in another forum, Konfrontasi officer Beb Vuyk recalled the group's frustration with Wright's color-based preoccupations during the conversation that followed his lecture.[33] According to Vuyk's narrative of the postlecture meal, Wright asked if Studieclub leader Takdir Alisjahbana felt inferior to people with white skin. Alisjahbana did not appreciate the question but was polite in implying he felt no such feelings. Wright asked the same question of prominent Indonesian writer Sitor Situmorang. Situmorang answered in the negative and spoke sharply. Emphasizing Situmorang's anger, Vuyk noted, "Raising one's voice in such a way to convey harsh truths to a guest is highly unusual in Indonesia" ("Weekend" 809). Vuyk also recalled that when Wright suggested Indonesians ought to feel a kinship with the Japanese because "they are also a colored race," "there were several among us who laughed out loud" (809). Situmorang had just reminded Wright that the Japanese, during their brutal Second World War occupation, had attempted to promote race- and color-consciousness in Indonesia: "They tried to spread it among us as well. They had little success, and absolutely none at all among the intellectuals" (809). Describing another occasion, Vuyk recalled the "unpleasant feeling" she had when Wright used the notion of color to explain to a group of Indonesians that he felt at home among them (806).

Also important to accessing Wright's ambivalent Indonesian reception is an interview documented in the cultural and literary magazine *Siasat*. Appearing in the periodical's important *Gelanggang* column as "Pertjakapan dengan Richard Wright" (Conversation with Richard Wright), the interview was most likely conducted by the column's main editor, prominent writer and cultural figure Asrul Sani.[34] Sani was inclined to have Wright represented evenly in his column. The interview touched on Harriet Beecher Stowe's *Uncle Tom's Cabin*, which Wright described as "nothing more than a 'document humain.'" Wright claimed Stowe's novel "doesn't say anything" (Sudjatmoko and Sani 23). The interview also touched on Wright's recently published novel *The Outsider*. The interviewer noted that the novel's theme, inspired by the author's associations with existentialists such as Jean-Paul Sartre and Simone de Beauvoir, differed strikingly from Wright's previous work. Wright's new subject was "no longer the issue of racial discrimination." Rather *The Outsider* asked how a person, after his convictions and superstitions had been purged, could "become a liberated human being" (22). The interviewer, commenting on his conversation with Wright, remarked, "Even though Richard Wright has described himself as an expert in poverty, there is not much trace of poverty and bitterness in the clear lines of his face. To look at him, to note his solid build and hear his uninhibited laughter, you would think he was a writer whose past was bathed in jasmine and rosewater. It's only his books that reveal the opposite was in fact the case." Then, as if to attenuate what might be read as a denial of what Wright claimed as his authentic knowledge of the wretched of the earth, the interviewer speculated that Wright's cheerfulness was perhaps a "shield against the humiliations that have been inflicted upon him" (22). Though seemingly innocuous, many of this interview's themes figured prominently into Sani's subsequent and harsh critiques of Wright.

Summarizing Wright's stay in Indonesia, Anas Ma'ruf of the monthly art magazine *Seni* expressed no discomfort regarding Wright's professed sense of brotherhood with Indonesians. Yet rather than discussing Wright as part of the 1950s-era Afro-Asian postcolonial world, Ma'ruf situated Wright in reference to nineteenth-century African American expatriate Victor Séjour and his circle: "[Wright's] escape [to Paris] reminds us of the time when the Louisana negroes sent their sons to Paris to study drama, music, and to associate with independent artists. . . . Many of the young men who were sent did not return to America, because it was not yet free from that cursed practice of discrimination based on skin color." Within Ma'ruf's article, Wright was analogous not to Indonesians but to earlier African American expatriates. His relationship to the Indonesian intelligentsia was not color based but instead based on Wright's interest in meeting with several famous artists and intellectuals in preparation to write an article (Ma'ruf). A young and well-known Indonesian poet had told Wright that Americans and Europeans tended to visit Indonesia and return home only to write inaccurate accounts of Indonesia's people and places (Wright, "Jakarta" 190). Undoubtedly, these cultural arbiters looked with anticipation toward reading what their guest would write about them after returning to Paris.

After leaving Indonesia, Wright published a handful of articles about his Indonesian travels in the CCF magazines *Encounter*, *Preuves*, *Der Monat*, and *Cuadernos*.[35] He also published English- and French-language collections of these articles in book form: *The Color Curtain* and *Bandoeng, 1,500,000,000 d'hommes*. Especially in published form as *The Color Curtain*, Wright's Indonesian writings have been extensively discussed elsewhere, and such discussions have cleared the way for heightened focus on the reception of these works among the intellectuals whom Wright met in Indonesia. An awareness of this reception is necessary to any approach seeking to access Wright's Indonesian travels vis-à-vis US diplomacy's state-private network. Examining Wright's Indonesian reception reveals that in conscripting Wright as a covert public diplomat, the CCF was unable to construct a direct cultural bridge between the United States and Indonesia. Rather, Wright's reception presents a view of US hipster diplomacy meeting the limits of its own fraught faith in the potential for the trope of blackness to function as the United States' universal mode of communication with non-Western constituencies.

The most famous response to Wright's writings on Indonesia has been the angry letter Mochtar Lubis wrote after reading "Indonesian Notebook," Wright's August 1955 *Encounter* article. "Indonesian Notebook" had privileged scenes emphasizing color prejudice among Indonesians. In one scene, Wright waits behind a white reporter while seeking a press card. The Indonesian official who is granting the cards stonewalls the white US reporter, while Wright gets his press card at once. Within the article, Wright receives special treatment because Indonesian faces are "as dark as" his. The article suggests that the white reporter's treatment by the official was analogous to the racist treatment Wright himself had received in the US South (28). "Indonesian Notebook" also includes a scene in which a famous Indonesian novelist, taking pride in his brown skin, spitefully calls the Japanese "those *yellow* monkeys" (31). Wright's erstwhile hosts saw such accounts as offensive and inaccurate. Published in *Encounter*'s March 1956 issue, Lubis's letter protested, "while [Wright] was here in Indonesia he had been looking through 'coloured-glasses,' and had sought behind every attitude he met colour and racial feeling." Relaying the reactions of "one of the best-known Indonesian novelists . . . and others," the letter continued: "They are all amazed to read Mr. Wright's notebook in which Mr. Wright quotes them saying things which they never had said, or to which they did not put meaning as accepted by Mr. Wright" (Lubis, "Through").

Lubis's letter has been referenced in several treatments of Wright in Indonesia, but a focus on public diplomacy's effects and reception enlighteningly reveals the letter to be a mosaic of quotations, absorbing and transforming specific texts and performances associated with Wright's Indonesian travels.[36] Lubis's phrase "'coloured-glasses'" is especially relevant on this point. In placing the phrase within quotation marks, Lubis might have been acknowledging his metaphor's hackneyed quality, as it cites and resignifies the phrase *rose-colored glasses* in English or *rooskleurige bril* in Dutch. But the quotation marks also seem to allude to Wright's previous words and performances. One of the key moments during which Wright presented color as a uniting heuristic was at the conclusion of his Konfrontasi lecture. Again, Wright had offered his audience a promise: "Look at us and know us and you will know yourselves, for *we* are *you*, looking back at you from the dark mirror of our lives!" As previously noted, Wright earlier had used this phrase to address a white readership. In 1941, he had relied on the darkness of a mirror to account for the minor difference of skin color in spite of overwhelming correspondences between black and white Americans. Fourteen years later, however, as Wright cited this metaphor at the conclusion of a lecture in Indonesia, the trope of the mirror continued to propose a commonality of experience (now between African Americans and Indonesians), while the mirror's darkness seemingly sought to elide racial difference by emphasizing the dark bodies of both Wright and his hosts. Drawing on the image of Wright's gaze as emanating from a *dark mirror*, Lubis's "coloured-glasses" metaphor recurs to the image of tinted glass to account for the way that Wright permitted dark skin to become a major index of transnational commonality.

The dark mirror's transformation from darkly reflective to darkly refractive glass may be a function of the way *Konfrontasi* mediated Wright's lecture. Though Wright gave his lecture in English, the Studieclub's journal offered an intriguing translation of his final metaphor of the dark mirror. In the Indonesian version, the English phrase *dark mirror* became *katja gelap*.[37] This translation is bivalent. On one hand, *katja gelap* continues to convey the image of a dark mirror, but the phrase also conveys the image of a dark pane of glass. Within this second, translation-evoked image, Wright no longer stands within a dark mirror as the Indonesians' reflection; he now stands on the other side of a dark window or pane of glass, incapable of accurately seeing his Indonesian hosts because the glass permits access only to their obscured refractions. In advancing the *coloured-glasses* metaphor in the pages of *Encounter*, Lubis was implicitly siding with the refractive and distorting interpretive possibilities made available by *Konfrontasi*'s ambiguous translation of Wright's assertion of transnational connection.

As for the dark mirror/window's transformation into a pair of glasses, a final tessera helps constitute Lubis's citational mosaic. Wright carried a few newspaper clippings with him when he left Indonesia.[38] One of these clippings was from Lubis's *Indonesia Raya* and contained a photograph of Wright upon his arrival in Indonesia. Another clipping was from a newspaper summarizing one of *Indonesia Raya*'s articles on Wright. Notably, both clippings were illustrated with photographs of Wright wearing dark glasses (figs. 4 and 5). These were certainly the most prominent—and perhaps the only—photographs of Wright that appeared in the daily press during his visit. It would seem strange if, in arriving at his metaphor for Wright's transnational *méconnaissance*, Lubis did not join these images with Wright's tropes of color and the dark mirror, layering the press photographs into the self-consciously citational phrase "'coloured-glasses.'"[39] But Wright, as Bill V. Mullen has indicated, was interested in a Western version of Indonesia (65–66), and he did not recognize Lubis's accusation as one that drew on his own Indonesian performances. In the same issue of *Encounter*, Wright responded to his host: "No. I did not see Indonesia through 'coloured-glasses.'" "Think hard, my friend Lubis, and you will recall the discussions that took place in your car as we drove through the Java mountains" ("Mr. Wright").

For Wright's former hosts, however, it was less a matter of recall and more a matter of accurate interpretation. As Vuyk later explained, Wright had indeed received his press card ahead of the white reporter—but this was because Lubis, his escort, was a friend of the official. And the "yellow monkeys" phrase was actually Situmorang's quotation of a Javanese village chief ("Weekend" 810). Regardless of who claimed the phrase *yellow monkeys*, however, Wright's Western glasses did not equip him to access the epithet through the *longue durée* of Javanese history. Indonesians brought ancient cultural baggage to the term *yellow monkey* when it emerged during the Second World War as a dehumanizing description of the Japanese. Popularly, it was recalled that the twelfth-century Javanese prophet Jayabaya had predicted that Java would spend centuries dominated by a "white buffalo." Eventually, however, a "yellow monkey" would arrive to expell the buffalo. During Java's domination by the Netherlands, the Dutch were interpreted as the "white buffalo,"

FIGURE 4. Richard Wright's arrival in Jakarta. (Courtesy of the Beinecke Rare Book and Manuscript Library, Yale University)

and when the Japanese arrived to expel the Dutch during the war, they seemed to correspond to the long-awaited "yellow monkey."[40] Of course, Wright and his Western readers saw the racist epithet to the exclusion of the prophetic epithet.

But in Indonesia, Wright's reputation (and consequently his efficacy as a public diplomat) suffered less from the question of *yellow monkeys* and more from his international representations of Indonesian sanitary practices. Lubis had worried about Wright's perception of Indonesian sanitation from the second day of the visit. Of his first night in Jakarta, Wright wrote in his journal of being lodged in a room that smelled like a water closet ("Jakarta" 98). In the morning, Wright must have complained, because that very day an article appeared in Lubis's *Indonesia Raya*. With great embarassment, the article reported that Wright had been placed in substandard quarters in which "the stench of the latrine

FIGURE 5. Richard Wright in Indonesia. (Courtesy of the Beinecke Rare Book and Manuscript Library, Yale University)

reached [his hotel] room." The article argued that Bandung Conference organizers must provide adequate rooms to individuals who have such a "great impact on mankind." The article concluded, "We hope this suggestion will receive consideration, for the good name of our government as well as for the good name of Indonesia itself" ("Satu"). Shortly thereafter, the story of Wright's substandard room was picked up by a second newspaper.[41] If Wright's hosts worried about such incidents finding representation abroad, then their fears were realized months later when they read their would-be brother's report to the world. Wright did not relay the story of his hotel room, but he expounded in what was for his Indonesian readers uncomfortable detail on topics scatological. In cadences bordering on colonial paternalism, Wright told *Encounter* readers, "I saw a young man squatting upon the bank of the canal, defecating in broad daylight into the . . . swirling waters; I saw another, then another." "Then I saw young women washing clothes only a few yards from them. . . . A tiny boy was . . . dipping his toothbrush into the canal" ("Indonesian" 26). Wright further explained that even "middle-class Indonesian bathrooms" were "strange contraptions indeed." "Instead of toilet paper, the Indonesians use water; a small bucket of water is placed in each toilet. Toilet paper is hard to come by, having to be imported from Europe" (28).

For a Western readership in the 1950s, Wright's accounts simply may have reinforced a colonial view of Asia's filthy teeming millions, but in Indonesia these accounts further drained Wright's reservoir of goodwill. Shortly after Lubis wrote his letter to *Encounter*, Asrul Sani published a harsh discussion of Wright in *Siasat*. Referencing Wright's visit to Indonesia, Sani reminded readers that after his return to Paris, Wright had reported in the French magazine *Preuves* that "Indonesian latrines contain only a bottle or bucket of water because Indonesians can no longer afford to import expensive European toiletpaper to clean themselves after using the restroom" (146). Evidently, Wright's unflattering representation of Indonesian sanitary practices played a role in Sani's decision to offer several antagonistic revisions of the balanced assessment of Wright he earlier had published in the *Gelanggang* column. Remarking on Wright's account of Indonesian latrines, Sani wrote, "This was just ignorance/supidity. . . . But "The Outsider" is a failure of judgment. And failures of this kind are very dangerous for a writer" (146–47). Whereas in 1955 Sani's column had been content to discuss *The Outsider*'s thematic elements, his 1956 article ranked Wright's novel among "the greatest failures in literature": "those lofty works produced by writers . . . who, in one way or another, are endeavoring to show that they are dealing with complex and profound personal issues" (142). In 1955, Sani's column had speculated on Wright's complexity, suggesting that even though Wright appeared to have a past "bathed in jasmine and rosewater," his "uninhibited laughter" might simply be "a shield." But in 1956, as Sani recalled his 1955 meeting with Wright, the *Gelanggang* editor claimed that "whoever speaks with him will immediately be astonished by the amount of 'naivety' in him." Sani now claimed that a laugh like Wright's was uncommon among intellectuals and indicative of a soul that was "straight as a bamboo tube," "unburdened by the kinds of complications that we generally find in representatives of peoples with very powerful traditions and who, as a result, come into this world with almost unbearable burdens" (141).

And just as Lubis had antagonistically redeployed a phrase Wright used during the Konfrontasi gathering, Sani's article now absorbed and transformed a term Wright had used in his earlier *Gelanggang* interview. During the interview, Wright had described *Uncle Tom's Cabin* as a *document humain* and claimed that the book "doesn't say anything." Now Sani began his essay with a discussion of the *document humain* as a genre. The *document humain*, Sani explained, promotes "sympathetic feeling" toward its characters but finally fails in its striving for the highest level of "value." Though hastening to add that Wright must be respected, Sani now asserted that many of Wright's books, including *Native Son* and *Black Boy*, should be classified as *documents humain* (140). The negative will generated by Wright's CCF-sponsored travel writing functioned to bring Sani's views into homology with those of James Baldwin, who also drew unflattering comparisons between *Native Son* and *Uncle Tom's Cabin*.[42]

Sani's and Lubis's discontent with Wright's travel writing were far from unique within the Indonesian community. Lubis's letter to *Encounter* professed to give voice to the disappointment of many of "the people with whom Mr. Wright . . . [came] into contact in Indonesia" ("Through"). Beb Vuyk's comments on this point offer further insight into the Indonesian intellectuals' negative response to Wright's cultural diplomacy. Describing the articles Wright published in the CCF magazines, Vuyk wrote, "He took on himself the role of a sort of father confessor, to whom numerous Indonesians had confessed feelings of bitterness and unease that came out of a racial-inferiority complex. Each confession contained a short, well-constructed anecdote, and each penitent was discreetly referred to by an initial, such as 'Student A' and 'Engineer P,' so that however suspicious we might have been about the authenticity of most of these 'confessions,' we were powerless to do anything about it" ("Weekend" 810). The Indonesian intelligentsia felt such discontent with Wright's representations of them that when Indonesia's Council for Deliberations on National Culture (BMKN) decided to devote both of its May 1956 newsletters to summarizing Wright's French-language book on his Indonesian travels, reviewer Frits Kandou prefaced the articles by explaining, "It is not our intention to sling mud, but only to offer a summary of all of Wright's experiences and impressions while in Indonesia. To avoid misunderstanding, this summary is presented to the reader as completely as possible, and we allow Wright himself to speak as much as possible" (8: 1). In other words, if Indonesian intellectuals recognized themselves in the BMKN newsletter and felt insulted by how they were represented, they should remember that these were Wright's representations and not those of the BMKN. After this disclaimer, and without extensive editorializing, Kandou's articles summarize the conversations that Wright alleged took place between himself and his Indonesian interlocutors. But even Kandou's measured summaries refuse to permit at least one of Wright's points to go unanswered. In Kandou's concluding comments, he claims that the book's portrayal of Indonesian sanitary practices was "entirely off target," which offered "proof that [Wright's] attitude is not completely objective." Returning to the issue that provoked Sani, Kandou explained that the absence of toilet paper reflected not poverty but Islamic tradition (9: 4).

Intriguingly, the writer who should have been Wright's greatest Indonesian ally was at this time an editor of the newsletter that published Kandou's review. Pramoedya Ananta Toer, who had taken inspiration from Wright and praised his "bitter realism," is not known to have made any direct comment on Wright's visit or his writings on Indonesia.[43] Hence, Toer's apparent involvement in publishing Kandou's summaries—with their opening disclaimer and concluding discussion of sanitation—may be the closest we will come to commentary from the figure whose literary reputation the Indonesian government had formerly linked strongly with Wright. If Wright's Indonesian travels were orchestrated to build stable transnational bridges with people of color, then the unrealized personal alliance between Wright and Toer might be viewed as hipster diplomacy's failure to make use of the most promising of bridgeheads.[44]

Diplomatic Shuttles and Historical Models

While visiting Indonesia as a hip-to-mat and covertly funded public diplomat, Wright apprehended the postcolonial world via a historical model he carried from his days as a communist. In his journal, he conceptualized Indonesia vis-à-vis the Marxian historical trope of uneven development ("Jakarta" 131), and he noted that the only people who could understand the historical complexity of the postcolonial situation were former communists (218). He saw his postcommunist view of history as superior to the view held by American foreign policy, which he believed lacked a theory capable of producing accurate insight into the events transpiring among Asian and African nations and peoples. When Americans saw disturbances in the world of color, Wright explained, they sought cures through cultural exchanges, particularly student exchanges. From Wright's perspective, the United States' ahistorical and unintellectualized emphasis on cultural exchange offered little more than a nostrum (145).

Yet even if Wright did not recognize it, a conversation he had with the US ambassador to Indonesia indicated that US diplomacy indeed possessed historical models on which it based its interactions with the postcolonial world. In his journal, Wright recorded that the ambassador told him that ten percent of Indonesian students who participated in American cultural exchanges felt profound resentment toward the United States upon returning to Indonesia. This was a necessary risk, the ambassador explained ("Jakarta" 194). Like the Indonesian exchange students, Wright himself was a shuttle within a crisscrossing global network of exchanges resulting in a very large number of individual cultural interactions. According to the US ambassador's representation of public diplomacy, Wright was a participant in a diplomatic model that was indeed historical, using linear statistical extrapolation to explain the development of affinity and resentment vis-à-vis the procession of events through time. According to this model, a certain number of diplomatic successes may be linearly predicted based on a corresponding set of diplomatic failures. Wright, in this view, contributed to the necessary set of disillusionments that statistically enabled US public diplomacy's larger successes.[45]

But contrary to the US ambassador's intimations, American public diplomacy's historical model was neither linear (with success and failure functionally tied) nor binary (with success and failure the sole available outcomes). Among US public diplomacy's more sophisticated operatives, the model was fractal in a way that sought to make use of the chaotics of cultural exchange. Theoretically, of course, the United States wished to see cultural exchanges result in unambiguous ideological victories, but CIA agent Michael Josselson and his collaborating magazine editors saw that real outcomes and processes could be much more complex. As revealed in the CCF's June 1955 meeting minutes, the CCF found controversy highly attractive. It actively sought to publish "controversial articles, or articles made controversial by inviting discussion and counter-attack." The minutes reveal that the CCF editors "paid a call on Richard Wright who had just returned from South-East Asia. He reported at length on his impressions of the rise of Asian nationalism and especially a 'new and dangerous racism' with strong mystical-religious elements." Evidently seeing the type of controversial subject matter they sought to promote, Josselson and the editors "felt that the Richard Wright treatment of Bandung and Indo[n]esia might provide the proper point of departure."[46] If Wright was a point of departure, however, the path to success in public diplomacy was far from linear, and arrival was far from assured. Wright's travel writings, and the responses they prompted in Indonesia, looped through the *longue durée* of Javanese history and coiled through Wright's 1940s publications and communist past. These East-West interactions were fractured and became rough in *Konfrontasi*'s translation and Lubis's sardonic absorptions and transformations. The cultural exchange came to a false dead end in the pages of *Encounter*, as Wright seemed to put an end to the conversation by dismissing Lubis's complaints. Unbeknownst to Wright, the citational legacy continued in important Indonesian periodicals.

In assessing the vagaries of cultural exchange, it is difficult to establish causality. But Wright's interactions with the Indonesian intelligentsia apparently were some of the first that the CCF orchestrated in Indonesia, and these controversial incidents swirled in the eddies and were caught in the currents of subsequent cultural flows.[47] Wright's CCF-sponsored visit probably helped strengthen the network of Indonesian contacts necessary for the 1956 establishment of "an 'interim committee' of the CCF" in Jakarta (Hill 73). This committee's members included Wright's hosts Alisjahbana and Lubis, the latter of whom came to lead a CCF book-translation program (Steele 39). One also wonders about the potentially tangled relationship between Wright's trip and the emergence of the magazine *Konfrontasi*, from 1958 to 1960, as a publisher of "a steady trickle of translated articles" from the CCF magazine *Preuves* (Foulcher 51). Furthermore, the alliance of convenience that Wright forged with the CCF in exchange for travel funding paved the way for Wright, after returning to Europe, to give other CCF-supported lectures and to field CCF requests that he "be good enough to give [the CCF] (*as quickly as possible*) the addresses" he had for such "Negro intellectuals" as Amos Tutuola and Ralph Ellison.[48] Yet within this chaotic diplomatic model, the CCF's later exertions on Wright and Indonesian intellectuals need not be considered definitive triumphs or arrivals for US public diplomacy. In 1960, as Indonesia entered the intensely nationalist and anti-imperialist era of the final Sukarno years, *Konfrontasi*'s involvement in Cold War politics became a liability resulting in the magazine's demise. This same year, with Wright under constant harassment by a US government that would not trust him in spite of his efforts at cooperation, his life also came to an end.[49]

Wright's troubled 1950s participation in US public diplomacy finds a genealogy in the earlier New Negro writer-diplomats, who were prominent among the black writers Wright described as artistic ambassadors. Similar to Douglass and Langston, Wright in Indonesia offered a view of the black ambassadorial figure as having power to revise and reconstitute the United States' domestic and international status. Analogous to Johnson and his compromise with US imperialism in Latin America, Wright purchased his opportunity to witness the Bandung Conference in exchange for provisional absorption into the US program for hipster diplomacy. Like Ellis and Downing in Africa, Wright had ambiguous ties to the United States. Yet this ambiguity, which earlier was symptomatic of the United States' disregard for its black representatives, was now a reflection of a US diplomacy experimenting with the hip-to-matic positionalities and practices developed during New Negro work in diplomacy. Offered by a hip-to-mat and public diplomat, Wright's Konfrontasi lecture positioned him not only as an independent spokesperson for African America and the United States but also as a representative embodiment of the decolonizing constituencies that Du Bois and Gibbs Hunt represented via the personages of yellow, black, and brown wise men. These correspondences between Wright and earlier black internationalists reveal that although Wright in "Blueprint for Negro Writing" had sought to clear the ground of New Negro pretensions toward artistic ambassadorship, he himself became a complicit and resistant shuttle for the modes of black ambassadorship that contributed to the neoliberalizing edifice of aesthetic and international representation that found construction after the Second World War.

Epilogue: Hipster Diplomacy's Fall and Barack Obama's Forms of Things Unknown

In 2002, as President George W. Bush moved toward authorizing the US invasion of Iraq, Jamaican American calypso singer and political activist Harry Belafonte took aim at the black members of Bush's inner circle. In an interview with San Diego radio station KFMB, Belafonte offered an incisive description of the first black US secretary of state: "In the days of slavery, there were those slaves who lived on the plantation and there were those slaves that lived in the house. . . . You got the privilege of living in the house if you served the master. . . . Colin Powell's committed to come into the house of the master. When Colin Powell dares to suggest something other than what the master wants to hear, he will be turned back out to pasture" (Purdum). A short time later, Belafonte elucidated: "I'd like to see both [Colin Powell] and [National Security Advisor] Condoleezza Rice show some moral backbone, show some courage, show some commitment to principles that are far higher than those being espoused by their boss" ("Powell"). Responding to Belafonte's allegorical description of his work as the head of the Bush State Department, Powell remarked, "If Harry had wanted to attack my politics, that was fine. . . . If he wanted to attack a particular position I hold, that was fine. But to use a slave reference, I think, is unfortunate and is a throwback to another time and another place that I wish Harry had thought twice about using" (Purdum).

In spite of Powell's desire to keep the debate within the parameters of present positions and politics, both Powell and Belafonte were operating within racial, diplomatic, and wider geopolitical milieus shot through with other times and places. If on one hand the Iraq invasion seemed allusive to two centuries of medieval crusades,[1] then on the other hand Powell and Belafonte were recipients of various diplomatic scripts innovated by the artistic ambassadors of the New Negro era. As a calypso singer turned US critic and United Nations goodwill ambassador, Belafonte bore a marked resemblance to the character Matthew, from Du Bois's *Dark Princess*, who certifies his speech before the international committee by first garnering its respect through song. Belafonte's drive toward independence of voice—reflected in his skepticism regarding the "master's" performance imperatives—situated him within a hip-to-matic tradition that emerged among the black writer-diplomats and flowered with W. E. B. Du Bois and Ida Gibbs Hunt's work on the Pan-African Congresses. In the follow-up to his flap with Powell, Belafonte's words converged perfectly with those of Langston Hughes's self-appointed and freewheeling hip-to-mat. "The platform that I have as an artist," Belafonte told one reporter, "the work that I do at the United Nations, sits above suspicion because I have no agenda, so to speak, I don't serve a political party" ("Belafonte").

Powell, meanwhile, was enacting the culmination of the early black diplomats' vision for a US State Department in which people of African descent could rise to the highest positions. Powell's situation at the pinnacle of the US diplomatic institution was the conclusion of African American diplomacy's long script of reversal, which was vividly written over a century earlier when Frederick Douglass represented himself in *Life and Times* as moving from a state of ontological ineligibility for US citizenship to a position in which he represented the US president in Haiti. Powell's achievement was the long-deferred resolution of a drama whose exposition and rising action had involved the State Department's racially sinister apathy toward the petitions for promotion it received from applicants such as George Washington Ellis and James Weldon Johnson. But as is indicated by Belafonte's warning that Powell was obligated to say "what the [president] wants to hear," the first African American secretary of state still needed to watch his words out of a concern similar to Archibald Grimké's trepidation in Santo Domingo—his chickens might come home to roost. Powell may have broken racial barriers, but (in Belafonte's view) diplomacy's structural barriers regarding freedom of expression remained overbearingly in place.

Though the two men's 2002 affiliations and positions would have placed them at odds, Powell nonetheless resembled the hip-to-matic Belafonte in critical ways. To be sure, as Powell reveals in his autobiography, the secretary of state's prior military career had conditioned him to living "Army-like," going "through the chain of command" and "abid[ing] by the decision" issued by the superior (275). But Powell was also well known as an independent thinker among Bush's neoconservative advisers. He exhibited what Michael L. Clemons has described as the "tendency . . . toward foreign policy dissent" that has been part of the African American internationalist tradition (146). In a unilateralist atmosphere, Powell maintained enough of a hip-to-matic ethos that commentators frequently singled him out for his independence of voice, with the *Los Angeles Times*'s Ronald Brownstein remarking, "Powell has had a difficult time in [the Bush] administration. . . . He's had a lot of sparring . . . but he is in a strong position, ultimately, because the president needs him. He is . . . an important symbol to constituencies both at home and abroad of a commitment . . . to working with other nations and that gives him a kind of independent power base that I don't think anybody else in the Cabinet truly has" (qtd. in "Does"). Like the Congress for Cultural Freedom, which cultivated a hipster diplomacy that placed value on Richard Wright's reputation as a hip-to-matic symbol, the Bush administration relied on Powell's symbolic status as an independent voice by sending him to offer his much-derided speech and PowerPoint presentation to the UN Security Council on 5 February 2003.[2] As a famously independent black secretary of state presented the Security Council with a white administration's inaccurate narrative of Iraq's nonexistent weapons of mass destruction, the epoch of hipster diplomacy reached its apogee and began a precipitous decline. On an international scale corresponding to the embarrassing event's international visibility, independence of voice was lost as blackness's essentialized and utopian attribute. American blackness's putative independence, which traditionally has emerged from what Wright described as a third point of view, had now functioned to lend gravitas to the Bush administration's factually misguided rationale for invading Iraq.

When Condoleezza Rice succeeded Powell as the second black US secretary of state, her confirmation hearing before the Senate Committee on Foreign Relations indicated that observers should not expect her to symbolize anything substantially different from what a white secretary of state might symbolize.[3] Indeed, her loyalty to the Bush administration was beyond suspicion. She was committed to "never let[ting any exploitable] distance develop between" herself and the president (Rice 292), and she spoke with him daily as a means of airing "differences privately and early" (293). The lack of public dissent produced by these commitments evoked an abiding image of Rice as "almost never want[ing] to take dissenting views to the president" (Goldman).[4] As Rice appeared to eschew foreign policy dissent and to toe the administration's line with perfection, Japanese foreign minister Taro Aso offered tellingly racialized commentary on US diplomatic efforts. Aso asserted that US diplomats were perpetually unable to solve problems in the Middle East because of their blue eyes and blond hair: "Japan is doing [in the Middle East] what Americans can't do. . . . Japanese are trusted. It would probably be no good to have blue eyes and blond hair. Luckily, we Japanese have yellow faces." Aso explained that unlike blond hair and blue eyes, "yellow faces" had "never been involved in exploitation [in the Middle East], or been involved in fights or fired machine guns" (McCurry). Aso's statement on eye and hair color was widely portrayed as a gaffe, and several commentators relished the irony as they pointed to Condoleezza Rice as evidence that the Japanese foreign minister had offered an ill-informed explanation for US difficulties in the Middle East.[5] Yet Rice's apparent absence from Aso's racialized musings on diplomacy did not grow out of a simple failure to recognize the blackness of the chief US diplomat. Rather, his comments were symptomatic of public and international perception of Rice as a high-fidelity medium rather than a resignifying metaphor; diplomatically, she appeared to excel at conveying the Bush administration's message without permitting herself as an ambassadorial vehicle to reinflect that message. This image of Rice was a far cry from the Bush-Powell height of hipster diplomacy, and it signified a major shift in—if not a complete end of—a diplomatic tack begun by a Cold War United States that made a practice of deploying African American men and women internationally to speak in seemingly independent ways on behalf of US interests.

In hipster diplomacy's wake, Barack Obama's election as the forty-fourth US president has been a landmark event in the history of African Americans' relation to US diplomacy and the United States' relation to the international world. As the first black president of the United States (notwithstanding Toni Morrison's 1998 bestowal of this title on Bill Clinton),[6] President Obama in many ways may actualize the multitenored representational vehicle that Richard Wright in Indonesia could project but not fully perform. While Obama's election to the office of president certifies his representational status in relation to the United States, the multiple heritages woven through his biography connect him metonymically to numerous ethnic, racial, cultural, and religious constituencies throughout the world. Obama has publicly constructed his ties to these constituencies in his memoir, *Dreams from My Father: A Story of Race and Inheritance*, originally published in 1995 in recognition of his election as the first black president of the *Harvard Law Review* and republished upon his emergence in 2004 as a figure projected to ascend to the US presidency. In the memoir's 2004 preface, Obama tells readers, "I have seen . . . the desperation and disorder of the powerless: how it twists the lives of children on the streets of Jakarta or Nairobi in much the same way as it does the lives of children on Chicago's South Side, how narrow the path is for them between humiliation and untrammeled fury" (x–xi). Yet Obama has not simply seen this desperation touristically. His "family," as he notes in the 1995 introduction, is "stretched across oceans and continents" (xvii).

Obama's familial and experiential links to the planet's desperate populations find vivid representation in *Dreams*, which presents readers with the view of a figure who, even as he becomes a consummate member of the United States' power elite, draws spiritual energy from locales and cultures traditionally associated with colonized peoples and the wretched of the earth. The memoir narrates Obama's birth to a white American mother and a black Kenyan father in Hawaiʻi, a site with a "recent history" of imperial conquest, aborted treaties, corrupt plantation practices, and Japanese internment camps (23). *Dreams* describes Obama's relocation with his mother and Indonesian stepfather to Jakarta, where at the age of six, Obama takes "less than six months to learn Indonesia's language, its customs, and its legends" (36). With Indonesian children, he runs "the streets . . . hustling odd jobs, catching crickets, battling swift kites with razor-sharp lines" (36). He survives measles (36) and eats dog meat, snake meat, and roasted grasshoppers (37). Later, his education continues when he works as a community organizer in Chicago's South Side, where he finds a spiritual family (295), and when he visits his late father's family in Kenya, where he finds siblings, aunts, and cousins living in an overcrowded apartment (317). Accepted to Harvard Law School, Obama longingly thinks of his past, wishing he were somehow "still in Indonesia running barefoot along a paddy field, . . . part of a chain of other brown boys chasing after a tattered kite" (290). Within the memoir, Obama takes the sensibilities of a third-world kite runner to Harvard's privileged libraries (437).

While Obama's early education in international powerlessness often has been a liability among pundits within the United States,[7] this education apparently has been an asset in his efforts to repair the United States' distressed relations with international and transnational constituencies.

Delivering his June 2009 speech "A New Beginning" at the University of Cairo, Obama drew on the transnational and transcultural narratives elaborated in his memoir: "I'm a Christian, but my father came from a Kenyan family that includes generations of Muslims. As a boy, I spent several years in Indonesia and heard the call of the azaan at the break of dawn and at the fall of dusk. As a young man, I worked in Chicago communities where many found dignity and peace in their Muslim faith." Placing emphasis on his middle name and his racial difference from what Aso identified as the blue-eyed tradition of US diplomacy, Obama drew applause by reminding his audience that "much has been made of the fact that an African American with the name Barack Hussein Obama could be elected President." He went on to present "black people in America" and their "peaceful and determined insistence upon the ideals at the center of America's founding" as a template in his imperative that "Palestinians . . . abandon violence." In Obama's speech, African Americans' nonviolent achievement of "full and equal rights" became part of a story that can be told by people "from South Africa to South Asia; from Eastern Europe to Indonesia." Not simply because of these transnational narratives, but in ways that would have been less likely in their absence, many people in the Muslim world greeted "A New Beginning" with enthusiasm, approval, and hope ("New"). Delivering a follow-up speech a year and a half later, Obama spoke at the University of Indonesia. Here, he continued to advocate "a new beginning between the United States and Muslims around the world." Recalling his childhood in Jakarta, he reminded his audience of his familial connections to Indonesia and praised "the spirit of religious tolerance that is enshrined in Indonesia's Constitution." Asserting that "we must build bridges" between the people of the United States and Indonesia, he announced to applause that "we have committed to double the number of American and Indonesian students studying in our respective countries. We want more Indonesian students in American schools, and we want more American students to come study in this country" ("Remarks").

Of course, Obama's approach to diplomacy has not sprung up sui generis. *Dreams* offers a glimpse into its familial and cultural genealogies. In the memoir, Obama's father arrives in the United States as part of a student exchange program (9),[8] and while living in Indonesia, Obama sometimes accompanies his mother to her work at the American embassy, where she teaches English to Indonesian businessmen (28–30, 43). Just as significant as his familial routes in cultural diplomacy, Obama's teenage readings in African American literature induct him into discussions surrounding diplomacy's central issues of power, national allegiance, and rhetorics of directness and compromise. In high school, Obama begins to see "a new map of the world" in which black people "were always playing . . . by the white man's rules," and he gathers "books from the library—Baldwin, Ellison, Hughes, Wright, DuBois" (85). These writers each lead him to the same anguish: "Even DuBois's learning and Baldwin's love and Langston's humor eventually succumbed . . . , each man finally forced to withdraw, one to Africa, one to Europe, one deeper into the bowels of Harlem" (86).

Within *Dreams*, as Obama contemplates the transnational flights of some of the United States' most famous artistic ambassadors and hip-to-mats, this earlier generation of black US writers makes a bodily and uncanny appearance. As a young man, Obama receives counsel from "a poet named Frank," "a contemporary of Richard Wright and Langston Hughes," who lives in a run-down area of Waikiki (76). Commenting on Obama's plans to attend college, an elderly version of African American writer Frank Marshall Davis weighs in on what James Weldon Johnson earlier dealt with as the dichotomy between compromise and directness, between diplomacy and truth telling. Frank calls college an "advanced degree in compromise." "You're going there to get *trained*," Frank tells Obama. "They'll train you so good, you'll start believing what they tell you about equal opportunity and the American way." Obama asks, "So what is it you're telling me—that I shouldn't be going to college?" In response Frank offers an alternative to both compromise and directness: "You've got to go. I'm just telling you to keep your eyes open. Stay awake" (97). At college, Obama struggles with what it means to remain uncompromised—to remain "indeed still awake" (100)—and comes to a realization: "You might be locked into a world not of your own making, . . . but you still have a claim on how it is shaped" (111). Obama's cultural routes and familial roots in diplomacy have thematic resonance throughout the remainder of *Dreams*, and they bleed into the texts of his work and legacy as a president and arbiter of international relations.

As an elected official rather than a participant in the tradition of appointed black emissaries, Obama's diplomacy is not strictly beholden to any mandate or history. His actions on the international stage may be loosely attentive to US public opinion, but he is not obligated to follow any particular script. He is likewise distanced from the exigencies of previous black performances in US diplomacy and internationalism more generally. Obama's diplomatic performances may allude to hip-to-macy, but his power position as a US president precludes a traditional hip-to-matic performance. The humility that characterizes his international work may in certain structural ways resemble the tradition of artistic ambassadorship, and he indeed may not fulfill Belafonte's messianic vision for the first black US president.[9] But Obama's work seeks to create a polyvocal and alert alternative to the genre of compromise that too often has rationalized itself as diplomacy. Students of black internationalism do well to mirror this humility and alertness in assessing Obama's ongoing performances and their unfolding geopolitical ramifications. Recognizing the beginnings of something new—the beginnings of a transition from a loose structure of feeling to a more evident cultural formation[10]—we might recur to a phrase used by Richard Wright while lecturing in Indonesia just twelve years before Obama arrived in Jakarta: Wright described African American folk cultures and "migratory voices" as "Forms of Things Unknown" ("American" 13). The complexities of Obama's diplomatic Forms of Things Unknown may not find pat and transhistorical answers in the performances of African America's early artistic ambassadors and hip-to-mats, but full critical access to his engagements with the world will depend on an apprehension of a black past that deeply inflects the major currents of early twenty-first-century internationalism. This is a past forged by the New Negro writer-diplomats who negotiated and innovated the persistent interanimations of literary, racial, and international representation.

Notes

Introduction

1. In 1988, Henry Louis Gates, Jr., framed this era as extending from 1895 to 1925 ("Trope" 131). More recently, Gates has collaborated with Gene Andrew Jarrett to edit *The New Negro*, an anthology taking 1892 through 1938 as its frame.

2. Caroline Gebhard and Barbara McCaskill follow Chesnutt in describing a "Post-Bellum–Pre-Harlem" era extending from the collapse of Reconstruction in 1877 to the end of the First World War.

3. Before this era, in 1845, William Alexander Leidesdorff, who had African and other ancestries, was appointed US vice consul in Yerba Buena, Mexico, which is now San Francisco, California (Dawson).

4. The United States sent a continuous stream of black ministers to Liberia from 1871 through the 1940s. It sent black ministers to Haiti from 1869 to 1913. From the 1860s through the 1930s, the United States sent about thirty black ministers to Haiti and Liberia (J. Miller 8–9). During this same era, about fifty African Americans worked as US consuls, with the number at four in 1880, peaking at seventeen during the Roosevelt administration, and decreasing to three during Wilson's presidency (Blakely, "Black" 1, 11–12). On black work in the US consular service, see Justesen; and Blakely, "Black." For historical work on black US diplomats after the Second World War, see Krenn.

5. Du Bois stayed in Liberia in this capacity from 22 December 1923 to 22 January 1924 (D. Lewis, *W. E. B. Du Bois: Fight* 118–27).

6. While a majority of these connections are documented in subsequent chapters, a few are not. On Downing as Douglass's godson, see "Henry F. Downing," in the *Amsterdam News*; on Francis Grimké as Ida Gibbs Hunt's pastor and friend, see Alexander 77; on Angelina and Archibald Grimké's attendance at the Gibbs-Hunt wedding, see Alexander 104–06; on Anderson and Washington's efforts to replace William Hunt with Johnson, see *BTWP* 10: 495–96.

7. On Obama's *Dreams from My Father* (1995), see Roth; Morrison, "Toni"; Dolisane-Ebosse; and T. Green, 103–32.

8. For instance, a phrase from Du Bois's anti-imperialist writings affords the title of Amy Kaplan's *The Anarchy of Empire in the Making of U.S. Culture* (1, 12–16), and Du Bois and Zora Neale Hurston are featured as anti-imperialist writers (though Hurston unevenly so) in John Carlos Rowe's *Literary Culture and U.S. Imperialism* (195–216, 253–91).

Part I: Representative Characters

1. In 1903, Du Bois described the project of the race's "Talented Tenth": "developing the Best of [the] race that they may guide the Mass away from the contamination and death of the Worst, in their own and other races" ("Talented" 33).

2. On presentability, see Gates, "Trope" 129.

3. This stanza may be found in Johnson's edited collection *The Book of American Negro Poetry* 89.

4. For Johnson's account of writing this poem while working as a consul, see his *Along This Way* 289–91.

5. For work that, like my own, explores New Negro literary representation's convergences with other modes of representation, see Nadell; and Carroll.

1 / The Negro Beat

1. On black US ministers to Haiti, see Padgett. On black ministers in Liberia, see Skinner 63–94. On black consuls, see Justesen; and Stafford.

2. Norma Brown refers to the tradition of calling Haiti and Liberia the "Negro beat" (i). Michael Krenn's work uncovers a more general "Negro circuit." Based on interviews, Krenn lists "Negro circuit" posts as Liberia, the Azores, the Canary Islands, and Madagascar (25). During the late nineteenth and early twentieth centuries, other posts within the circuit included Santo Domingo, a handful of consulates in West Africa, a handful of consulates in Central and South America, and a few plum positions at small consulates in Europe.

3. McDowell's "In the First Place" offers a critique of Douglass's place as the representative father of the African American literary tradition. Gates's "From Wheatley to Douglass" traces Douglass's ascendancy as achieved through Phillis Wheatley's effacement.

4. See Himelhoch; Sears; Brantley; Pitre; Goldstein; Dayan 166–71; and Nwankwo 129–52. Norma Brown edited Douglass's diplomatic dispatches.

5. Gates observes that the title "representative colored man" was "a designation that Douglass . . . seems to have encouraged" ("Trope" 129). Even before the Civil War, Douglass was preoccupied with representational questions. "It is evident we must be our own representatives and advocates," he asserted (*Life and Writings* 1: 281). For more on Douglass and representation, see Moses, "Where"; and W. Martin 253–78.

6. Ellis to Theophile T. Allain, 29 Dec. 1913, IMGP, Box 1, Folder 1-2.

7. Derrida discusses the "threat of perversion" (147) attendant to the representative, who is a "supplement" revealing that the original "can accomplish itself, only by allowing itself to be filled through . . . proxy" (145).

8. On prestige and skin, see Levine 13. On masculinity, see Carby's *Race Men* and Ross's *Manning the Race*. On New Negro racial uplift, see Jarrett 73–99. Also on New Negro race representation, see Ross's "The New Negro Displayed."

9. Even after resurgent post-Reconstruction prejudice edged black leaders out of prominent political positions, black Americans continued as US ministers to Haiti and Liberia (McFeely 335). For more on the State Department's unique willingness to employ African Americans as high ranking officials, see N. Brown i.

10. Traditionally, only the high rank of ambassador is imbued with representative character, and no African American diplomat held the rank of ambassador until after the era with which this study is primarily concerned. However, during the era with which I am concerned, it was held that "whatever [diplomats'] title of dignity, . . . they are, each and all, . . . the unquestionable representatives *pro tanto* of the sovereignty of the United States" (Ogdon 146). It is evident that black US ministers had a sense of their representative character, which was also generally recognized by the US public.

11. Douglass was sent to Haiti without his exequatur and from Port-au-Prince had to request repeatedly before the State Department sent his diplomatic credentials; see Douglass, *Black Diplomat* 1: 5 and 19–21. In *Life and Times*, Douglass elides these complications, refusing to permit the State Department to disrupt the representative image he actively sought to evoke.

12. Gibbs does not directly tell readers his autobiography was written in Madagascar, but *Shadow and Light* indicates as much when Gibbs includes a letter from Madagascar's governor-general, who mentions having "read with great pleasure [Gibbs's] biographical sketch" (307).

13. John Stephens Durham to Whitefield McKinlay, 6 Jan. 1897, CGWP.

14. This letter to the editor, titled "Not Representative of Her Race," was signed by Durham and J. W. Mans. Another black US consul, C. C. Astwood, also publicly disagreed with Wells ("Lynching of Negroes"). On Wells's British antilynching campaign, see Silkey.

15. On women in the Foreign Service, see A. Wright; and McGlen and Sarkees 62–66. Operating outside of official internationalism has enabled women such as Wells to assume more radical approaches to international relations, and black women have often asserted representative status and thus challenged male-oriented office-holding as a model for race representation.

16. Bercovitch describes the genre of the auto-American-biography as "the celebration of the representative self as America, and of the American self as the embodiment of a prophetic universal design" (136).

17. I refer to the chiasmus famously included in Douglass's 1845 *Narrative*: "You have seen how a man was made a slave; you shall see how a slave was made a man" (60).

18. For references to similar newspaper articles, see Himelhoch 176.

19. Herman Crouze to Grover Cleveland, 27 Mar. 1891, Applications and Recommendations for Public Office, 1797–1901: Administration of Cleveland and Harrison, 1885–1893, Frederick Douglass Folder, RG 59. This letter was written in recommendation that Douglass receive a second appointment as minister to Haiti.

20. Unless otherwise noted, Durham's biography is taken from Wynes.

21. On transculturation, see Pratt 6.

22. Durham's novel resonates with what Ann duCille and Claudia Tate discuss as the politically significant marriage plots common in African American women's writing of the era. Yet far from participating in the "sexual reticence" (duCille 10) of what Tate describes as "black Victorian love stories" (*Domestic* 5), *Diane* represents its heroine with what Dickson Bruce calls "an eroticism that had never been used by

a black [US] writer before" (*Black* 134). Clearly, *Diane* owes its greatest debt to a Latin American literary tradition in which "erotic passion was . . . the opportunity . . . to bind together heterodox constituencies" (Sommer 14).

23. On Martí's meeting with Gómez and his stay in Santo Domingo, see Zéndegui 170, 184–86; and Mañach 301–04. On Durham's trip to Santo Domingo, see dispatches dated 12 and 13 August 1892 in *DUSMH* (roll 26) and dispatch 76 in *Despatches from the State Department to US Ministers to Haiti, Sept. 8, 1891 to Nov. 14, 1893*, Diplomatic Records from Haiti, Vol. 039, RG 84.

24. My translation.

25. Martí to Manuel de. J. Galván, 19 Sept. 1894, included in Galván 5; my translation. For a gloss of *Enriquillo*, see Luis 128.

26. Durham to Chesnutt, 14 Sept. 1898, CWCC.

27. *Diane*'s generic disjunctions seem to have contributed to Durham's difficulties in finding a publisher. Durham wrote to Chesnutt, "It will [appear] in *Lippincotts*. I trust that you will look over it and tell me frankly what is the matter with it. Something is wrong with it for I cannot get a publisher for the thing in book form." 15 Oct. 1901, CWCC.

28. "Heil dir im Siegerkranz" was the unofficial German national anthem until 1918. It shares a melody with Britain's "God Save the Queen" and the United States' "My Country, 'Tis of Thee."

29. Here I allude to Washington's 1900 *A New Negro for a New Century*, which, like *Diane*, foregrounded black performance in the Caribbean. Washington drew attention to the performances of black US soldiers in the Spanish-American War as indicative of African Americans' fitness as US citizens (36–71).

30. Durham to Whitefield McKinlay, 1 Sept. 1902, CGWP.

31. In the black diplomatic context, the masculinism of US internationalism was affirmed by Langston, who explained the "feelings of earnest, patriotic, manly pride" that possessed him upon thinking of his role as "the American diplomat" (357–58).

2 / Passing into Diplomacy

1. Few studies take more than a passing interest in Johnson's overlapping diplomatic and literary work in Latin America. For important exceptions, see Levy 121–47; Goldsby, "Keeping" and *Spectacular* 164–213; and Stecopoulos 53–76. W. Gibbs offers a thorough, nonliterary discussion of Johnson's consulships.

2. Johnson to A. S. Halstead, Dispatch 53, 30 Sept. 1909, in *American Consulate Corinto: Legation Correspondence, July 11, 1908–August 4, 1912*, Consular Records from Corinto, Nicaragua. Vol. 015, RG 84.

3. Johnson to State Department, Dispatch 186, 14 Nov. 1910, in *American Consulate Corinto: Dispatches to Department, July 2, 1908–August 1, 1912*, Consular Records from Corinto, Nicaragua. Vol. 012, RG 84.

4. On Johnson's involvement in these activities, see Johnson, *Along* 252–89; and Johnson to Grace Nail Johnson, 31 Aug. 1912, JWJP, Series III, Box 41, Folder 22. See also LaFeber, *American* 246.

5. Johnson to Grace Nail Johnson, 26 June 1912, JWJP, Series III, Box 41, Folder 22.

6. From the midst of a revolution in Nicaragua, Johnson wrote to Grace Nail, "Well, there's no 'comic opera' about it. The bombardment of Managua was terrible" (17 Aug. 1912, JWJP, Series III, Box 41, Folder 22). While the quote denies the

revolution's similarities to a "comic opera," it suggests that Johnson and Grace Nail likely had previous conversations in which they made the comparison that Johnson denied in the letter. This likelihood is supported by Johnson's later comment on Latin American revolutions: "The seriousness of the frequent Latin-American revolutions has been greatly over-emphasized. The writer has been in the midst of three of these revolutions and must confess that the treatment given them on our comic opera stage is very little farther removed from the truth than the treatment which is given in the daily newspapers. Not nearly so bloody as reported, their interference with people not in politics is almost negligible" ("Self-Determining" 227).

7. Quotes from "Down by the Carib Sea" are taken from the poem's second section, "*Los Cigarillos.*"

8. Houston Baker observes that the narrator "resolves to be a race man at [this] commencement speech" (*Singers* 21). J. Martin Favor notes that the narrator holds Shiny as "a model of African American deportment" as he "looks at Shiny's [black] skin and uses it to connect with the [black] folk" (37).

9. See Olmsted 82.

10. For other interpretations of black indirection as hypocrisy, see Du Chaillu 136; Crummell 79; and Day 229–30.

11. See Emerson's remark, "A foolish consistency is the hobgoblin of little minds" ("Self-Reliance" 58), and Whitman's equally famous question and answer, "Do I contradict myself? Very well then . . . . I contradict myself" (87).

12. Allison Heisch explains, "Long after Phillips's death black students memorized ["Toussaint L'Ouverture"] and recited it on occasions such as school graduations. Thus, . . . [Phillips's] second (and more enduring) audience was an audience of black people—largely students" (237).

13. Many others described Washington's tactics as diplomacy; see for instance *BTWP* 5: 136. Interestingly, Johnson used the term "diplomatic" to describe the performance of Charles Anderson, a black politician and advocate of Johnson's advancement within the consular service. Johnson to Grace Nail Johnson, 6 Apr. 1912, JWJP, Series III, Box 41, Folder 21.

14. See "Diploma."

15. See *American Consulate Corinto: Business Letters, 1909, 1910, 1911*, Consular Records from Corinto, Nicaragua. Vol. 021, RG 84.

16. See Fabi 100; Pisiak 93; Sollors 264–66; and Andrews xvi. The link between Johnson's anonymity and the novel's marketing is supported by a 26 June 1912 letter to Grace Nail Johnson in which James Weldon Johnson wrote that the secret of the book's authorship needed to be kept: if it were known that the author were a "colored man who could not be the character in the book," public interest would decline. 26 June 1912, JWJP, Series III, Box 41, Folder 22. Jacqueline Goldsby's analysis has insightfully complemented marketing concerns with diplomatic contexts, arguing that Johnson's maintenance of anonymity was both a marketing tactic ("Keeping" 257) and a means of denying gestures of friendship to State Department officials who themselves had denied Johnson's request for a promotion (262). Following Goldsby in exploring the novel's diplomatic contexts, and without undercutting marketing as a significant factor, I seek to complicate our approach to what Johnson himself described as the drawn-out decision to publish anonymously (*Along* 238).

17. For Tarry on collecting material, see K. Smith 282.

18. Even as the section on "Correspondence with the Press" forbade Johnson from corresponding on the topic of international politics with private individuals, newspapers, or other periodicals, the section also noted that this "prohibition does not extend to literary articles or subjects not connected with politics" (*Regulations* 172). My argument here is not that Johnson was officially prohibited from signing his name to his novel but that he was operating according to the more cautious rule of thumb expressed by John W. Foster.

19. See McMurry 145–49; and Sundquist, Introduction xviii.

20. John W. Foster recalled a US diplomat whose candid commentary found its way into the press. Neither the president nor the State Department censured the indiscretion, but a hostile House of Representatives condemned the diplomat (120–21). An understanding of the varied volatilities of differing political factions may explain Johnson's willingness to reveal his authorship to certain State Department officials while concealing it in other contexts. See Wilbur J. Carr to Johnson, 8 Oct. 1912, JWJP, Series I, Box 5, Folder 82.

21. See Goellnicht; Ruotolo; and Kawash 135–55.

22. Johnson to William Jennings Bryan, 1 Sept. 1913, JWJP, Series I, Box 4, Folder 71.

23. On Johnson as a "good talker" and his recruitment as a "coup d'état," see Levy 184–85.

24. See Johnson's "A Poor Rule" and "Haiti and Mexico."

Part II: Lost Theaters

1. On the presence of McKay and other Caribbean writers in Alain Locke's *The New Negro*, see Charras. On McKay's relation to the US-based New Negro establishment, see Karem 170–82. On the relation between McKay as a New Negro and a traveler in the Soviet Union, see K. Baldwin 25–85.

2. For other work treating *Banjo* and black transnationalism, see Rosenberg; and Smethurst.

3. Gilroy describes the politics of fulfillment as "immanent within modernity" (*Black* 37), but the politics of immanence I am describing would not, as Gilroy outlines, make demands of modernity in terms of modernity's "own rhetoric" (37) or see itself as playing modernity at "its own game" (38). Rather than making demands or offering competition, the politics of immanence drives performances that implicitly undercut the notion of modernity as having its *own* rhetoric or game that somehow does not always already involve blackness.

4. On Ida Gibbs and William Henry Hunt at the consulate in Saint-Étienne, see Alexander 138–214.

5. In 1924, Du Bois described William Hunt in the pages of the *Crisis*: "At St. Etienne the most popular man in town—the head of the French and Foreign Club, the chief sportsman, the guest of a hundred hosts, and the welcomed of all business men—is one of us—Hunt, the only American Consul of Negro descent in Europe. The State Department is worried over Hunt. He deserves a promotion and they dare not promote him" ("Sketches" 203).

3 / Diplomatic and Modern Representations

1. Ellis to Theophile T. Allain, 29 Dec. 1913, IMGP, Box 1, Folder 1-2.

2. See Skinner 63–94.

3. John H. Smythe, known for his work as minister to Liberia from 1878 to 1885, drew on a familiarity with Africa as he introduced Daniel Webster Davis's 1895 dialect collection *Idle Moments*. Alexander Priestly Camphor and Richard C. Bundy (consular officers in Liberia during the early 1900s) had literary aspirations for their West African folklore collections.

4. On colonial modernity, see Young 374–78; and Mignolo, "Geopolitics." I take colonial modernity to encompass the formations arising from the global interactions of peoples brought into contact by colonialism, which had a temporal trajectory of centuries. In this chapter, I am specifically addressing colonial modernity's late nineteenth- and early twentieth-century manifestations.

5. On modernist primitivism, see Clifford; H. Foster; Sweeney; and North 37–99.

6. In subsequently referring to "misrepresentation" and representational disjunction, this chapter does not mean to imply the possibility of a direct or true imitative relationship between signs and things. Using this language, however, is important to understanding the cultural forms in question on their own terms.

7. See especially *Crisis* issues during 1918.

8. Harrison refers to *The Leopard's Claw* and *The American Cavalryman*, novels by Ellis and Downing.

9. Unless otherwise noted, Ellis's general biographical information is from Fleming and Logan.

10. Ellis to W. E. B. Du Bois, 15 July 1908, IMGP, Box 1, Folder 1-2.

11. Walter Neale to Ellis, 25 Apr. 1914, IMGP, Box 1, Folder 1-4.

12. Before and after Park's review, Ellis employed psychology to understand conflict between black and white Americans as well as between African populations and colonial governments. See his "Liberia in the Political Psychology of West Africa," "Psychic Factors in the New American Race Situation," and "The Psychology of American Race Prejudice."

13. Gruesser rightly observes that the novel strives for accuracy on questions of geography, native practices, and flora and fauna (17).

14. The subtitle includes the printer's error "psyschic." In the quote, I have corrected this error.

15. The origins of this illustration are unclear. Ellis may have requested or drawn the image. The other book released by Ellis's publisher (International Authors' Association) does not bear a cover illustration (see Dillon).

16. For sleep-talking, see Ellis, *Leopard's* 133. For dream-based memory recovery, see 139. For loss of memory and speech, see 101 and 160.

17. This quote is from Ellis's 1919 article "Liberia in the New Partition of West Africa" (251), which repeats from his 1912 article "Liberia in the Political Psychology of West Africa" (55).

18. For other significant scenes involving leopards, see for instance Ellis, *Leopard's* 55–56 and 58.

19. Such works include Joseph Conrad's *Heart of Darkness*, Sigmund Freud's *Totem and Taboo*, and Gertrude Stein's "Melanctha."

20. On the leopard's claw as fetish, see Ellis, *Leopard's* 106.

21. See O'Neill's *The Emperor Jones* and *All God's Chillun Got Wings*.

22. Michael North notes the aesthetic and political pitfalls that black modernists faced when Anglo-American modernists used misrepresentative racial stereotypes to

arrive at "the most radical representational strategies of English-language modernism" (i).

23. See "Pulled"; and "Leopard."

24. Neale to Ellis, 30 Jan. 1913, IMGP, Box 1, Folder 1-3.

25. See advertisement "New Race Literature" (IMGP, Box 1, Folder 1-4). No reviews of *The Leopard's Claw* are included among Ellis's papers; besides the recent scholarship of V. Williams and Gruesser, the novel is mentioned by Harrison 352 and J. Hughes 36.

26. For Downing's biographical information, I draw on Contee unless otherwise noted.

27. Downing to G. L. Rives, 3 Oct. 1888, *DUSCSP*, Roll 5, Vol. 4.

28. Downing to James D. Porter, 18 Nov. 1887, *DUSCSP*, Roll 4, Vol. 4.

29. Downing to the Department of State, 29 Jan 1888, containing Downing's report to G. L. Rives, 12 Jan. 1888, *DUSCSP*, Roll 5, Vol. 4.

30. I allude to Warren's essay "Frederick Douglass's *Life and Times*: Progressive Rhetoric and the Problem of Constituency."

31. Downing to George L. Rives, 30 Dec. 1887, *DUSCSP*, Roll 4, Vol. 4.

32. Downing to James D. Porter, 14 Nov. 1887, *DUSCSP*, Roll 4, Vol. 4.

33. Downing to His Excellency [Grover Cleveland], 18 Nov. 1888, *GCP*, Series 2, Reel 65.

34. Downing to G. L. Rives, 18 Aug. 1888, *GCP*, Series 3, Reel 124.

35. Downing to G. L. Rives, 31 Jan. 1888, *DUSCSP*, Roll 5, Vol. 4.

36. Though Downing's weekly paper is not known to exist in any archives, it was mentioned in his obituary ("Henry Downing"). His involvement in the National Colored People's Protective Association (as chairman of the Executive Committee) is alluded to in "Testimonials," DF, 341.112 D75. The association "aimed to fight against southern outrages such as lynchings, peonage, and disfranchisement" (Reed 127).

37. On Downing's involvement with Dunbar and Coleridge-Taylor, see Downing, "Samuel Coleridge Taylor" 267. The London *Times* noted Downing's Pan-African Conference speech in "Pan-African Conference." Downing wrote the lyrics for "Where the Paw-Paw Grows," composed by Montague Ring (pseudonym of Amanda Aldridge). J. Green mentions that Downing was one of Nina's only associates during this time (252).

38. See Downing's incomplete novella "A Black and White Tangle."

39. Downing's leadership of the Players and Playwrights Association is mentioned in Downing to Reginald McKenna, 11 Apr. 1915, DF, 341.112 D75. On organizations similar to Downing's, see "Unacted Authors' Association"; and "Amateur."

40. *The African Times*'s reviews of Downing's play *The Arabian Lovers* appear in the August and November–December 1913 issues. For reference to other praise for Downing's dramatic work, see "Race Playwright."

41. For Downing's account of his plays' scheduling at the Royal Court Theatre, see Downing to Reginald McKenna, 11 Apr. 1915, DF, 341.112 D75. In corroboration of Downing's account of his plays' cancellation, the *Times* ceased announcing performances at the Royal Court between 10 June 1914 and 17 Sept. 1915 (see "Play"; and "News"). For a discussion of Downing's performance history, see B. Roberts 279–80.

42. For descriptions of Downing's other plays, see B. Roberts 273 and 282.

43. Though Johnston had earlier worked to appropriate swaths of African land, he was by 1911 deemed sufficiently sympathetic to interracial unity that he was invited to

be a member of the Universal Races Central Executive Committee ("Report" 29). Like Terminus, however, the *African Times* suggested that Johnston's prejudice ran deeper than he acknowledged ("Mrs. Besant").

44. Booker T. Washington had Johnston as a visitor at Tuskegee in 1908 (Johnston). As early as 1909, Du Bois arranged for Johnston to be on the board of advisers for his proposed "Encyclopaedia Africana" (Du Bois, *Dusk* 322). Ellis became a Fellow of Britain's Royal Geographical Society at Johnston's recommendation (Fleming 211).

45. On created African chiefs, see also Mamdani 22–23.

46. With the term "reconstructed," I allude to Henry Louis Gates, Jr.'s use of the term *reconstruction* to refer to the advancement of the New Negro as a trope to supersede the image of the Old Negro ("Trope" 129–31).

47. See Sheean 186; and Wells 143.

48. After Hemingway took inspiration from Stein and modeled his writing on Cézanne's paintings, he wrote to Stein, "[Writing] used to be easy before I met you. Certainly was bad, Gosh, I'm awfully bad now but it's a different kind of bad" (qtd. in Knight 123–24). On modernism and the bad, see Mao and Walkowitz.

49. On Downing's return to Manhattan and settlement in Harlem, see B. Roberts 278–80.

4 / Metonymies of Absence and Presence

1. See J. Stephens 332; Schroeder 94–95; and C. Allen 63.

2. "A Biographical Sketch of Archibald H. Grimké," draft, ArGP, Box 39-2, Folder 50. For an overview of Archibald's consulship, see D. Bruce, *Archibald* 64–77.

3. See Scott 358; and Carruth.

4. *Rachel* had four known performances, either amateur or semiprofessional: on 3–4 March 1916 under direction of the Washington, DC–area NAACP; on 26 April 1917 at the Neighborhood Playhouse in New York City; and on 24 May 1917 in Cambridge, Massachusetts (Hull 119). As a book published in 1920, *Rachel* "commanded considerably more attention" (Hull 121).

5. On 18 October 1894, Archibald left Angelina with Charlotte and Francis Grimké at their home in Washington, DC. Francis was Archibald's brother. For Archibald's reference to his departure, see Archibald Grimké to Edwin F. Uhl, 29 Oct. 1894, *DUSCSD*, Roll 15.

6. "Archibald H. Grimké," undated holograph. ArGP, Box 39-2, Folder 51.

7. See Markovitz; and Goldsby, *Spectacular.*

8. On Grimké's conceptualization of lynching and silence, see Hirsch 466–67.

9. Archibald Grimké to Home Ones, 16 Mar. 1895, FGP, Box 40-3, Folder 112. During Archibald's first year abroad, he wrote numerous letters addressed to "Home Ones," a group including Angelina as well as Francis and Charlotte, with whom Angelina was staying. To "Home Ones," he explained, "I cannot write to each of you separate letters, & I know that you . . . will be willing to receive one for all." Archibald Grimké to Home Ones, 28 Oct. 1894, FGP, Box 40-3, Folder 110.

10. Archibald Grimké to Home Ones, 22 Jan. 1895, FGP, Box 40-3, Folder 119. Quotes from these letters are taken from discussions in which Archibald worries that either his comments on international affairs or Dominican cultural customs may jeopardize his status as a consul. When looking at Dominican life, he wanted to play the role of "reformer," but a role in racial uplift was precluded by his role as consul.

11. Archibald's friend T. McCants Stewart was openly criticizing Grover Cleveland, and in the subsequently quoted newspaper article, Archibald references having read "the letter" from Stewart to Cleveland. On 15 September 1894, Stewart had written to Cleveland, "Under your present administration, we are suffering from cruel lynchings in the South and from unjust discrimination in the public service throughout the nation" (*GCP*, Series 2, Reel 87).

12. See Spivak 280–90.

13. Reflective of counterfactual history's special usefulness in considering international relations, the collection *Unmaking the West* concludes by noting that questions of politics and war "are particularly appropriate for counterfactual analysis" (Parker and Tetlock 365). For an example of counterfactual history's relationship to imaginative literature, see Niall Ferguson's "Virtual History: Towards a 'Chaotic' Theory of the Past," which sees models for counterfactualization in writers including Ray Bradbury, Robert Musil (3), Jorge Luis Borges, Stéphane Mallarmé, and Robert Frost (71).

14. Untitled and undated outline in ArGP, Box 39-2, Folder 52.

15. Archibald Grimké to Angelina Grimké, 25 Nov. 1894, AnGP, Box 38-4, Folder 65; and Archibald Grimké to Angelina Grimké, 7 Feb. 1895, AnGP, Box 38-4, Folder 66.

16. Archibald Grimké to Angelina Grimké, 25 Nov. 1894, AnGP, Box 38-4, Folder 65.

17. Archibald Grimké to Angelina Grimké, 26 Apr. [1895], AnGP, Box 38-4, Folder 66; Archibald Grimké to Angelina Grimké, 23 Aug. 1897, AnGP, Box 38-4, Folder 67; and Archibald Grimké to Angelina Grimké, 20 Dec. 1897, AnGP, Box 38-4, Folder 67.

18. Archibald Grimké to Home Ones, 27 Feb. 1895, FGP, Box 40-3, Folder 112.

19. Archibald Grimké to Angelina Grimké, 4 Nov. 1897, AnGP, Box 38-4, Folder 67.

20. Archibald Grimké to Angelina Grimké, 4 Jan. 1898, AnGP, Box 38-4, Folder 68.

21. Archibald Grimké to Home Ones, 8 Nov. 1894, FGP, Box 40-3, Folder 115; and Archibald Grimké to Home Ones, 8 Jan. 1895, FGP, Box 40-3, Folder 116.

22. Archibald Grimké to Angelina Grimké, 25 Apr. 1895, AnGP, Box 38-4, Folder 66.

23. Here, all editions of *Rachel* have represented the refrain's second line as "Out from that sea," even though the lullaby's standard text (as well as the play's previous rendition of this text) has the line as "Out upon that sea." I have replaced *from* with *upon* because, based on a handwritten draft of *Rachel*, the *from* appears to be a printer's error. See "Blessed Are the Barren," AnGP, Box 38-13, Folder 222.

24. Archibald Grimké to Home Ones, 8 Nov. 1894, FGP, Box 40-3, Folder 115.

25. See "The Neighborhood Playhouse" and "Rachel: A Play of Protest, by Angelina W. Grimké," AnGP, Box 33-13, Folder 225.

26. In the late nineteenth and early twentieth centuries, travel was a preferred prescription for men suffering from "neurasthenia," a diagnosis comprehending various nervous disorders brought on by overwork and stress (Showalter 65–66). In *Up from Slavery*, Booker T. Washington has a journey paid for by friends who "noticed that [he] seemed unusually tired" and insisted he go on a trip to Europe (159).

27. See Egan.

28. See Meier 123; and J. Stephens 333.

29. I refer to spirituals such as "Oh, Mary Don't You Weep," "Mary Had a Baby," and "Hail Mary." On Mary and universal motherhood in the United States, see Hurll xiii.

30. Archibald Grimké to Home Ones, 22 Jan. 1895, FGP, Box 40-3, Folder 119.

31. Archibald Grimké to Home Ones, 22 Jan. 1895, FGP, Box 40-3, Folder 119.

32. In another letter, Archibald continued peering through the dark glass of modern eyes to see the reality beyond. He wrote of attending a Catholic mass, during which he "saw some young girls kneeling in the . . . striking manner of Holbein, that singular blending which that old Master lived to depict." Archibald Grimké to Home Ones, 1 Feb. 1895, FGP, Box 40-3, Folder 111.

33. Of course, *Rachel* is not the originator of this tradition. The previously mentioned African American spirituals operate according to a similar logic.

34. See John Henry Newman's "Mary Is the 'Rosa Mystica,' the Mystical Rose" in his *Prayers, Verses, and Devotions* (168–69).

35. Archibald Grimké to Home Ones, 14 Apr. 1895, FGP, Box 40-3, Folder 113.

36. Archibald Grimké to Angelina Grimké, 10 May 1898, AnGP, Box 38-4, Folder 68.

37. James Weldon Johnson to Grace Nail Johnson, 8 May 1912, JWJP, Series III, Box 41, Folder 21; and James Weldon Johnson to Grace Nail Johnson, 26 June 1912, JWJP, Series III, Box 41, Folder 22.

38. Here I draw on Joseph Roach's notion of *surrogation*, described as a performative "substitution" that generates anxiety and subsequent "failures of memory" (6).

39. Archibald Grimké to Angelina Grimké, 6 Oct. 1897, AnGP, Box 38-4, Folder 67; and Archibald Grimké to Angelina Grimké, 21 Feb. 1898, AnGP, Box 38-4, Folder 68.

40. For more on Hubbard, see "Lady Vice-Consul."

Part III: Hip-to-macy

1. For Hughes's involvement in a diplomatic conflict between the United States and Soviet Union, see McDowell, "Conversations" 292–93. For Hughes's account of speaking at the same event with the wife of a US consul in Japan, see his *I Wonder as I Wander* 242–43. For Hughes's address at the opening of the US Information Agency Library in Accra, Ghana, see his "American Interest in African Culture."

2. See Pease; Rowe et al.; and Kaplan, "Left."

3. For a useful discussion of the move from national to transnational geography, see Dimock, "Planet" 3.

4. On US imperialism, see Kaplan, *Anarchy*; on the global South, see for instance Stecopoulos; on the borderland, see Anzaldúa; on Americanity, see Saldívar; on the Atlantic world, see Gilroy, *Black*; on the Pacific Rim, see Wilson; on the hemisphere, see Levander and Levine; on the planet, see Dimock, *Through*.

5 / Diplomats but Ersatz

1. On Du Bois at the Pan-African Conference of 1900, see D. Lewis, *W. E. B. Du Bois: Biography* 248–51. For Du Bois as founder and secretary and Gibbs Hunt as assistant secretary, see Du Bois's "The Pan-African Congress" 271–72.

2. Du Bois used this phrase in his essay "Pan-Africa in Portugal." Here, he recounts his activities during the PAC sessions and remarks, "The American Minister [to Portugal] . . . wish[ed] to see me and I called and had a pleasant meeting." Then, preparing readers for future accounts of his postsession travels to Liberia, Du Bois states, "And now as a sort of ambassador of Pan-Africa I turn my face toward Africa." Skinner recounts that Du Bois was turning to Africa because he had arranged to be appointed

(for the span of a month) Calvin Coolidge's "Special Envoy" with the rank of "Envoy Extraordinary and Minister Plenipotentiary" in attendance at the Liberian president's inauguration (491–98). In fact, his meeting with the US minister in Portugal was "a courtesy call" as "one senior official representing the United States to another" (D. Lewis, *W. E. B. Du Bois: The Fight* 116).

3. In William Hunt's unpublished autobiography, "From Cabin to Consulate," he explains how Ida Gibbs's advocacy helped him receive his consular appointment (64).

4. For biographical information on the Hunts, see Alexander, as well as Blakely's "Hunt, Ida Alexander Gibbs" and "Hunt, William H[enry]."

5. Quote taken from D. Lewis, *W. E. B. Du Bois: Biography* 575.

6. See Du Bois's "The Pan African Congress" 271 and his "The Third Pan-African Congress."

7. See D. Lewis, *W. E. B. Du Bois: Biography* 561.

8. In other editions of *The Republic*, see Book 10, 601d. The development of Kautilya's character (as well as Matthew's) is informed by dialogues in *The Republic*. This becomes clear as Matthew and Kautilya debate the merits of "democracy" and "oligarchy" (Du Bois, *Dark* 283–87), continuing the dialogue in *The Republic*, Book 8.

9. Ida Gibbs Hunt to W. E. B. Du Bois, 11 Feb. 1924, *DBP*, Reel 13, Frames 835–36.

10. Quote taken from the PAC's 1923 meeting program, "The Pan-African Congress: Third Biennial Sessions," WHHP, Box 55-3, Folder 56.

11. For Gibbs Hunt and the Booklovers Club, see Crowder 172.

12. In Gibbs Hunt's speech titled "Reading," she spoke of writing poetry and of manuscripts' rejection and acceptance as if she had personal experience (25–27). She is known to have used at least one pseudonym, "Iola Gibson." In concluding an apparently unpublished piece titled "The New Sphere of Woman," she signed her name "Iola Gibson" and noted that this is "a pen name sometimes used by Ida Gibbs Hunt" (8). She also used this pen name to sign "After the Rhinelander Case," a letter to the editor of the European edition of the *New York Herald*. In 1931, she submitted work to Du Bois that she said was "signed [with] a 'nom de plume' which I have used sometimes." Ida Gibbs Hunt to W. E. B. Du Bois, 24 Jan. 1931, *DBP*, Reel 34, Frame 1184. However, the *Crisis* never includes any work by "Iola Gibson," which may suggest that Du Bois consistently declined her work or perhaps that she sometimes used a pseudonym besides "Iola Gibson." Du Bois published Gibbs Hunt's article "The Hurricane" under her own name.

13. For the narrative of how copies of Gibbs Hunt's poems found their way into the Kendrick-Brooks Family Papers, I draw on conversations with Adele Logan Alexander. Alexander's *Parallel Worlds* discusses "To France" as written during the months of preparing for the 1919 PAC meetings (175). Given the two poems' similar rhetorical strategies, my assumption is that Gibbs Hunt wrote "To Belgium" during the same time period that she wrote "To France."

14. For instance, Du Bois's "The Pan-African Congress" reproduces the PAC's resolutions to be presented at the Paris Peace Conference (273). His "The Second Pan-African Congress" references a "Special Committee to visit the Assembly of the League of Nations" (119).

15. This international formation runs counter to what Edwards describes as vagabond internationalism (198).

16. This phrasing (qtd. in Malanczuk 75) was first included in the 1933 Montevideo

Convention on the Rights and Duties of States, but diplomatic recognition has long played an important role in the legitimization of states, as seen in *The Education of Henry Adams*, when Adams (recounting the scene of his father's ambassadorship to England) describes the national validation that the Southern States gained when the British foreign secretary "received the rebel emissaries," which implied a "recognition of [the Confederacy's] independence" (115). This international commonplace is not far from Kautilya's mind when she acknowledges that Bwodpur lacks sovereignty as long as it "sent no [diplomatic] ministers to foreign lands" (Du Bois, *Dark* 229).

17. Such proclamations include Du Bois's "To the World" and his "Manifesto to the League of Nations," published in the *Crisis* in 1921.

18. On "Jesus Christ in Texas" and "The Coming of John," see Moses, *Black* 142–43.

19. See for instance Mullen 20–21; and Ahmad, *Landscapes* 165–66.

20. Monica L. Miller suggests that the scene is designed to bring the novel into "engagement with actual pieces of art" (155).

21. See Du Bois's "Third Pan-African Congress" (121).

22. See Du Bois's "Pan-African Congress" (274) and his "Third Pan-African Congress" (121–22).

23. Ida Gibbs Hunt to W. E. B. Du Bois, 12 July 1918, *DBP*, Reel 6, Frames 579–81.

24. See Ahmad, "More" 778; Moses, *Black* 148; and Mullen 14.

25. For reference to the UNIA's ambassadors, see Garvey 2: 295–96; and 5: liv and 568.

26. Garvey in 1922 used the notion of diplomacy to rationalize his own dialogue with the Klan: "The Universal Negro Improvement Association . . . must be led by diplomacy; . . . it does not pay us in America to offend any organized group of whi[te] men" (4: 725).

27. I allude to Karl Marx's quotation, famously borrowed by Edward Said as an epigraph for *Orientalism*. Years after publishing *Dark Princess*, Du Bois overtly expressed this concern, observing that at an upcoming United Nations meeting, "colonial peoples will, for the most part, be represented either by the nations owning or governing them or at best by representatives chosen by these master nations." He resented that "not a single person of Negro descent will have any voice save in the case of Ethiopia and Liberia, which are free nations" (qtd. in Krenn 11).

28. See Ida Gibbs Hunt to W. E. B. Du Bois, 5 July 1928, and W. E. B. Du Bois to Ida Gibbs Hunt, 3 Aug. 1928, *DBP*, Reel 25, Frames 742–43.

29. After the London session of the Third Pan-African Congress, Du Bois visited the Hunts in Saint-Étienne. Du Bois wrote of this event at least three times in the *Crisis*. See Du Bois's "Sketches," "Journey," and "Pan-Africa in Portugal."

30. Lillie Mae Hubbard to Du Bois, 17 Feb. 1929, *DBP*, Reel 28, Frames 716–18; Lillie Mae Hubbard to Du Bois, 2 May 1929, *DBP*, Reel 28, Frames 720–22.

6 / The Practice of Hip-to-macy

1. On this diplomatic milieu, see W. Roberts 37.

2. On the definition and origins of public diplomacy, see Tuch 3–38; and W. Roberts 44. On soft power, see especially Nye 44–55.

3. See Dudziak 6–17.

4. On jazz diplomacy, see Von Eschen, *Satchmo*. On radio distribution and jazz programs, see Von Eschen, *Satchmo* 15–16. Borstelmann offers an enlightening

discussion of Voice of America's celebratory broadcasting on the success of *Brown v. Board of Education* (93–94). On Anderson, see Keiler 261–92.

5. In "I Choose Exile," Wright reveals that US officials worried his unofficial commentary on race could damage the United States' image (8).

6. Wright to Paul Reynolds, 4 Feb. 1955. MFP, Box 31, Folder 2 (Richard Wright Letters Project [3 of 4]).

7. Wright to Paul Reynolds, 4 Feb. 1955. In this letter, the emphasis with which Wright handles the *official* aspect of his freelance status resonates with Frances Stonor Saunders's description of one CCF insider as "America's official unofficial cultural propagandist" (64).

8. On the CCF's outing as a CIA front, see Coleman 219–34.

9. On Wright as a strictly independent journalist unworried by CCF funding, see Fabre 417; and Webb 381. On this point, several subsequent treatments of Wright in Indonesia have followed Webb's and Fabre's influential biographical accounts. Important treatments of *The Color Curtain* include V. Smith; Mullen 43–71; Hakutani; Stecopoulos 145–58; and Singh. For general treatments of Wright's Indonesian travels, see Fabre 416–25; Gayle 256–61; Rowley 462–69; and King 240–41.

10. As New Negro hip-to-macy branched into US public diplomacy's hipsterism after the Second World War, the loose ties between the state and its cultural representatives came to provide for the "individual right to freedom of action, expression, and choice" that David Harvey emphasizes as one of the neoliberal state's hallmarks (64).

11. On this influence, see also Sukartiah 95.

12. Thanks to Eric Teng, Anggita Putri, and Keith Foulcher for help with Indonesian translations.

13. Josselson to Wright, 23 Feb. 1955, IACFR, Series 2, Box 304, Folder 11. On Josselson as CCF director and CIA officer, see Saunders 153–56; and Coleman 6.

14. For Lubis's comments, see Passin 134–35.

15. *Harian Rakjat* described segregated schools with headlines such as "Inilah Demokrasi Amerika!" (This Is American Democracy!), "Negro di Amerika" (The Negro in America), and "Nasib Negro di AS" (The Fate of the Negro in the US).

16. Wright's essay appears as the third chapter of *Kegagalan "Tuhan"-Komunis*, translated by L. E. Hakim.

17. *Siasat* commented on Wright's contribution to *The God That Failed*. *Siasat* also directed readers to Wright's novel *The Outsider*, summarized as presenting the Communist Party's worst victims as those who most vociferously deny their victimhood (Sudjatmoko and Sani). Wright's contribution to the anticommunist anthology was also mentioned in the newspaper article "Richard Wright & Bau Kakus Dikamar."

18. The hazy difference between official CCF employment and Wright's officially designated freelance status is illustrated in an apparent misstep by *Indonesia Raya*, which upon Wright's arrival published a front-page photograph of him with a caption identifying him with the CCF, as "Correspondent for Encounter magazine" ("Telah").

19. Wright to Reynolds, 4 Feb. 1955. For propaganda reasons, the United States also was expediting passports for several independent African American reporters to attend the conference (Gordon 300). See also Plummer 248.

20. On the United States' orchestration of independent expression that served foreign policy ends, see Saunders 252–78; and Von Eschen, "Who's" 116–17.

21. On the distinction between a representative delegate and a representative symbol, see R. Williams, *Keywords* 268.

22. For further details on Studieclub Konfrontasi, see Roberts and Foulcher 799–801.

23. English translations from the French are taken from the lecture as published in *White Man, Listen!*

24. The *Temps Modernes* lecture was a translation of Wright's "Speech for a White Audience" (Cobb 239). The 1957 version was included in the emphatically titled *White Man, Listen!*

25. The superscript 2s in this quote are present in the original. According to the conventions of written Indonesian at this time, the superscript 2 functioned to pluralize a noun.

26. The 1957 lecture contains this quotation, but the 1948 and 1955 versions do not. It seems Wright informally tested the line at the end of the Konfrontasi lecture.

27. See RWP, MSS 3, Box 31, Folder 433. Thanks to David Hill and Keith Foulcher for sending handwriting samples for comparison.

28. See Passin 38–44.

29. For insight into the likely texture of this conversation on industrialization, see Lubis, *Twilight* 122–24. Wright's hosts would have been less concerned about the general menaces of industrialization and more concerned about Wright's specific ideas on the role of dictators in industrialization.

30. See Wright, "Tradition" 79.

31. On cultures of US imperialism, I refer to work inspired by such essays as Amy Kaplan's 1993 "'Left Alone with America.'" On studies in black internationalism, Paul Gilroy's *The Black Atlantic* has been foundational.

32. The quote is taken from Cohn 409. For more on public diplomacy and cultural bridges, see Tuch 70; and Zolov 219–20.

33. For background on Vuyk's account, see Roberts and Foulcher.

34. On the *Gelanggang* column, see Teeuw 115. The interview appeared under the names of Sudjatmoko and Sani, as editors. Given the continuities between the interview and Sani's later writing on Wright, it seems most likely that Sani interviewed Wright.

35. On these essays, see Davis and Fabre 89–90. The editors of the CCF magazines were "free to make such selections as they like for one or more articles" (Lasky).

36. Here I draw on Julia Kristeva's famous discussion of intertextuality (66).

37. While in English the word *dark* may describe both skin and mirrors or glass more generally, the word *gelap* (*Konfrontasi*'s translation of *dark*) would not seem to have preserved the English word's bicontextual meaning in 1950s Indonesia. During this era, *katja gelap* corresponded to the English *dark glass*, but the phrase *kulit gelap* does not yet seem to have emerged as idiomatic for *dark skin*. E-mail communication with Keith Foulcher, 31 Dec. 2011.

38. Clippings are in RWP, MSS 3, Box 29, Folder 416.

39. Elsewhere, Lubis's friend Beb Vuyk also discussed Wright's perspective on Africa as indebted to Wright's unique lenses or glasses ("Black").

40. One source offers this version of the prophecy: "For ten generations a great white buffalo will plough the rice fields. . . . When the people have finally accepted the Divine Will . . . , God . . . will send them an ally. A little yellow monkey . . . will

rule over [Java] for the life of one maize plant" (Huie 6). For a midcentury Indonesian source reading the Japanese as Jayabaya's "yellow monkey," see Mataram 32 and 61–68. Pramoedya Ananta Toer recalled, "Everyone, myself included, was preoccupied with the predictions found in *Jangka Jayabaya*" (*Mute's* 156).

41. See "Richard Wright & Bau Kakus Dikamar."

42. See Baldwin's "Everybody's Protest Novel." Sani knew of Baldwin's essay in 1955 but misunderstood it as suggesting *Native Son* was an advancement over *Uncle Tom's Cabin* (Sudjatmoko and Sani 22).

43. On Pramoedya Ananta Toer as an editor of *Sebaran B.M.K.N.*, I draw on Astuti Ananta Toer's inclusion of *Sebaran*'s editorial introduction in Pramoedya Toer's collected essays, *Menggelinding I* (448–49). Currently writing the first comprehensive literary biography of Toer, Hilmar Farid notes that to his knowledge, Toer "never wrote nor spoke about meeting with Wright" (e-mail communication, 4 Dec. 2008).

44. Of course, Wright's Indonesian travel could have uses in public diplomacy beyond creating cultural bridges with Indonesians. Jean-Paul Freyss, of Voice of America, wrote to Wright's publisher on USIA stationery. Claiming his letter had nothing to do with Voice of America, he was grateful for the opportunity to write a review of *The Color Curtain*, thus giving him the chance to make Wright's book better known internationally. Freyss to Peguy Amend, 23 Apr. 1956, RWP, Box 31, Folder 442.

45. For useful commentary on statistics in a literary context, see Dimock, *Through* 55–56.

46. See Lasky.

47. In considering this chaotic model, I benefit from John Ernest's discussion of a classic scenario in chaos theory: the leaf controlled by complex currents as it floats on a stream (471–72).

48. Jean-José Marchand to Wright, 21 Dec. [1955, 1956, or 1957?], RWP, Box 31, Folder 433. On Wright's CCF-supported lecture on the psychology of oppressed peoples, see Kinnamon 371.

49. On *Konfrontasi*'s decline and Wright's death, I draw on Foulcher 53–54; and Gayle xv.

Epilogue

1. For one of many comparisons between the Crusades and the US invasion of Iraq, see Pinkerton.

2. See Powell, "Remarks."

3. On Rice's confirmation hearing, see Allen, Tillery, and Walton.

4. Andrew Goldman's phrase summarizes his reading of Donald Rumsfeld's memoir, *Known and Unknown*, which represents Rice's emphasis on "bridging and consensus" (329).

5. See Drezner; and Porter.

6. See Morrison, "Talk."

7. This domestic trend is emblematized by some of former Arkansas governor Mike Huckabee's puzzlingly inaccurate 2011 commentary: "If you think about it, [Obama's] perspective as growing up in Kenya with a Kenyan father and grandfather . . . is very different than ours because he probably grew up hearing that the British were a bunch of imperialists who persecuted his grandfather" (Madison).

8. On the State Department's eventual support for the program, see Dobbs.

9. On humility and Obama's internationalism, see Lizza 55. Undoubtedly unaware of Wright's criticism of the artistic ambassadors' conciliatory tones, former Massachusetts governor Mitt Romney described Obama's international stance in terms of a so-called American Apology Tour, characterized by a "reluctance to speak out with confidence for American ideals abroad" (27). For Belafonte's dissatisfaction, see Belafonte 441.

10. See R. Williams, *Marxism* 133–34.

Works Cited

Adams, Henry. *The Education of Henry Adams*. 1918. Ed. Ernest Samuels. Boston: Houghton Mifflin, 1973. Print.

Ahmad, Dohra. *Landscapes of Hope: Anti-colonial Utopianism in America*. New York: Oxford UP, 2009. Print.

———. "'More than Romance': Genre and Geography in *Dark Princess*." *ELH* 69 (2002): 775–803. *Project Muse*. Web. 26 July 2010.

Alexander, Adele Logan. *Parallel Worlds: The Remarkable Gibbs-Hunts and the Enduring (In)significance of Melanin*. Charlottesville: U of Virginia P, 2010. Print.

Allen, Carol Dawn. *Peculiar Passages: Black Women Playwrights, 1875 to 2000*. New York: Lang, 2005. Print.

Allen, Josephine A. V., Alvin Tillery, Jr., and Hanes Walton, Jr. "The Making of African American Foreign Policymakers: Senate Confirmation Hearings on Secretaries of State Colin Powell and Condoleezza Rice." *African Americans in Global Affairs: Contemporary Perspectives*. Ed. Michael L. Clemons. Lebanon, NH: UP of New England, 2010. 118–43. Print.

"The Amateur Players' Association." *Times* [London] 12 May 1908: 17. Print.

Anderson, Benedict. *Imagined Communities: Reflections on the Origin and Spread of Nationalism*. 1983. Rev. ed. London: Verso, 1991. Print.

Andrews, William L. Introduction. *The Autobiography of an Ex-Colored Man*. By James Weldon Johnson. New York: Penguin, 1990. vii–xxvii. Print.

Anzaldúa, Gloria. *Borderlands/La Frontera: The New Mestiza*. San Francisco: Aunt Lute, 1987. Print.

Austin, J. L. *How to Do Things with Words*. 1962. 2nd ed. Ed. J. O. Urmson and Marina Sbisà. Cambridge, MA: Harvard UP, 1975. Print.

Baker, Houston, Jr. *Modernism and the Harlem Renaissance*. Chicago: U of Chicago P, 1987. Print.

———. *Singers of Daybreak: Studies in Black American Literature*. Washington, DC: Howard UP, 1974. Print.

Bakhtin, M. M. *The Dialogic Imagination: Four Essays*. Ed. Michael Holquist. Trans. Caryl Emerson and Michael Holquist. Austin: U of Texas P, 1981. Print.

Baldwin, James. "Everybody's Protest Novel." 1949. *Notes of a Native Son*. Boston: Beacon, 1955. 13–23. Print.

Baldwin, Kate A. *Beyond the Color Line and the Iron Curtain: Reading Encounters between Black and Red, 1922–1963*. Durham, NC: Duke UP, 2002. Print.

Baraka, Amiri. "Somebody Blew Up America." 2001. *Somebody Blew Up America & Other Poems*. Philipsburg, St. Martin: House of Nehesi, 2004. 41–50. Print.

Belafonte, Harry, with Michael Shnayerson. *My Song: A Memoir*. New York: Knopf, 2011. Print.

"Belafonte Won't Back Down from Powell Slave Reference." *CNN* 14 Oct. 2002. Web. 28 May 2009.

Bercovitch, Sacvan. *The Puritan Origins of the American Self*. New Haven, CT: Yale UP, 1975. Print.

Bérubé, Michael. "American Studies without Exceptions." *PMLA* 118 (2003): 103–13. Print.

Bhabha, Homi K. "Introduction: Narrating the Nation." *Nation and Narration*. Ed. Homi K. Bhabha. London: Routledge, 1990. 1–7. Print.

———. *The Location of Culture*. London: Routledge, 1994. Print.

Blakely, Allison. "Black U.S. Consuls and Diplomats and Black Leadership, 1880–1920." *Umoja: A Scholarly Journal of Black Studies* ns 1.1 (1977): 1–16. Print.

———. "Hunt, Ida Alexander Gibbs." *Dictionary of American Negro Biography*. Ed. Rayford W. Logan and Michael R. Winston. New York: Norton, 1982. 336. Print.

———. "Hunt, William H[enry]." *Dictionary of American Negro Biography*. Ed. Rayford W. Logan and Michael R. Winston. New York: Norton, 1982. 336–37. Print.

Blum, Edward J. *W. E. B. Du Bois: American Prophet*. Philadelphia: U of Pennsylvania P, 2007. Print.

"Books by Prominent Negroes." Advertisement. *Crisis* July 1917: 149. Print.

Borstelmann, Thomas. *The Cold War and the Color Line: American Race Relations in the Global Arena*. Cambridge, MA: Harvard UP, 2001. Print.

Bourne, Randolph S. "Trans-national America." *Atlantic Monthly* July 1916: 86–97. Print.

B[raithwaite], W[illiam] S[tanley]. "The Poems of James Weldon Johnson." *Boston Evening Transcript* 12 Dec. 1917: part 2, 9. Print.

Brantley, Daniel. "Black Diplomacy and Frederick Douglass' Caribbean Experiences, 1871 and 1889–1891: The Untold Story." *Phylon* 45 (1984): 197–209. Print.

Breeden, James O., ed. *Advice among Masters: The Ideal in Slave Management in the Old South*. Westport, CT: Greenwood, 1980. Print.

Brown, Norma. Introduction. *A Black Diplomat in Haiti: The Diplomatic Correspondence of U.S. Minister Frederick Douglass from Haiti, 1889–1891*. Vol. 1. Ed. Norma Brown. Salisbury, NC: Documentary, 1977. i–v. Print.

Brown, William Wells. *The Escape; or, A Leap for Freedom*. 1858. Ed. John Ernest. Knoxville: U of Tennessee P, 2001. Print.

Bruce, Dickson D., Jr. *Archibald Grimké: Portrait of a Black Independent*. Baton Rouge: Louisiana State UP, 1993. Print.

———. *Black American Writing from the Nadir: The Evolution of a Literary Tradition, 1877–1915*. Baton Rouge: Louisiana State UP, 1989. Print.

Bruce, John E. "The Spirit of Diane." *Colored American: A National Negro Newspaper* 19 Apr. 1902: 1, 4. *Chronicling America: Historic American Newspapers*. Web. 7 Feb. 2012.

Bunche, Ralph J. *A Brief and Tentative Analysis of Negro Leadership*. Ed. Jonathan Scott Holloway. New York: NYU P, 2005. Print.

Bundy, Richard C. "Folk-Tales from Liberia (in Abstract)." *Journal of American Folk-lore* 32 (1919): 406–27. *JSTOR*. Web. 15 July 2010.

Burke, Edmund. "Speech to the Electors of Bristol on Being Elected (Nov. 1774)." *The Political Philosophy of Edmund Burke*. Ed. Iain Hampsher-Monk. London: Longman, 1987. 108–11. Print.

Camphor, Alexander Priestly. *Missionary Story Sketches: Folk-lore from Africa*. 1909. Freeport, NY: Books for Libraries, 1971. Print.

Carby, Hazel V. *Race Men*. Cambridge, MA: Harvard UP, 1998. Print.

Carroll, Anne Elizabeth. *Word, Image, and the New Negro: Representation and Identity in the Harlem Renaissance*. Bloomington: Indiana UP, 2005. Print.

Carruth, Mary C. "Grimké, Angelina Weld." *The Oxford Companion to African American Literature*. Ed. William L. Andrews et al. New York: Oxford UP, 1997. 329. Print.

"Casual Comment." *Dial: A Semi-monthly Journal of Literary Criticism, Discussion, and Information* 1 July 1913: 9–12. Print.

Charras, Françoise. "The West Indian Presence in Alain Locke's *The New Negro* (1925)." *Temples for Tomorrow: Looking Back at the Harlem Renaissance*. Ed. Geneviève Fabre and Michel Feith. Bloomington: Indiana UP, 2001. 270–87. Print.

Cheng, Anne Anlin. *The Melancholy of Race: Psychoanalysis, Assimilation, and Hidden Grief*. New York: Oxford UP, 2001. Print.

Chesnutt, Charles W. *Frederick Douglass*. Boston: Small, 1899. Print.

———. *The Marrow of Tradition*. 1901. Ed. Eric Sundquist. New York: Penguin, 1993. Print.

Clemons, Michael L. "Colin L. Powell and the Iraq War: Bureaucratic Actor and Foreign Policy Dissenter." *African Americans in Global Affairs: Contemporary Perspectives.* Ed. Michael L. Clemons. Lebanon, NH: UP of New England, 2010. 144–68. Print.

Clifford, James. "Histories of the Tribal and the Modern." *Art in America* Apr. 1985: 164–77, 215. Print.

Cobb, Nina Kressner. "Richard Wright and the Third World." *Critical Essays on Richard Wright.* Ed. Yoshinobu Hakutani. Boston: Hall, 1982. 228–39. Print.

Cohn, Deborah. "Combatting Anti-Americanism during the Cold War: Faulkner, the State Department, and Latin America." *Mississippi Quarterly* 59 (2006): 395–413. *Ebsco.* Web. 27 July 2010.

Coleman, Peter. *The Liberal Conspiracy: The Congress for Cultural Freedom and the Struggle for the Mind of Postwar Europe.* New York: Free, 1989. Print.

Congress for Cultural Freedom (CCF). "Manifesto of Congress for Cultural Freedom (Berlin, 1950)." *The Liberal Conspiracy: The Congress for Cultural Freedom and the Struggle for the Mind of Postwar Europe.* By Peter Coleman. New York: Free, 1989. 249–51. Print.

Conrad, Joseph. *Heart of Darkness.* 1902. Mineola, NY: Dover, 1990. Print.

"Consul Grimke [*sic*]." *Washington Evening Star* 24 Sept. 1894: 1. Print.

Contee, Clarence G., Sr. "Downing, Henry F[rancis]." *Dictionary of American Negro Biography.* Ed. Rayford W. Logan and Michael R. Winston. New York: Norton, 1982. 188–89. Print.

Cox, Oliver C. "Leadership among Negroes in the United States." *Studies in Leadership: Leadership and Democratic Action.* Ed. Alvin W. Goulder. New York: Harper, 1950. 228–71. Print.

Crowder, Ralph L. "Booklovers Club." *Encyclopedia of the Harlem Renaissance.* Vol. 1. Ed. Cary D. Wintz and Paul Finkelman. New York: Routledge, 2004. 172–73. Print.

Crummell, Alexander. *Civilization and Black Progress: Selected Writings of Alexander Crummell on the South.* Ed. J. R. Oldfield. Charlottesville: U of Virginia P, 1995. Print.

Dash, J. Michael. *Haiti and the United States: National Stereotypes and the Literary Imagination.* 2nd ed. New York: St. Martin's, 1997. Print.

Davis, Charles T., and Michel Fabre. *Richard Wright: A Primary Bibliography.* Boston: Hall, 1982. Print.

Dawson, Horace G., Jr. "First African-American Diplomat." *Foreign Service Journal* Jan. 1993: 42–45.

Day, Charles William. *Five Years' Residence in the West Indies.* Vol. 2. London: Colburn, 1852. Print.

Dayan, Joan. "A Few Stories about Haiti, or, Stigma Revisited." *Research in African Literatures* 35.2 (2004): 157–72. *JSTOR.* Web. 15 July 2010.

Deleuze, Gilles, and Félix Guattari. *Anti-Oedipus: Capitalism and Schizophrenia.*

Trans. Robert Hurley, Mark Seem, and Helen R. Lane. Minneapolis: U of Minnesota P, 1983. Print.

Derrida, Jacques. *Of Grammatology*. Trans. Gayatri Chakravorty Spivak. Baltimore: Johns Hopkins UP, 1997. Print.

Dillon, Nell C. *Love's Toll*. New York: International Authors' Association, 1917. Print.

Dimock, Wai Chee. "Planet and America, Set and Subset." *Shades of the Planet: American Literature as World Literature*. Ed. Wai Chee Dimock and Lawrence Buell. Princeton, NJ: Princeton UP, 2007. 1–16. Print.

———. *Through Other Continents: American Literature across Deep Time*. Princeton, NJ: Princeton UP, 2006. Print.

"Diploma." *Oxford English Dictionary*. 2nd ed. 1989. Print.

Dirlik, Arif. "The End of Colonialism? The Colonial Modern in the Making of Global Modernity." *boundary 2* 32.1 (2005): 1–31. *Dukejournals*. Web. 25 Sept. 2007.

"Distinguished Colored Men." Chromolithograph. New York: Muller, 1883. Library of Congress Prints and Photographs Division, Washington, DC. *LoC Online Catalogue*. Web. 15 July 2010.

Dixon, Thomas. *The Leopard's Spots: A Romance of the White Man's Burden—1865–1900*. New York: Grosset, 1902. Print.

Dobbs, Michael. "Obama Overstates Kennedys' Role in Helping His Father." *Washington Post* 30 Mar. 2008: A01. Web. 12 June 2009.

"Does Powell Have Solid Standing on Bush's Foreign Policy Team?" *CNN* 10 May 2003. Web. 29 May 2009.

Dolisane-Ebosse, Cécile. Rev. of *Dreams from My Father*, by Barack Obama. Trans. R. H. Mitsch. *Research in African Literatures* 41.1 (2010): 190–92. *Project Muse*. Web. 27 Apr. 2010.

Douglass, Frederick. *A Black Diplomat in Haiti: The Diplomatic Correspondence of U.S. Minister Frederick Douglass from Haiti, 1889–1891*. 2 vols. Ed. Norma Brown. Salisbury, NC: Documentary, 1977. Print.

———. *Life and Times of Frederick Douglass*. 1893. *Autobiographies*. Ed. Henry Louis Gates, Jr. New York: Library of America, 1994. 453–1045. Print.

———. *The Life and Writings of Frederick Douglass*. 5 vols. New York: International, 1950. Print.

———. *Narrative of the Life of Frederick Douglass, an American Slave*. 1845. *Autobiographies*. Ed. Henry Louis Gates, Jr. New York: Library of America, 1994. 1–102. Print.

Downing, Henry Francis. *The American Cavalryman: A Liberian Romance*. New York: Neale, 1917. Print.

———. *The Arabian Lovers; or, The Sacred Jar*. London: Griffiths, 1913. Print.

———. "A Black and White Tangle." *African Times and Orient Review* July, Aug., Sept., Oct., Nov.–Dec. 1913: 23–29, 67–74, 116–21, 161–65, 259–61. Print.

———. *A New Coon in Town: A Farcical Comedy Made in England.* [London]: n.p., 1914. Print.

———. "Samuel Coleridge Taylor." *Messenger* July, Sept., and Oct. 1926 and Jan. 1927: 200, 266–67, 298, 319, 8–9. Print.

Drake, St. Clair, and Horace R. Cayton. *Black Metropolis: A Study of Negro Life in a Northern City.* New York: Harcourt, 1945. Print.

Dreiser, Theodore. "Nigger Jeff." 1901. *The Best Short Stories of Theodore Dreiser.* Cleveland, OH: World, 1956. Print.

Drezner, Daniel W. "Has Taro Aso Ever Met Condoleezza Rice?" *FP: Foreign Policy* 22 Mar. 2007. Web. 28 May 2009.

Du Bois, W. E. B. *Black Folk, Then and Now: An Essay in the History and Sociology of the Negro Race.* New York: Holt, 1939. Print.

———. "Criteria of Negro Art." *Crisis* Oct. 1926: 290–97. Print.

———. *Dark Princess: A Romance.* 1928. Intro. Claudia Tate. Jackson: UP of Mississippi, 1995. Print.

———. *Dusk of Dawn: An Essay toward an Autobiography of a Race Concept.* New York: Harcourt, 1940. Print.

———. "An Essay toward a History of the Black Man in the Great War." *Crisis* June 1919: 63–87. Print.

———. "Jesus Christ in Texas." *Darkwater: Voices from within the Veil.* 1920. New York: Schocken, 1969. 123–33. Print.

———. "The Journey of W. E. B. Du Bois." *Crisis* May 1924: 31. Print.

———. "Manifesto to the League of Nations." *Crisis* Nov. 1921: 18. Print.

———. "Of the Coming of John." *The Souls of Black Folk.* 1903. Ed. Brent Hayes Edwards. New York: Oxford UP, 2008. 153–66. Print.

———. "Pan-Africa in Portugal." *Crisis* Feb. 1924: 170. Print.

———. "The Pan-African Congress." *Crisis* Apr. 1919: 271–74. Print.

———. "A Pile of Books." *Crisis* Feb. 1915: 198–200. Print.

———. "A Second Journey to Pan-Africa." *New Republic* 7 Dec. 1921: 39–42. Print.

———. "The Second Pan-African Congress." *Crisis* July 1921: 119–20. Print.

———. "Sketches from Abroad." *Crisis* Mar. 1924: 203–05. Print.

———. *The Souls of Black Folk.* 1903. Ed. Brent Hayes Edwards. New York: Oxford UP, 2008. Print.

———. "The Talented Tenth." *The Negro Problem: A Series of Articles by Representative American Negroes of To-day.* New York: Pott, 1903. 33–75. Print.

———. "The Third Pan-African Congress." *Crisis* Jan. 1924: 120–22. Print.

———. "To the World (Manifesto of the Second Pan-African Congress)." *Crisis* Nov. 1921: 5–10. Print.

Du Chaillu, Paul. B. *A Journey to Ashango-land: And Further Penetration into Equatorial Africa.* New York: Harper, 1871. Print.

duCille, Ann. *The Coupling Convention: Sex, Text, and Tradition in Black Women's Fiction.* New York: Oxford UP, 1993. Print.

Dudziak, Mary L. *Cold War Civil Rights: Race and the Image of American Democracy.* Princeton, NJ: Princeton UP, 2000. Print.

Dunbar, Paul Laurence. "Representative American Negroes." *The Negro Problem: A Series of Articles by Representative American Negroes of To-day.* New York: Pott, 1903. 189–209. Print.

Durham, John S. "Address of Hon. J. S. Durham, Ex-Minister to Haiti." *In Memoriam: Frederick Douglass.* Philadelphia: Yorston, 1897. 219–21. Print.

———. "Anecdotes from the Antilles." *Lippincott's Monthly Magazine* Sept. 1899: 474–80. Print.

———. "Confessions of a Man Who Did." *Southern Workman and Hampton School Record* May 1899: 168–72. Print.

———. *Diane, Priestess of Haiti. Lippincott's Monthly Magazine* Apr. 1902: 385–466. Print.

Dyson, Walter. Rev. of *Negro Culture in West Africa,* by George W. Ellis. *Journal of Negro History* 1 (1916): 95–96. Print.

Edwards, Brent Hayes. *The Practice of Diaspora: Literature, Translation, and the Rise of Black Internationalism.* Cambridge, MA: Harvard UP, 2003. Print.

Egan, Bill. "Europe and the Harlem Renaissance: 4—Paris." *Encyclopedia of the Harlem Renaissance.* Vol. 1. Ed. Cary D. Wintz and Paul Finkelman. New York: Routledge, 2004. 349–52. Print.

Ellis, George W. *The Leopard's Claw.* New York: International Authors' Association, 1917. Print.

———. "Liberia in the New Partition of West Africa." *Journal of Race Development* 9 (1919): 247–67. Print.

———. "Liberia in the Political Psychology of West Africa." *Journal of the Royal African Society* 12.45 (1912): 52–70. *JSTOR.* Web. 21 Sept. 2006.

———. *Negro Culture in West Africa.* New York: Neale, 1914. Print.

———. "Psychic Factors in the New American Race Situation." *Journal of Race Development* 7 (1917): 467–88. Print.

———. "The Psychology of American Race Prejudice." *Journal of Race Development* 5 (1915): 297–315. Print.

Ellison, Ralph. *Invisible Man.* 1952. New York: Vintage, 1980. Print.

Embassy of Indonesia. *The Cultural Life of Indonesia: Religion, the Arts, Education.* Washington, DC: H. K. Press, 1951. Print.

Emerson, Ralph Waldo. *Representative Men: Seven Lectures.* 1850. Boston: Osgood, 1876. Print.

———. "Self-Reliance." 1841. *Essays.* Boston: Houghton Mifflin, 1883. 47–87. Print.

Ernest, John. "Representing Chaos: William Craft's *Running a Thousand Miles for Freedom.*" *PMLA* 121 (2006): 469–83. Print.

Fabi, M. Giulia. *Passing and the Rise of the African American Novel.* Urbana: U of Illinois P, 2001. Print.

Fabre, Michel. *The Unfinished Quest of Richard Wright*. Trans. Isabel Barzun. New York: Morrow, 1973. Print.

Fauset, Jessie Redmon. *Comedy: American Style*. 1933. New York: Negro Universities Press, 1969. Print.

———. "Impressions of the Second Pan-African Congress." *Crisis* Nov. 1921: 12–18. Print.

Favor, J. Martin. *Authentic Blackness: The Folk in the New Negro Renaissance*. Durham, NC: Duke UP, 1999. Print.

Ferguson, Niall. "Virtual History: Towards a 'Chaotic' Theory of the Past." *Virtual History: Alternatives and Counterfactuals*. Ed. Niall Ferguson. New York: Basic, 1999. 1–90. Print.

Fishkin, Shelley Fisher. "Crossroads of Cultures: The Transnational Turn in American Studies—Presidential Address to the American Studies Association, November 12, 2004." *American Quarterly* 57.1 (2005): 17–57. *Project Muse*. Web. 28 Mar. 2007.

Fleming, John E. "George Washington Ellis and Africa, 1902–1910." Diss. Howard U, 1972. Print.

Fleming, John E., and Rayford W. Logan. "Ellis, George Washington." *Dictionary of American Negro Biography*. Ed. Rayford W. Logan and Michael R. Winston. New York: Norton, 1982. 211–12. Print.

Foley, Barbara. *Spectres of 1919: Class and Nation in the Making of the New Negro*. Urbana: U of Illinois P, 2003. Print.

"Foreword." *African Times and Orient Review* July 1912: iii–iv. Print.

Foster, Hal. "The 'Primitive' Unconscious of Modern Art." *October* 34 (1985): 45–70. Print.

Foster, John W. *The Practice of Diplomacy: As Illustrated in the Foreign Relations of the United States*. Boston: Houghton Mifflin, 1906. Print.

Foulcher, Keith. "Bringing the World Back Home: Cultural Traffic in *Konfrontasi*, 1954–1960." *Heirs to World Culture: Being Indonesian, 1950–1965*. Ed. Jennifer Lindsay and Maya H. T. Liem. Leiden, Netherlands: KITLV, 2012. 31–56. *KITLV*. Web. 2 Jan. 2012.

Freud, Sigmund. *Moses and Monotheism*. 1939. Trans. Katherine Jones. New York: Vintage, 1967. Print.

———. *Totem and Taboo: Resemblances between the Psychic Lives of Savages and Neurotics*. 1913. Mineola, NY: Dover, 1998. Print.

Friedman, Susan Stanford. "Periodizing Modernism: Postcolonial Modernities and the Space/Time Borders of Modernist Studies." *Modernism/modernity* 13 (2006): 425–43. Print.

Galván, Manuel de Jesús. *Enriquillo: Leyenda Histórica Dominicana (1503–1533)*. 1882. México, DF: Porrúa, 1976. Print.

Garvey, Marcus. *The Marcus Garvey and Universal Negro Improvement Association Papers*. Ed. Robert A. Hill. 7 vols. Berkeley: U of California P, 1983–1991. Print.

Gates, Henry Louis, Jr. "From Wheatley to Douglass: The Politics of Displacement." *Frederick Douglass: New Literary and Historical Essays.* Ed. Eric J. Sundquist. Cambridge: Cambridge UP, 1990. 47–65. Print.

———. *The Signifying Monkey: A Theory of African-American Literary Criticism.* New York: Oxford UP, 1988. Print.

———. "The Trope of a New Negro and the Reconstruction of the Image of the Black." *Representations* 24 (1988): 129–55. *JSTOR.* Web. 12 Sept. 2009.

Gates, Henry Louis, Jr., and Gene Andrew Jarrett. Introduction. *The New Negro: Readings on Race, Representation, and African American Culture, 1892–1938.* Princeton, NJ: Princeton UP, 2007. 1–20. Print.

Gayle, Addison. *Richard Wright: Ordeal of a Native Son.* Garden City, NY: Anchor, 1980. Print.

Gebhard, Caroline, and Barbara McCaskill. Introduction. *Post-Bellum, Pre-Harlem: African American Literature and Culture, 1877–1919.* New York: NYU P, 2006. 1–14. Print.

George, Rosemary Marangoly. *The Politics of Home: Postcolonial Relocations and Twentieth-Century Fiction.* Berkeley: U of California P, 1999. Print.

"George W. Ellis Issues 'The Leopard's Claw.'" *Chicago Defender* 6 July 1918: 15. Print.

Gibbs, Mifflin Wistar. *Shadow and Light: An Autobiography, with Reminiscences of the Last and Present Century.* 1902. Lincoln: U of Nebraska P, 1995. Print.

Gibbs, William E. "James Weldon Johnson: A Black Perspective on 'Big Stick' Diplomacy." *Diplomatic History* 8 (1984): 329–47. Print.

Gibbs Hunt, Ida [signed Iola Gibson]. "After the Rhinelander Case." *New York Herald* 10 Dec. 1925, European ed.: 4. Print.

———. "The Hurricane." *Crisis* Jan. 1929: 9, 24–26. Print.

——— [signed Iola Gibson]. "The New Sphere of Woman." KBFP, Box 13, Folder 8. Print.

———. "The Price of Peace." *Journal of Negro History* 23 (1938): 79–86. *JSTOR.* Web. 26 July 2010.

———. "Reading" (address likely given at M Street School ca. 1899). WHHP, Box 55-4, Folder 78. Print.

———. Rev. of *The American Cavalryman,* by Henry Francis Downing. *Journal of Negro History* 3 (1918): 444–45. *JSTOR.* Web. 7 Feb. 2005.

———. "To Belgium." KBFP, Box 13, Folder 8. Print.

———. "To France." KBFP, Box 13, Folder 8. Print.

Gillman, Susan. *Blood Talk: American Race Melodrama and the Culture of the Occult.* Chicago: U of Chicago P, 2003. Print.

Gilroy, Paul. *The Black Atlantic: Modernity and Double Consciousness.* Cambridge, MA: Harvard UP, 1993. Print.

———. *Small Acts: Thoughts on the Politics of Black Cultures.* London: Serpent's Tail, 1993. Print.

Gloster, Hugh M. *Negro Voices in American Fiction.* 1948. New York: Russell and Russell, 1965. Print.

Goellnicht, Donald C. "Passing as Autobiography: James Weldon Johnson's *The Autobiography of an Ex-Coloured Man.*" *African American Review* 30 (1996): 17–33. Print.

Goldman, Andrew. "Nobody Puts Condoleezza Rice in a Corner." *New York Times* 26 Apr. 2011. Web. 24 May 2011.

Goldsby, Jacqueline. "Keeping the 'Secret of Authorship': A Critical Look at the 1912 Publication of James Weldon Johnson's *Autobiography of an Ex-Colored Man.*" *Print Culture in a Diverse America.* Ed. James P. Danky and Wayne A. Wiegand. Urbana: U of Illinois P, 1998. 244–71. Print.

———. *A Spectacular Secret: Lynching in American Life and Literature.* Chicago: U of Chicago P, 2006. Print.

Goldstein, Leslie Friedman. "Racial Loyalty in America: The Example of Frederick Douglass." *Western Political Quarterly* 28 (1975): 463–76. Print.

Gordon, Eugene. "Seven Years since Bandung." *Freedomways: A Quarterly Review of the Negro Freedom Movement* 2.3 (1962): 298–306. Print.

Gourdine, Angeletta. "The *Drama* of Lynching in Two Blackwomen's Drama, or Relating Grimké's *Rachel* to Hansberry's *A Raisin in the Sun.*" *Modern Drama* 41 (1998): 533–45. Print.

Gramsci, Antonio. "The Intellectuals." *Selections from the Prison Notebooks.* Ed. and trans. Quintin Hoare and Geoffrey Nowell Smith. New York: International, 1971. 5–23. Print.

Green, Jeffery P. *Black Edwardians: Black People in Britain, 1901–1914.* London: Cass, 1998. Print.

Green, Tara T. *A Fatherless Child: Autobiographical Perspectives of African American Men.* Columbia: U of Missouri P, 2009. Print.

Griggs, Sutton E. *Imperium in Imperio.* 1899. Miami, FL: Mnemosyne, 1969. Print.

Grimké, Angelina W. "A Biographical Sketch of Archibald H. Grimke [*sic*]." *Opportunity* Feb. 1925: 44–47. Print.

———. *Rachel: A Play in Three Acts.* 1920. College Park, MD: McGrath, 1969. Print.

———. "'Rachel': The Play of the Month." 1920. *Selected Works of Angelina Weld Grimké.* Ed. Carolivia Herron. New York: Oxford UP, 1991. 413–16. Print.

———. "To My Father upon His Fifty-Fifth Birthday." *Selected Works of Angelina Weld Grimké.* Ed. Carolivia Herron. New York: Oxford UP, 1991. 61–63. Print.

Gruesser, John Cullen. *Black on Black: Twentieth-Century African American Writing about Africa.* Lexington: UP of Kentucky, 2000. Print.

"Haiti's Broken Promise." *New York Times* 25 Mar. 1891: 5. *ProQuest.* Web. 15 July 2010.

Hakim, L. E., trans. *Kegagalan "Tuhan"-Komunis*. Bandung: "Front Anti Komunis" Indonesia, [Feb.] 1955. Print.

Hakutani, Yoshinobu. "*The Color Curtain*: Richard Wright's Journey into Asia." *Richard Wright's Travel Writings: New Reflections*. Ed. Virginia Whatley Smith. Jackson: UP of Mississippi, 2001. 63–77. Print.

Halttunen, Karen. *Confidence Men and Painted Women: A Study of Middle-Class Culture in America, 1830–1870*. New Haven, CT: Yale UP, 1982. Print.

Harlan, Louis R. *Booker T. Washington: The Wizard of Tuskegee, 1901–1915*. New York: Oxford UP, 1983. Print.

Harrison, Hubert. *A Hubert Harrison Reader*. Ed. Jeffrey B. Perry. Middletown, CT: Wesleyan UP, 2001. Print.

Harvey, David. *A Brief History of Neoliberalism*. New York: Oxford UP, 2005. Print.

Heisch, Allison. "Wendell Phillips (1811–1884)." *Instructor's Guide for the Heath Anthology of American Literature*. 3rd ed. Ed. Paul Lauter. Boston: Houghton Mifflin, 1998. 236–39. Print.

Henriques, Guy. "Paris Diary: Witch-Hunting." *Tribune: Voice of the Left* [London] 14 May 1954: 3. Print.

"Henry Downing." *New York Times* 21 Feb. 1928: 21. Print.

"Henry F. Downing." *New York Amsterdam News* 29 Feb. 1928: 20. Print.

Herskovits, Melville J. *The Myth of the Negro Past*. 1941. Boston: Beacon, 1958. Print.

Hildreth, Richard. *Archy Moore, the White Slave; or, Memoirs of a Fugitive*. 1855. New York: Miller, 1857. Print.

Hill, David T. *Journalism and Politics in Indonesia: A Critical Biography of Mochtar Lubis (1922–2004) as Editor and Author*. London: Routledge, 2010. Print.

Himelhoch, Myra. "Frederick Douglass and Haiti's Mole St. Nicolas." *Journal of Negro History* 56 (1971): 161–80. *JSTOR*. Web. 15 July 2010.

Hirsch, David A. Hedrich. "Speaking Silences in Angelina Weld Grimké's 'The Closing Door' and 'Blackness.'" *African American Review* 26 (1992): 459–74. Print.

Horwitz, Richard P. "Coming to Terms with International American Studies." *The Fulbright Difference, 1948–1992*. Ed. Richard T. Arndt and David Lee Rubin. New Brunswick, NJ: Transaction, 1993. 459–68. Print.

Hughes, John Milton Charles. *The Negro Novelist: A Discussion of American Negro Novelists, 1940–1950*. New York: Citadel, 1953. Print.

Hughes, Langston. "American Interest in African Culture (Address at Opening of New USIS Center and Library, Accra, 29 June, 1962)." LHP, Box 483, Folder 12221. Print.

———. "Christ in Alabama." 1931. *The Collected Poems of Langston Hughes*. Ed. Arnold Rampersad. New York: Knopf, 1994. 143. Print.

———. *I Wonder as I Wander: An Autobiographical Journey.* 1956. Intro. Arnold Rampersad. New York: Hill, 1993. Print.

———. "The See-Saw of Race." 1946. *Langston Hughes and the* Chicago Defender: *Essays on Race, Politics, and Culture, 1942–1962.* Ed. Christopher C. De Santis. Urbana: U of Illinois P, 1995. 31–32. Print.

———. *Simple's Uncle Sam.* New York: Hill, 1965. Print.

Huie, Shirley Fenton. *The Forgotten Ones: Women and Children under Nippon.* Pymble, Australia: HarperCollins, 1992. Print.

Hull, Gloria T. *Color, Sex, & Poetry: Three Women Writers of the Harlem Renaissance.* Bloomington: Indiana UP, 1987. Print.

Hunt, William Henry. "From Cabin to Consulate: The Autobiography of William H. Hunt." Ed. and intro. Harold T. Pinkett. Unpublished ms.; copy held in Adele Logan Alexander's private collection. Print.

Hurll, Estelle M. *The Madonna in Art.* Boston: Page, 1898. Print.

Hurston, Zora Neale. *Tell My Horse: Voodoo and Life in Haiti and Jamaica.* 1938. New York: HarperPerennial, 1990. Print.

"Inilah Demokrasi Amerika!" *Harian Rakjat* 7 Apr. 1955: 1. Print.

"Items from Philadelphia." *New York Times* 8 Mar. 1902: BR12. *ProQuest.* Web. 15 July 2010.

Jackson, Miles M. "Letters to a Friend: Correspondence from James Weldon Johnson to George A. Towns." *Phylon* 29 (1968): 182–98. Print.

Jameson, Fredric. *Postmodernism, or, The Cultural Logic of Late Capitalism.* Durham, NC: Duke UP, 1991. Print.

Jarrett, Gene Andrew. *Representing the Race: A New Political History of African American Literature.* New York: NYU P, 2011. Print.

Jefferson, Thomas. *Notes on the State of Virginia.* 1784. Ed. William Peden. Chapel Hill: U of North Carolina P, 1955. Print.

Jenkins, Candice M. *Private Lives, Proper Relations: Regulating Black Intimacy.* Minneapolis: U of Minnesota P, 2007. Print.

Johnson, James Weldon. *Along This Way: The Autobiography of James Weldon Johnson.* 1933. New York: Da Capo, 2000. Print.

———. *The Autobiography of an Ex-Colored Man.* 1912. Ed. William L. Andrews. New York: Penguin, 1990. Print.

———, ed. *The Book of American Negro Poetry.* New York: Harcourt, 1922. Print.

———. "Down by the Carib Sea." *Fifty Years & Other Poems.* Boston: Cornhill, 1917. 30–36. Print.

———. *Fifty Years & Other Poems.* Boston: Cornhill, 1917. Print.

———. "Haiti." *New York Age* 5 Aug. 1915: 4. Print.

———. "Haiti and Mexico." *New York Age* 16 Mar. 1916: 4. Print.

———. "The Haitian Situation." *New York Age* 12 Aug. 1915: 4. Print.

———. "Internationalization." *New York Age* 8 Feb. 1919: 4. Print.

———. "The Monroe Doctrine in Latin America." *New York Age* 5 Apr. 1919: 4. Print.

———. "Once More Haiti." *New York Age* 29 Oct. 1914: 4. Print.

———. "A Poor Rule." *New York Age* 20 Jan. 1916: 4. Print.

———. Preface. *The Book of American Negro Poetry*. Ed. James Weldon Johnson. New York: Harcourt, 1922. vii–xlviii. Print.

———. "Self-Determining Haiti." 1920. *Social, Political, and Literary Essays*. Ed. Sondra Kathryn Wilson. Vol. 2 of *The Selected Writings of James Weldon Johnson*. New York: Oxford UP, 1995. 207–43. Print.

———. "The Truth about Haiti." 1920. *Social, Political, and Literary Essays*. Ed. Sondra Kathryn Wilson. Vol. 2 of *The Selected Writings of James Weldon Johnson*. New York: Oxford UP, 1995. 244–52. Print.

Johnston, Harry. "The Negro in America." *Times* [London] 15 Jan. 1909: 6. Print.

Jonas, Lucien. "Les Nouveaux Rois Mages." *L'Illustration* 26 Dec. 1914: 502–03. Print.

Jönsson, Christer, and Karin Aggestam. "Trends in Diplomatic Signalling." *Innovation in Diplomatic Practice*. Ed. Jan Melissen. New York: St. Martin's, 1999. 151–70. Print.

Justesen, Benjamin R. "African-American Consuls Abroad, 1897–1909." *Foreign Service Journal* Sept. 2004: 72–76. Print.

Kandou, Frits. "Kesan-kesan Richard Wright tentang Indonesia." *Sebaran B.M.K.N: Diedarkan oleh Badan Musjawarat Kebudajaan Nasional* 8 [ca. 15 May 1956] and 9 [ca. 31 May 1956]: 1–4 and 1–4. Print.

Kaplan, Amy. *The Anarchy of Empire in the Making of U.S. Culture*. Cambridge, MA: Harvard UP, 2002. Print.

———. "'Left Alone with America': The Absence of Empire in the Study of American Culture." *Cultures of United States Imperialism*. Ed. Amy Kaplan and Donald E. Pease. Durham, NC: Duke UP, 1993. 3–21. Print.

Karem, Jeff. *The Purloined Islands: Caribbean-U.S. Crosscurrents in Literature and Culture, 1880–1959*. Charlottesville: U of Virginia P, 2011. Print.

Kawash, Samira. *Dislocating the Color Line: Identity, Hybridity, and Singularity in African-American Narrative*. Stanford, CA: Stanford UP, 1997. Print.

Keiler, Allan. *Marian Anderson: A Singer's Journey*. Urbana: U of Illinois P, 2002. Print.

Kelley, Robin D. G. *Freedom Dreams: The Black Radical Imagination*. Boston: Beacon, 2002. Print.

Kennedy, Liam, and Scott Lucas. "Enduring Freedom: Public Diplomacy and U.S. Foreign Policy." *American Quarterly* 57 (2005): 309–33. *Project Muse*. Web. 28 Apr. 2010.

King, Richard. "Richard Wright: From the South to Africa—and Beyond." *Look Away! The U.S. South in New World Studies*. Ed. Jon Smith and Deborah Cohn. Durham, NC: Duke UP, 2004. 227–50. Print.

Kinnamon, Kenneth. *A Richard Wright Bibliography: Fifty Years of Criticism and Commentary, 1933–1982*. New York: Greenwood, 1988. Print.

Knight, Christopher J. *The Patient Particulars: American Modernism and the Technique of Originality.* Lewisburg, PA: Bucknell UP, 1995. Print.

Krasner, David. *A Beautiful Pageant: African American Theatre, Drama, and Performance in the Harlem Renaissance, 1910–1927.* New York: Palgrave, 2002. Print.

Krenn, Michael L. *Black Diplomacy: African Americans and the State Department, 1945–1969.* Armonk, NY: Sharpe, 1999. Print.

Kristeva, Julia. *Desire in Language: A Semiotic Approach to Literature and Art.* Ed. Leon S. Roudiez. Trans. Thomas Gora, Alice Jardine, and Leon S. Roudiez. New York: Columbia UP, 1980. Print.

"Lady Vice-Consul." *Ebony* Apr. 1960: 43–46. Print.

LaFeber, Walter. *The American Age: United States Foreign Policy at Home and Abroad since 1750.* New York: Norton, 1989. Print.

———. *Inevitable Revolutions: The United States in Central America.* 2nd ed. New York: Norton, 1993. Print.

Langston, John Mercer. *From the Virginia Plantation to the National Capitol; or, The First and Only Negro Representative in Congress from the Old Dominion.* Hartford, CT: American, 1894. Print.

Lasky, Melvin J. "Report on 3rd Editorial Meeting." Berlin, 2 June 1955. IACFR, Series 2, Box 241, Folder 6. Print.

Lemke, Sieglinde. *Primitivist Modernism: Black Culture and the Origins of Transatlantic Modernism.* New York: Oxford UP, 1998. Print.

"The Leopard and the Mouse." *New York Times* 3 Aug. 1906: 7. *ProQuest.* Web. 15 July 2010.

Levander, Caroline F., and Robert S. Levine, eds. *Hemispheric American Studies.* New Brunswick, NJ: Rutgers UP, 2008. Print.

Levine, Robert S. *Martin Delany, Frederick Douglass, and the Politics of Representative Identity.* Chapel Hill: U of North Carolina P, 1997. Print.

Levy, Eugene D. *James Weldon Johnson: Black Leader, Black Voice.* Chicago: U of Chicago P, 1973. Print.

Lewis, David Levering. *W. E. B. Du Bois: Biography of a Race, 1868–1919.* New York: Holt, 1993. Print.

———. *W. E. B. Du Bois: The Fight for Equality and the American Century, 1919–1963.* New York: Holt, 2000. Print.

———. *When Harlem Was in Vogue.* 1979. New York: Penguin, 1997. Print.

Lewis, R. W. B. *The American Adam.* Chicago: U of Chicago P, 1955. Print.

"Literary Notes." *Albany Law Journal* Apr. 1902: 140. *HeinOnline.* Web. 20 July 2010.

Lizza, Ryan. "The Consequentialist: How the Arab Spring Remade Obama's Foreign Policy." *New Yorker* 2 May 2011: 44–55. Print.

Locke, Alain. "The New Negro." *The New Negro.* Ed. Alain Locke. Intro. Arnold Rampersad. 1925. New York: Touchstone-Simon, 1997. 3–16. Print.

Lubis, Mochtar. "Through Coloured Glasses?" *Encounter* Mar. 1956: 73. Print.

———. *Twilight in Djakarta.* 1963. Trans. Claire Holt. Singapore: Millet, 2011. Print.

Luis, William. "The Caribbean Novel." *The Cambridge Companion to the Latin American Novel.* Ed. Efraín Kristal. New York: Cambridge UP, 2005. 125–41. Print.

"Lynching of Negroes." *Washington Post* 12 Aug. 1894: 6. Print.

MacPhee, A. Marshall. *Kenya.* New York: Praeger, 1968. Print.

Madison, Lucy. "Mike Huckabee: Obama Grew Up in Kenya." *CBSnews.com* 1 Mar. 2011. Web. 26 May 2011.

Mailer, Norman. *Advertisements for Myself.* New York: Putnam, 1959. Print.

Malanczuk, Peter. *Akehurst's Modern Introduction to International Law.* 7th rev. ed. London: Routledge, 1997. Print.

Mamdani, Mahmood. *Citizen and Subject: Contemporary Africa and the Legacy of Late Colonialism.* Princeton, NJ: Princeton UP, 1996. Print.

Mañach, Jorge. *Martí: Apostle of Freedom.* Trans. Coley Taylor. New York: Devin-Adair, 1950. Print.

Mans, J. W., and John S. Durham. "Not Representative of Her Race." *New York Times* 30 Apr. 1894: 2. *ProQuest.* Web. 15 July 2010.

Mao, Douglass, and Rebecca L. Walkowitz. "Introduction: Modernisms Bad and New." *Bad Modernisms.* Ed. Douglass Mao and Rebecca L. Walkowitz. Durham, NC: Duke UP, 2006. 1–17. Print.

Markovitz, Jonathan. *Legacies of Lynching: Racial Violence and Memory.* Minneapolis: U of Minnesota P, 2004. Print.

Martí, José. "Nuestra America." *Obras Completas / José Martí.* Vol. 6. Havana: Editorial Nacional, 1963. 15–23. Print.

Martin, Waldo E., Jr. *The Mind of Frederick Douglass.* Chapel Hill: U of North Carolina P, 1984. Print.

M[a'ruf], A[nas]. "Richard Wright di Indonesia." *Seni: Bulanan Kesenian* July 1955: 333. Print.

Marx, Karl, and Frederick Engels. *The German Ideology: Part One, with Selections from Parts Two and Three and Supplementary Texts.* Ed. C. J. Arthur. New York: International, 2001. Print.

Mataram, Tjantrik. *Peranan Ramalan Djojobojo dalam Revolusi Kita.* 1948. Bandung: Masa Baru, 1966. Print.

McCurry, Justin. "Blue Eyes, Blond Hair: That's US Problem, Says Japanese Minister." *Guardian* 23 Mar. 2007. Web. 26 May 2011.

McDowell, Deborah E. "Conversations with Dorothy West." *The Harlem Renaissance Re-examined.* Ed. Victor A. Kramer. New York: Whitson, 1997. 285–303. Print.

———. "In the First Place: Making Frederick Douglass and the Afro-American Narrative Tradition." *Critical Essays on Frederick Douglass.* Ed. William L. Andrews. Boston: Hall, 1991. 192–214. Print.

McFeely, William S. *Frederick Douglass.* New York: Norton, 1991. Print.

McGlen, Nancy E., and Meredith Reid Sarkees. *Women in Foreign Policy: The Insiders.* New York: Routledge, 1993. Print.

McKay, Claude. *Banjo.* 1929. New York: Harcourt, 1970. Print.

McMurry, Linda O. *To Keep Waters Troubled: The Life of Ida B. Wells.* New York: Oxford UP, 1998. Print.

Meier, Joyce. "The Refusal of Motherhood in African American Women's Theater." *MELUS* 25 (2000): 117–39. Print.

Mignolo, Walter D. "Citizenship, Knowledge, and the Limits of Humanity." *American Literary History* 18 (2006): 312–31. *Project Muse.* Web. 15 Apr. 2010.

———. "The Geopolitics of Knowledge and the Colonial Difference." *South Atlantic Quarterly* 101 (2002): 57–96. *Project Muse.* Web. 15 July 2010.

Miles, Robert, and Malcolm Brown. *Racism.* 2nd ed. London: Routledge, 2003. Print.

Miller, Jake C. *The Black Presence in American Foreign Affairs.* Washington, DC: UP of America, 1978. Print.

Miller, Monica L. *Slaves to Fashion: Black Dandyism and the Styling of Black Diasporic Identity.* Durham, NC: Duke UP, 2009. Print.

"Miss Lillie Mae Hubbard." *Crisis* Jan. 1929: 42. Print.

Morrison, Toni. "The Talk of the Town: Comment." *New Yorker* 5 Oct. 1998. Web. 29 May 2009.

———. "Toni Morrison on Bondage and a Post-racial Age." *National Public Radio* 10 Dec 2008. Web. 27 Apr. 2010.

Moses, Wilson Jeremiah. *Black Messiahs and Uncle Toms: Social and Literary Manipulations of a Religious Myth.* Rev. ed. University Park: Pennsylvania State UP, 1993. Print.

———. "Where Honor Is Due: Frederick Douglass as Representative Black Man." *Prospects* 17 (1992): 177–89. Print.

"Mrs. Besant, Sir Harry Johnston and Sir Charles Bruce." *African Times and Orient Review* Sept. 1912: 79–80. Print.

Mullen, Bill V. *Afro-Orientalism.* Minneapolis: U of Minnesota P, 2004. Print.

Nadell, Martha Jane. *Enter the New Negroes: Images of Race in American Culture.* Cambridge, MA: Harvard UP, 2004. Print.

"Nasib Negro di AS." *Harian Rakjat* 15 Apr. 1955: 3. Print.

"Negro di Amerika." *Harian Rakjat* 13 Apr. 1955: 1. Print.

"A New Beginning." *Wikipedia.* Web. 29 June 2011.

Newman, John Henry. *Prayers, Verses, and Devotions.* 1843. San Francisco: Ignatius, 1989. Print.

"News in Brief." *Times* [London] 17 Sept. 1915: 11. Print.

North, Michael. *The Dialect of Modernism: Race, Language, and Twentieth-Century Literature.* New York: Oxford UP, 1994. Print.

Nwankwo, Ifeoma Kiddoe. *Black Cosmopolitanism: Racial Consciousness and Transnational Identity in the Nineteenth-Century Americas.* Philadelphia: U of Pennsylvania P, 2005. Print.

Nye, Joseph S., Jr. *Soft Power: The Means to Success in World Politics.* New York: PublicAffairs, 2004. Print.

Obama, Barack. *Dreams from My Father: A Story of Race and Inheritance.* 1995. New York: Three Rivers, 2004. Print.

———. "A New Beginning." *The White House* 4 June 2009. Web. 4 June 2009.

———. "Remarks by the President at the University of Indonesia in Jakarta, Indonesia." *The White House* 10 Nov. 2010. Web. 31 May 2011.

Ogdon, Montell. *Juridical Bases of Diplomatic Immunity: A Study in the Origin, Growth and Purpose of the Law.* Washington, DC: Byrne, 1936. Print.

Oliver, Lawrence J. "'Jim Crowed' in Their Own Countries: James Weldon Johnson's *New York Age* Essays on Colonialism during the Wilson Years." *Critical Essays on James Weldon Johnson.* Ed. Kenneth M. Price and Lawrence J. Oliver. New York: Hall-Simon, 1997. 209–22. Print.

Olmsted, Frederick Law. *The Cotton Kingdom: A Traveller's Observations on Cotton and Slavery in the American Slave States.* 1861. Ed. Arthur M. Schlesinger. New York: Da Capo, 1996. Print.

O'Neill, Eugene. *All God's Chillun Got Wings.* 1924. *Nine Plays.* New York: Random House, 1959. 89–133. Print.

———. *The Emperor Jones.* 1920. *Nine Plays.* New York: Random House, 1959. 1–35. Print.

Padgett, James A. "Diplomats to Haiti and Their Diplomacy." *Journal of Negro History* 25 (1940): 265–330. *JSTOR.* Web. 15 July 2010.

"Pan-African Conference." *Times* [London] 26 July 1900: 11. Print.

Park, Robert E. Rev. of *Negro Culture in West Africa*, by George W. Ellis. *American Journal of Sociology* 20 (1915): 841–42. Print.

Parker, Geoffrey, and Philip E. Tetlock. "Counterfactual History: Its Advocates, Its Critics, & Its Uses." *Unmaking the West: 'What-If?' Scenarios That Rewrite World History.* Ed. Philip E. Tetlock, Richard Ned Lebow, and Geoffrey Parker. Ann Arbor: U of Michigan P, 2006. 363–92. Print.

Passin, Herbert, ed. *Cultural Freedom in Asia: The Proceedings of a Conference Held at Rangoon, Burma on February 17, 18, 19, and 20, 1955, and Convened by the Congress for Cultural Freedom and the Society for the Extension of Democratic Ideals.* Rutland, VT: Tuttle, 1956. Print.

Pease, Donald. "Re-thinking 'American Studies after US Exceptionalism.'" *American Literary History* 21 (2009): 19–27. *Project Muse.* Web. 28 Apr. 2010.

Phillips, Wendell. "Toussaint L'Ouverture." 1861. *Speeches, Lectures, and Letters.* Boston: Lee, 1894. 468–94. Print.

Pinkerton, James. "Century In, Century Out—It's Crusade Time." *Newsday* 3 Dec. 2003. Web. 29 June 2012.

Pisiak, Roxanna. "Irony and Subversion in James Weldon Johnson's *The Autobiography of an Ex-Colored Man.*" *Studies in American Fiction* 21 (1993): 83–96. Print.

Pitre, Merline. "Frederick Douglass and American Diplomacy in the Caribbean." *Journal of Black Studies* 13 (1983): 457–75. *JSTOR*. Web. 15 July 2010.

Plato. *The Republic*. Ed. G. R. F. Ferrari. Trans. Tom Griffith. Cambridge Texts in the History of Political Thought. Cambridge: Cambridge UP, 2000. Print.

"A Play on a Will." *Times* [London] 10 June 1914: 5. Print.

Plummer, Brenda Gayle. *Rising Wind: Black Americans and U.S. Foreign Affairs, 1935–1960*. Chapel Hill: U of North Carolina P, 1996. Print.

Porter, Keith. "Blond Hair + Blue Eyes = No Diplomat." *About.com* 26 Mar. 2007. Web. 28 May 2009.

Pound, Ezra. "The New Sculpture." *Egoist* 16 Feb. 1914: 67–68. Print.

Powell, Colin L. "Remarks to the United Nations Security Council." *U.S. Department of State Archive* 5 Feb. 2003. Web. 14 June 2012.

Powell, Colin L., with Joseph E. Persico. *My American Journey*. New York: Random, 1995. Print.

"Powell, Rice Accused of Toeing the Line." *FOX News* 22 Oct. 2002. Web. 28 May 2009.

Pratt, Mary Louise. *Imperial Eyes: Travel Writing and Transculturation*. London: Routledge, 1992. Print.

Puckett, Newbell Niles. *Folk Beliefs of the Southern Negro*. Chapel Hill: U of North Carolina P, 1926. Print.

"Pulled Leopard's Claws." *New York Times* 7 Sept. 1910: 20. *ProQuest*. Web. 15 July 2010.

Purdum, Todd S. "Powell Finesses a Sour Note from Harry Belafonte, 'a Friend.'" *New York Times* 10 Oct. 2002. Web. 28 May 2009.

"Race Playwright." *Chicago Defender* 17 July 1920: 6. Print.

Reed, Christopher Robert. *"All the World Is Here!" The Black Presence at White City*. Bloomington: Indiana UP, 2000. Print.

Regulations Prescribed for the Use of the Consular Service of the United States. Washington, DC: GPO, 1896. Print.

Reiss, Oscar. *Blacks in Colonial America*. Jefferson, NC: McFarland, 1997. Print.

"Report of the First Universal Races Congress." *African Times and Orient Review* July 1912: 27–30. Print.

Rev. of *The Arabian Lovers; or, The Sacred Jar*, by Henry Francis Downing. *African Times and Orient Review* Aug. 1913: 83. Print.

Rev. of *The Arabian Lovers; or, The Sacred Jar*, by Henry Francis Downing. *African Times and Orient Review* Nov.–Dec. 1913: 236–37. Print.

Rev. of *Negro Culture in West Africa*, by George W. Ellis. *Journal of Race Development* 5 (1915): 336. Print.

Rice, Condoleezza. *No Higher Honor: A Memoir of My Years in Washington*. New York: Crown, 2011. Print.

"Richard Wright & Bau Kakus Dikamar." Clipping crediting *Pedoman* 14 Apr. 1955. RWP, Box 29, Folder 416. Print.

Rimanelli, Marco. "The 1891–92 U.S.–Italian Diplomatic Crisis and War-Scare:

Foreign and Domestic Policies of the Harrison and di Rudiní Governments." *The 1891 New Orleans Lynching and U.S.-Italian Relations: A Look Back*. Ed. Marco Rimanelli and Sheryl L. Postman. New York: Lang, 1992. 183–285. Print.

———. "The New Orleans Lynching and U.S.-Italian Relations from Harmony to War-Scare: Immigration, Mafia, Diplomacy." *The 1891 New Orleans Lynching and U.S.-Italian Relations: A Look Back*. Ed. Marco Rimanelli and Sheryl L. Postman. New York: Lang, 1992. 106–82. Print.

Ring, Montague [Amanda Ira Aldridge]. "Where the Paw-Paw Grows." London: Ascherberg, 1907. Print.

Roach, Joseph. *Cities of the Dead: Circum-Atlantic Performance*. New York: Columbia UP, 1996. Print.

Roberts, Brian Russell. "Lost Theaters of African American Internationalism: Diplomacy and Henry Francis Downing in Luanda and London." *African American Review* 42 (2008): 269–86. Print.

Roberts, Brian Russell, and Keith Foulcher. "Richard Wright on Bandung, Beb Vuyk on Richard Wright." Introduction. "A Weekend with Richard Wright." By Beb Vuyk. Trans. Keith Foulcher. Ed. Brian Russell Roberts and Keith Foulcher. *PMLA* 126 (2011): 798–803. Print.

Roberts, Walter R. "What Is Public Diplomacy? Past Practices, Present Conduct, Possible Future." *Mediterranean Quarterly* 18.4 (2007): 36–52. *Duke-journals*. Web. 27 July 2010.

Robin, Ron. "Requiem for Public Diplomacy?" *American Quarterly* 57 (2005): 345–53. *Project Muse*. Web. 27 July 2010.

Romney, Mitt. *No Apology: The Case for American Greatness*. New York: St. Martin's, 2010. Print.

Rosenberg, Leah. "Caribbean Models for Modernism in the Work of Claude McKay and Jean Rhys." *Modernism/modernity* 11 (2004): 219–38. *Project Muse*. Web. 7 June 2011.

Ross, Marlon B. *Manning the Race: Reforming Black Men in the Jim Crow Era*. New York: NYU P, 2004. Print.

———. "The New Negro Displayed: Self-Ownership, Proprietary Sites/Sights, and the Bonds/Bounds of Race." *Claiming the Stones, Naming the Bones: Cultural Property and the Negotiation of National and Ethnic Identity*. Ed. Elazar Barkan and Ronald Bush. Los Angeles: Getty, 2002. 259–301. Print.

Roth, Philip. "Philip Roth Unbound: Interview Transcript." *Daily Beast* 30 Oct. 2009. Web. 27 Apr. 2010.

Rowe, John Carlos. *Literary Culture and U.S. Imperialism: From the Revolution to World War II*. New York: Oxford UP, 2000. Print.

Rowe, John Carlos, et al. Introduction. *Post-nationalist American Studies*. Ed. John Carlos Rowe. Berkeley: U of California P, 2000. 1–21. Print.

Rowley, Hazel. *Richard Wright: The Life and Times*. New York: Holt, 2001. Print.

Rumsfeld, Donald. *Known and Unknown: A Memoir.* New York: Sentinel, 2011. Print.

Ruotolo, Christina L. "James Weldon Johnson and the Autobiography of an Ex-Colored Musician." *American Literature* 72 (2000): 249–74. Print.

Said, Edward. *Orientalism.* 25th anniversary ed. New York: Vintage, 1994. Print.

Saldívar, José David. *Trans-Americanity: Subaltern Modernities, Global Coloniality, and the Cultures of Greater Mexico.* Durham, NC: Duke UP, 2012. Print.

Sani, Asrul. "Richard Wright: Seniman yang Jadi Intelektual." 25 Apr. 1956. *Surat-surat Kepercayaan.* Ed. Ajip Rosidi. Jakarta: Pustaka Jaya, 1997. 140–47. Print.

Sastroamidjojo, Ali. Foreword. *The Cultural Life of Indonesia: Religion, the Arts, Education.* By Embassy of Indonesia. Washington, DC: H. K. Press, 1951. vii–viii. Print.

"Satu Usul Perbaikan." *Indonesia Raya* 13 Apr. 1955: 3. Print.

Saunders, Frances Stonor. *The Cultural Cold War: The CIA and the World of Arts and Letters.* New York: New Press, 1999. Print.

Schroeder, Patricia R. "Remembering the Disremembered: Feminist Realists of the Harlem Renaissance." *Realism and the American Dramatic Tradition.* Ed. William W. Demastes. Tuscaloosa: U of Alabama P, 1996. 91–106. Print.

Scott, Laine A. "Grimké, Angelina Weld." *African American Lives.* Ed. Henry Louis Gates, Jr. New York: Oxford UP, 2004. 358–60. Print.

Sears, Louis Martin. "Frederick Douglass and the Mission to Haiti, 1889–1891." *Hispanic American Historical Review* 21 (1941): 222–38. *JSTOR.* Web. 15 July 2010.

Shaw, George Bernard. *Not Bloody Likely! And Other Quotations from Bernard Shaw.* Ed. Bernard F. Dukore. New York: Columbia UP, 1996. Print.

Sheean, Vincent. *Personal History.* Garden City, NY: Doubleday, 1937. Print.

Showalter, Elaine. *Hystories: Hysterical Epidemics and Modern Media.* New York: Columbia UP, 1997. Print.

"Siapa Mengapa." *Indonesia Raya* 4 May 1955: 2. Print.

Silkey, Sarah L. "Redirecting the Tide of White Imperialism: The Impact of Ida B. Wells's Antilynching Campaign on British Conceptions of American Race Relations." *Women Shaping the South: Creating and Confronting Change.* Ed. Angela Boswell and Judith N. McArthur. Columbia: U of Missouri P, 2006. 97–119. Print.

Singh, Amritjit. Afterword. *The Color Curtain: A Report on the Bandung Conference.* By Richard Wright. Jackson: UP of Mississippi, 1994. 223–45. Print.

Skinner, Elliot P. *African Americans and U.S. Policy toward Africa, 1850–1924: In Defense of Black Nationality.* Washington, DC: Howard UP, 1992. Print.

Smethurst, James. "The Red Is East: Claude McKay and the New Black

Radicalism of the Twentieth Century." *American Literary History* 21 (2009): 355–67. *Project Muse*. Web. 7 June 2011.

Smith, Katherine Capshaw. "From Bank Street to Harlem: A Conversation with Ellen Tarry." *The Lion and the Unicorn* 23 (1999): 271–85. *Project Muse*. Web. 28 Mar. 2007.

Smith, Virginia Whatley. "Richard Wright's Passage to Indonesia: The Travel Writer/Narrator as Participant/Observer of Anti-Colonial Imperatives in *The Color Curtain*." *Richard Wright's Travel Writings: New Reflections*. Ed. Virginia Whatley Smith. Jackson: UP of Mississippi, 2001. 78–115. Print.

Smythe, John H. Introduction. *Idle Moments: Containing Emancipation and Other Poems*. By Daniel Webster Davis. Baltimore: Educator, 1895. 3–6. Print.

Sollors, Werner. *Neither Black nor White yet Both: Thematic Explorations of Interracial Literature*. New York: Oxford UP, 1997. Print.

Sommer, Doris. *Foundational Fictions: The National Romances of Latin America*. Berkeley: U of California P, 1991. Print.

Spivak, Gayatri Chakravorty. "Can the Subaltern Speak?" *Marxism and the Interpretation of Culture*. Ed. Cary Nelson and Lawrence Grossberg. Urbana: U of Illinois P, 1988. 271–313. Print.

Stafford, Alphonso O. "Negro Representatives." *Boston Evening Transcript* 2 Oct. 1897: 15. Print.

Stecopoulos, Harilaos. *Reconstructing the World: Southern Fictions and U.S. Imperialisms, 1898–1976*. Ithaca, NY: Cornell UP, 2008. Print.

Steele, Janet. *Wars Within: The Story of* Tempo, *an Independent Magazine in Soeharto's Indonesia*. Jakarta: Equinox, 2005. Print.

Stein, Gertrude. "Melanctha." *Three Lives*. 1909. New York: Dover, 1994. 47–141. Print.

Stephens, Judith L. "Anti-Lynch Plays by African American Women: Race, Gender, and Social Protest." *African American Review* 26 (1992): 329–39. Print.

Stephens, Michelle Ann. *Black Empire: The Masculine Global Imaginary of Caribbean Intellectuals in the United States, 1914–1962*. Durham, NC: Duke UP, 2005. Print.

Stepto, Robert B. *From Behind the Veil: A Study of Afro-American Narrative*. Urbana: U of Illinois P, 1979. Print.

Stewart, Susan. *Crimes of Writing: Problems in the Containment of Representation*. New York: Oxford UP, 1991. Print.

Storm, William. "Reactions of a 'Highly-Strung Girl': Psychology and Dramatic Representation in Angelina W. Grimké's *Rachel*." *African American Review* 27 (1993): 461–71. Print.

Sudjatmoko, and Asrul Sani, eds. "Pertjakapan dengan Richard Wright." *Siasat: Warta Sepekan* 15 May 1955: 22–23. Print.

Sukartiah. "The Indonesian Literature." *Indonesië: Tweemaandelijks Tijdschrift Gewijd Aan Het Indonesisch Cultuurgebied* 5 (1951–1952): 93–96. Print.

Sundquist, Eric J. Introduction. *The Marrow of Tradition*. By Charles W. Chesnutt. New York: Penguin, 1993. vii–xliv. Print.

———. *To Wake the Nations: Race in the Making of American Literature*. Cambridge, MA: Harvard UP, 1993. Print.

Sweeney, Carole. *From Fetish to Subject: Race, Modernism, and Primitivism, 1919–1935*. Westport, CT: Praeger, 2004. Print.

"Synopsis." *Konfrontasi* May–June 1955: 25–28. Print.

Tarry, Ellen. *Young Jim: The Early Years of James Weldon Johnson*. New York: Dodd, 1967. Print.

Tate, Claudia. *Domestic Allegories of Political Desire: The Black Heroine's Text at the Turn of the Century*. New York: Oxford UP, 1992. Print.

———. *Psychoanalysis and Black Novels: Desire and the Protocols of Race*. New York: Oxford UP, 1998. Print.

Teeuw, A. *Modern Indonesian Literature*. The Hague, Netherlands: Nijhoff, 1967. Print.

"Telah Tiba di Jakarta." *Indonesia Raya* 14 Apr. 1955: 1. Print.

Toer, Pramoedya Ananta. "Definisi dan Keindahan dalam Kesusastraan." 1953. *Menggelinding I*. Ed. Astuti Ananta Toer. Jakarta: Lentera Dipantara, 2004. 173–79. Print.

———. *Menggelinding I*. Ed. Astuti Ananta Toer. Jakarta: Lentera Dipantara, 2004. Print.

———. *The Mute's Soliloquy: A Memoir*. Trans. Willem Samuels. New York: Hyperion, 1999. Print.

Tuch, Hans N. *Communicating with the World: U.S. Public Diplomacy Overseas*. New York: St. Martin's, 1990. Print.

Twain, Mark. "Diplomatic Pay and Clothes." 1899. *The $30,000 Bequest and Other Stories*. New York: Oxford UP, 1996. 398–413. Print.

"The Unacted Authors' Association." *Times* [London] 10 Mar. 1909: 13. Print.

"Unacted Plays." *African Times and Orient Review* July 1913: 43. Print.

Vickers, Adrian. *A History of Modern Indonesia*. Cambridge: Cambridge UP, 2005. Print.

Von Eschen, Penny M. *Satchmo Blows Up the World: Jazz Ambassadors Play the Cold War*. Cambridge, MA: Harvard UP, 2004. Print.

———. "Who's the Real Ambassador? Exploding Cold War Racial Ideology." *Cold War Constructions: The Political Culture of United States Imperialism, 1945–1966*. Ed. Christian G. Appy. Amherst: U of Massachusetts P, 2000. 110–31. Print.

Vuyk, Beb. "Black Power." *Indonesia Raya* 1 June 1955: 3. Print.

———. "A Weekend with Richard Wright." 1960. Trans. Keith Foulcher. Ed. Brian Russell Roberts and Keith Foulcher. *PMLA* 126 (2011): 803–12. Print.

Waldstein, Charles. *Greek Sculpture and Modern Art: Two Lectures Delivered to the Students of the Royal Academy of London*. Cambridge: Cambridge UP, 1914. Print.

Waligora-Davis, Nicole A. *Sanctuary: African Americans and Empire*. New York: Oxford UP, 2011. Print.

Walker, Jeffrey K. "Fiction versus Function: The Persistence of 'Representative Character' Theory in the Law of Diplomatic Immunity." *The Psychology of Diplomacy*. Ed. Harvey J. Langholtz and Chris E. Stout. Westport, CT: Praeger, 2004. 243–67. Print.

Walrond, Eric. *Tropic Death*. New York: Boni, 1926. Print.

Warren, Kenneth W. "Frederick Douglass's *Life and Times*: Progressive Rhetoric and the Problem of Constituency." *Frederick Douglass: New Literary and Historical Essays*. Ed. Eric J. Sundquist. Cambridge: Cambridge UP, 1990. 253–70. Print.

Washington, Booker T. *A New Negro for a New Century: An Accurate and Up-to-Date Record of the Upward Struggles of the Negro Race*. Chicago: American, 1900. Print.

———. *Up from Slavery*. 1901. Ed. William L. Andrews. Oxford: Oxford UP, 1995. Print.

Wayman, H. Harrison. "The Quaker City." *Colored American Magazine* Dec. 1903: 887–96. Print.

Webb, Constance. *Richard Wright: A Biography*. New York: Putnam, 1968. Print.

Weiss, John. "The Horrors of San Domingo." *Atlantic Monthly* Mar. 1863: 289–306. Print.

Wells, H. G. *The Soul of a Bishop*. New York: Macmillan, 1917. Print.

Wheatley, Phillis. "To the Right Honorable William, Earl of Dartmouth, His Majesty's Principal Secretary of State for North-America." 1773. *Complete Writings*. New York: Penguin, 2001. 39–40. Print.

Whitman, Walt. *Leaves of Grass*. 1855. New York: Vintage, 1992. Print.

Williams, Raymond. *Keywords: A Vocabulary of Culture and Society*. Rev. ed. New York: Oxford UP, 1985. Print.

———. *Marxism and Literature*. Oxford: Oxford UP, 1977. Print.

Williams, Vernon J., Jr. *Rethinking Race: Franz Boas and His Contemporaries*. Lexington: UP of Kentucky, 1996. Print.

Wilson, Rob. *Reimagining the American Pacific: From* South Pacific *to Bamboo Ridge and Beyond*. Durham, NC: Duke UP, 2000. Print.

"Would Curb Officials." *New York Times* 26 Feb. 1925: 3. Print.

Wright, Ann. "For the Record: Breaking through Diplomacy's Glass Ceiling." *Foreign Service Journal* Oct. 2005: 53–62. Print.

Wright, Richard. "American Negro Writing." *Konfrontasi* May–June 1955: 2–25. Print.

———. "Blueprint for Negro Writing." *New Challenge* 2 (1937): 53–65. Print.

———. *The Color Curtain: A Report on the Bandung Conference*. 1956. Jackson: UP of Mississippi, 1994. Print.

———. "Forerunner and Ambassador." Rev. of *The Big Sea: An Autobiography,* by Langston Hughes. *New Republic* 28 Oct. 1940: 600–01. Print.

———. "I Choose Exile." n.d. (ca. 1952). RWP, Box 6, Folder 110. Print.

———. "Indonesian Notebook." *Encounter* Aug. 1955: 24–31. Print.

———. "Jakarta—Asian and African Conference." Journal, 3 Feb. through early May 1955. RWP, Box 29, Folder 418. Print.

———. "The Literature of the Negro in the United States." *White Man, Listen!* Garden City, NY: Doubleday, 1957. 105–50. Print.

———. "Littérature Noire Américaine." Trans. René Guyonnet. *Les Temps Modernes* Aug. 1948: 193–221. Print.

———. "Mr. Wright Replies." *Encounter* Mar. 1956: 73. Print.

———. *The Outsider.* 1953. New York: HarperPerennial, 2003. Print.

———. "Retreat from Paradise." RWP, Box 31, Folder 433. Print.

———. "Seniman dan Masaalahnja." *Indonesia Raya* 21 May 1955: 5. Print.

———. "Tradition and Industrialization." *White Man, Listen!* Garden City, NY: Doubleday, 1957. 74–104. Print.

———. *12 Million Black Voices: A Folk History of the Negro in the United States.* New York: Viking, 1941. Print.

Wynes, Charles E. "John Stephens Durham, Black Philadelphian: At Home and Abroad." *Pennsylvania Magazine of History and Biography* Oct. 1982: 527–37. Print.

Young, Robert J. C. *Postcolonialism: An Historical Introduction.* Oxford, UK: Blackwell, 2001. Print.

Zéndegui, Guillermo de. *Ámbito de Martí.* n.p.: Sociedad Columbista Panamerica, 1954. Print.

Zolov, Eric. "¡Cuba sí, Yanquis no! The Sacking of the Instituto Cultural Méxicano-Norteamericano in Morelia, Michoacán, 1961." *In from the Cold: Latin America's New Encounter with the Cold War.* Ed. Gilbert M. Joseph and Daniela Spenser. Durham, NC: Duke UP, 2008. 214–52. Print.

Index